Environmental Impact Assessment

Environmental Impact Assessment

Ruthann Corwin
Patrick H. Heffernan
Robert A. Johnston
Michael Remy
James A. Roberts
D. B. Tyler

Freeman, Cooper & Company
1736 Stockton Street
San Francisco, CA 94133

Printed in the United States of America
Library of Congress Catalogue Card Number 75-17326
International Standard Book Number 0-87735-061-2

Contents

Preface

Earth Day, April 22, 1970, brought to the public attention facts that had been causing fears to simmer in the consciousness of scientists and students of the natural environment. Although we present a very brief background on environmental problems in the first chapter, this text is intended to give you a tool for solving problems rather than to create awareness of the problems. We expect that students of this text will have more than just a passing acquaintance with the issues raised before Earth Day and since.

Our readers probably have an overview of ecological problems from an introductory course or from books like Rachel Carson's *Silent Spring* (*1*)*, Paul Ehrlich's *Population Bomb* (*2*), and *Science and Survival* by Barry Commoner (*3*). You know, for example, what the accumulation of pesticides in food chains can mean for the animals at the top. You know what is meant by "the tragedy of the commons," as Garrett Hardin expressed it (*4*), and why we must find a way to bring public goods such as clean air and water into our accounting systems. You have some idea of the meaning of "ecosystem," and know about the one-way flow of energy and the cycling of nutrients in our biosphere. Some basic ecology is part of your background (*5*).

You have read some of the muckrakers and others who have looked at human use of resources and our destructiveness towards our landscapes (*6*). *The Hungry Planet* (*7*), *Famine 1975!* (*8*), *Limits to Growth* (*9*), or other books and articles have given you an appreciation of what rapid human population growth may mean for the future of this planet and humankind. Some of you may have read the views of the anti-doomsday writers, or those who feel that it is not numbers but the nature of our social and economic systems that is causing many of our present environmental problems (*10*). You are forming your own perspective on the causes and seriousness of issues, and the complexities of creating positive changes. A few of you are looking into interdisciplinary approaches to systems and communication to form a more holistic framework for your understanding of the issues (*11*).

---

* The numbers in parentheses are those of the references at the end of the preface.

In thinking about solutions, you might be contemplating a "land ethic" after reading Leopold's *Sand County Almanac* (*12*). Some of you may have looked into the origins of our present ethics, as Lynn White did in "The Historical Roots of Our Ecology Crisis" (*13*), or have begun to search out alternatives, both technological and socio-economic (*14*).

These references and many other good texts and collections of readings (*15*) cover the multitude of facts and trends, known damages, frightening predictions, and suggestions for change that make up the environmental literature. A good background in this literature guarantees your understanding of the meaningfulness of impact assessment as one way of approaching environmental problems: we must begin to think ahead to the effects of our decisions before taking actions which might have highly undesirable consequences somewhere or sometime else.

The value of such reading is not just in the view of the problems that it gives. The more one reads, the more one will become familiar with the past results of human actions, and with current efforts at prediction. No one book can cover all the possible impacts, but texts such as *Man's Impact on Environment* (*16*) or *Man's Role in Changing the Face of the Earth* (*17*) will begin to build your store of impacts to consider. Impact assessment is partly an exercise in recognition, in identification of those impacts which might occur. The more examples you are aware of, the more impacts you will be able to think of, and the closer you will come to identifying all the impacts that might occur as a result of a specific project or action.

1. Carson, Rachel. *Silent Spring*, Houghton Mifflin, Boston, 1962.
2. Ehrlich, Paul. *The Population Bomb*, Ballantine, N.Y., 1968.
3. Commoner, Barry. *Science and Survival*, Viking, N.Y., 1966.
4. Hardin, Garrett. "The Tragedy of the Commons," *Science*, Vol. 162, pp. 1243–1248, December, 1968.
5. For example: Kormondy, Edward J. *Concepts of Ecology*, Prentice-Hall, Englewood Cliffs, N.J., 1969.
   Odom, Eugene P. *Fundamentals of Ecology*, W. P. Saunders, Philadelphia, 1959.
   Man and the Ecosystem, a collection of articles from *Scientific American*, W. H. Freeman and Company, San Francisco.
6. For example: Marine, Gene. *America, The Raped*, Simon and Schuster, N.Y., 1969.
   Osborn, Fairfield. *Our Plundered Planet*, Pyramid, N.Y., 1968.
7. Borgstrum, Georg. *The Hungry Planet*, Macmillan, N.Y., 1965.
8. Paddock, William, and Paul Paddock. *Famine 1975!*, Little/Brown, Boston, 1967.
9. Meadows, Donella H., et al. *The Limits to Growth*, Universe Books, N.Y., 1972.

10. Maddox, John. *The Doomsday Syndrome—An Attack on Pessimism*, McGraw-Hill, N.Y., 1972.
    Mamdani, Mahmood. *The Myth of Population Control*, Monthly Review Press, N.Y., 1972.
    Ridgeway, James. *The Politics of Ecology*, Dutton, N.Y., 1971.
    Weisberg, Barry. *Beyond Repair, The Ecology of Capitalism*, Beacon Press, Boston, 1971.

11. Schultz, Arnold M. "The Ecosystem as a Conceptual Tool in the Management of Natural Resources," in Ciriacy-Wantrup, S. V., and James J. Parsons (eds.), *Natural Resources—Quality and Quantity*, University of California Press, Berkeley, 1967.
    Schick, Allen. "Systems Politics and Systems Budgeting," in Leslie L. Roos (ed.), *The Politics of Ecosuicide*, Holt, Rinehart and Winston, N.Y., 1971.
    Bateson, Gregory. *Steps to an Ecology of Mind*, Chandler, N.Y., 1972.
    Wilden, Anthony. *System and Structure*, Tavistock, London, 1972.

12. Leopold, Aldo. *A Sand County Almanac*, Oxford University Press, N.Y., 1966.

13. White, Lynn, Jr. "The Historical Roots of Our Ecology Crisis," *Science*, Vol. 155, pp. 1203–1207, March, 1967.

14. Caldwell, Lynton K. "The Ecosystem as a Criterion for Public Land Policy," *Natural Resource Journal*, Vol. 10, pp. 203–220, 1970.
    DeBell, Garret. *The Environmental Handbook*, Ballantine, N.Y., 1970.
    Portola Institute. *Whole Earth Catalog*, Menlo Park, Calif., 1968.
    Goldman, Marshall I. (ed.). *Controlling Pollution*, Prentice-Hall, Englewood Cliffs, N.J., 1967.
    Helfrich, H. W. (ed.), *Agenda for Survival*, Yale University Press, New Haven, Conn., 1970.
    McHarg, Ian. *Design with Nature*, Natural History Press, Garden City, N.Y., 1969.
    Goodman, Paul, and Percival Goodman. *Communitas*, Random House, N.Y., 1960 . . .
    and many more.

15. For example: Smith, Robert Leo (ed.). *The Ecology of Man: An Ecosystem Approach*, Harper & Row, N.Y., 1972.
    Shepard, Paul, and Daniel McKinley (eds.). *The Subversive Science*, Houghton Mifflin, Boston, 1969.

16. Detwyler, Thomas (ed.). *Man's Impact on Environment*, McGraw-Hill, N.Y., 1971.

17. Thomas, William L., Jr. (ed.). *Man's Role in Changing the Face of the Earth*, University of Chicago Press, Chicago, Illinois, 1956.

RUTHANN CORWIN

Editors' Foreword

This book and its authors reflect the variety of skills and temperaments required in environmental impact analysis. An engineer/biologist, a planner/systems analyst, a geographer, an attorney, an economist, and a journalist/political scientist have joined their talents to define and teach an embryonic and rapidly changing science. Each of us brings to this volume not only his or her special set of skills, but also a participation in and some responsibility for the evolution of the impact assessment process. All of us have worked in the day-to-day business of unravelling and documenting the results of civilization's contact with nature. All of us agree that the impact assessment process is only as good as those who perform it, and that it is changing as our knowledge of nature and skill with technology grow. By setting down in print what we have learned of how to perform this process and what we know of its evolution, we hope that we can encourage its growth and improvement and keep it changing for the better.

One person whose name does not appear in the table of contents is as much responsible for this book as those who wrote it, Dr. Stuart Cooney, Director of the Northern California Regional Instructional Television Consortium of Universities and Colleges. Stu brought us all together with Andy Sabhlock, Thelma Johnson, Clyde Ongaro, and Dr. Wes Jackson to produce a television study course on environmental impact reporting. The syllabus for the 26-segment course was the original basis for this book, and Dr. Cooney was its spiritual guide. Those with whom we worked on the course taught us a great deal about the process and how to communicate that knowledge. We thank them and appreciate the opportunity to have worked with them.

Another name that does not appear in the table of contents is that of Dr. Rolland Hauser of California State University at Chico. Rolli was a pleasure to work with in the television course and we were all disappointed when his labors at Chico made it impossible for him to continue with us on the book.

PATRICK H. HEFFERNAN
RUTHANN CORWIN

Environmental Impact Assessment

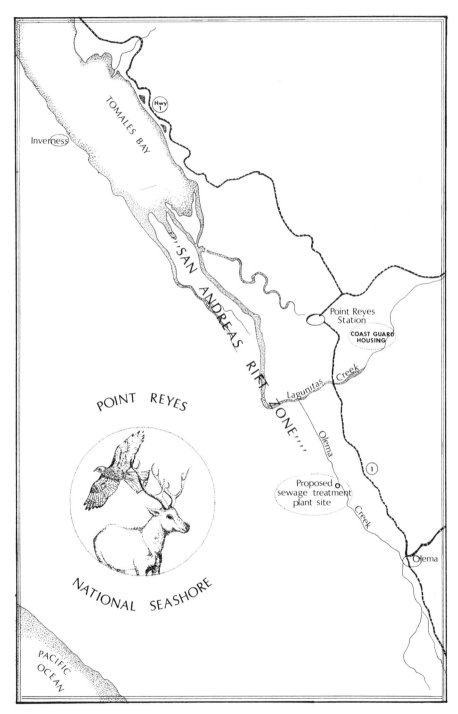

Fig. 1–1 Map of Point Reyes Station vicinity and Coast Guard project sites.

1 · Impact Assessment
Origin, Operation, and Outlook

Humans as Change Agents

Human nature compels us to alter the natural environment for our benefit and seems to allow us to discount the future harmful effects of our actions. No one who reflects upon our increase in lifespan, in personal comfort, and in material well-being can doubt that such alterations have created a better life for many. Less fortunate peoples have come to expect this progress and grow increasingly impatient with governments that do not provide it. But these improvements come with a serious cost in environmental problems that affect all people, and we are beginning to pay that cost now without realizing how great it is.

The purpose of impact assessment is to measure that cost before it is incurred so we can decide whether or not the promised benefits are worth their price. Impact assessment does not belittle the achievements of technology, but evaluates its impacts and determines which benefits are realizable with the least injury to society and to the environment. The question seems to be one of limits we must accept, both of affluence we can have in exchange for detrimental side-effects and of our knowledge and ability to predict these effects.

Human beings have not only increased their material well-being over the centuries, they have vastly increased the number and magnitude of impacts they

Ruthann Corwin, born in 1945, is a lecturer in Environmental Studies at the University of California at Santa Barbara and a principal in Resources, a public-interest consulting firm. She completed her Ph.D. work under the Interdisciplinary Graduate Program at the University of California, Berkeley, combining ecology, planning, and psychology in a systems framework. She served as Environmental Planner for the County of Marin, California. She is the author of *Environmental Impact Review* and currently conducts research in perception and values, environmental planning, and decision-making systems.

can create. Other species have also played roles in modifying the nature of their surroundings. Beavers create ponds; trees establish microclimates of light and moisture; some plants produce toxins which control surrounding species; herbivores alter plant communities through their grazing and browsing preferences. Many of these effects are limited in scale, but where they create broader changes, they span several generations, allowing the plants and animals and their physical environment to adapt to each other over time. The pressures of competition and predation, the existence of limiting factors in the immediately available energy sources and nutrient pool, the habitat requirements of species for protection and reproduction, for water and climatic factors, all establish carrying capacities of species, and limit the population increase of any one creature.

But humans have the peculiar ability to create changes too fast for our surroundings to keep pace. The ramifications of our actions are world-wide, from DDT in penguins and crab-eating seals in the Antarctic (*1*)* to CO_2 levels in the atmosphere (*2*). Our predators and competitors have proven no match for human hands and brains. At each stage in our cultural evolution, we have transcended the limiting factors of our environment. No longer bound by the present energy flow, we have extended our energy budget by drawing upon the ecological capital deposited in fossil fuels. The limits of nutrient cycling have been surpassed by the development of agriculture and mining, and technology has enabled human requirements to be met anywhere in the world.

Early hominids as hunters and food-gatherers were just one of the larger species evolving and being shaped by nature. Although the revolution of tool-using and tool-making gave migrating early humans access to a wide range of environments, the effects of their passage on the landscape were of small enough scale to allow disturbances to heal. Even so, it is thought that our present capability to exterminate other species goes back 40,000 years, when early man may have had his first significant impact on the environment through the extinction of many large late-Pleistocene mammals, such as the mammoth and sabertooth tiger, either by killing them directly or through competition or destruction of their habitats (*3*).

After the invention of tools, the domestication of plants and animals as the second major stage in our cultural evolution was a significant departure both in human numbers and in environmental impact. At the climax of the Mesolithic hunting and gathering phase 10,000 years ago, a total of perhaps 5 million people inhabited the earth (*4*). These peoples generally roamed large areas to find the sustenance available to them from the variety of the natural ecosystem.

* The numbers in italics refer to the references and notes at the end of the chapter.

Domestication concentrated edible species, expanding the energy budget and allowing for higher rates of survival. By about 4000 B.C., agricultural productivity had increased to the point where farms were beginning to support urban civilizations, such as ancient Ubaid in southern Mesopotamia. In 8,000 years of early farming, we multiplied the Mesolithic population 100 times, to over 500 million people.

The agricultural period represented the first major spending of ecological capital—nutrients built up in the soils of natural ecosystems squandered by exposure to sun, wind, and rain through over-grazing and poor agricultural practices. Long-term impacts of human action began to be created which would be felt by future generations. Present residents of the Middle Eastern "fertile crescent," where the agricultural revolution began, now suffer from the deforestation, soil deterioration, and erosion that is their legacy of 10,000 years of human habitation (5). In Iraq, the government is trying to reclaim the salt-poisoned soils of the Diyala River Basin, which has been a desert since the twelfth century (6).

A second expansion of the human energy budget began about 300 years ago with the advent of the scientific industrial revolution and large-scale use of fossil fuels and mineral resources. As a result of this progress, impacts were created that would have been impossible in earlier times: large rivers polluted by acid waters from mines, industrial wastes poured into the oceans and skies, radiation from atomic energy and bomb material production, loss of entire food chains through filling and polluting marshes and estuaries, poisons in our food and drink, fertile lands not only eroded but buried under paving to provide shelter and transportation.

By the turn of this century, demographers estimate we will number over 6 billion (4), an increase of more than 10 times the total population in only 350 years. The world's population is now about 4 billion. We are facing a population doubling time of only 35 years, as compared to twice as long during the first half of this century. At the present rate, by the end of this century the population will be facing a doubling time of less than 20 years. The most disturbing aspect is that our population is increasing at an increasing rate—from one percent to three percent per year in the past 50 years alone.

Perhaps it is possible to support another 10-fold increase in human numbers. The real questions we must face are the world-wide standards of living that we are willing to accept. Human inventiveness may enable us to extend our material endowment, provided we don't create side effects worse than those we are grappling with now from such advances as the automobile and nuclear energy. But it is questionable whether we can mobilize the resources necessary to support 50 billion people at a reasonable level, when we cannot now create the social mechanisms for adequate resource distribution throughout the world. What new forms of social organization will have to emerge? What human values will have to change?

Again we must recognize that in the present period of human culture, as in the last, we are living on the earth's capital. A mining-dependent life-style, especially in the developed nations where we spend 30–60 times as much energy for other purposes as we do for food (*4*), cannot afford to run out. "Find more" appears to be the basis for our present resource decision-making, as exemplified by our response to the so-called "energy crisis" of 1973.

But a growing number of citizens are questioning the presumption of tying our life-styles to the earth's supply of resources without considering their limits or the earth's ability to absorb the side effects of our activities. It no longer suffices for government to talk about full-scale energy resource exploitation, when there are many who are willing to trade a lower consumption level for uncontaminated coastlines, cleaner air, or freedom from fear of radiation hazards. One of the earliest concepts of impact assessment is the exploration of alternatives which must take such non-economic values into account.

It would be impossible here to describe all the impacts that man has created over the years. The list of areas of environmental impacts in Appendix II of the Council on Environmental Quality's guidelines to the National Environmental Policy Act (*22*), including air quality, weather modification, marine pollution, noise, radiation, and toxic materials, illustrates the fact that we have added a vast array of impacts to early man's original abilities to extinguish species, destroy plant communities, and accelerate soil erosion. New ones are being added every day, as witness some 250,000 new chemicals per year registered with Chemical Abstract Service. Only a small fraction of the chemicals in use have been tested, and those usually only for carcinogenicity. It has been estimated that to test all the new substances would require laboratory technicians equalling ten times the world's present population! And that would not be taking into account all the possible synergistic effects of two or more chemicals acting in combination.

It is clear that we need to slow the rate of our creation of new impacts until we can evaluate the effects of what we are doing now, or we will be in for some surprises that might turn science-fiction fantasy into unpleasant reality.

The NEPA Evolution

The Conservation Tradition

Environmental impact assessment did not spring fully grown from the heads of the congressmen and their aides who wrote the National Environmental Policy Act (NEPA). It is rather the latest in a recent tradition of legislative efforts to preserve environmental quality. However, NEPA represents a significant break with the early methods of conservation, a break with profound impacts on our perceptions, our governmental processes, and many of our institutions.

Current environmental awareness has its roots in the concept of preserving land from man's destructive activities. The American philosophy of government disposal of land to private interests dominated federal and state policy until 1872, when Yellowstone National Park was dedicated, the first such land reserve in the country. Yellowstone's creation was preceded by the work of a forerunner of impact assessment advocates, George Perkins Marsh, who wrote an early impact assessment text: *Man and Nature; or, Physical Geography as Modified by Human Action* (7). In the book, Marsh gave notice that in the past man has endangered his own existence through destruction of his environment.

Still, there was always more land "to the west" and people were not willing to listen to the lesson of impact assessment. What did occur, however, was a period of preservation and management of resources, the major thrust of early federal environmental policy. President Theodore Roosevelt and Gifford Pinchot, first Director of the Forest Service, closed millions of acres of rich land to private development at the turn of this century. Pinchot established the concept of multiple-use resource management and sustained yields of timber, forage, watershed, and recreation opportunities. John Muir and his followers advocated a more protective philosophy, that of preservation of lands and resources for their own sake. Muir's work culminated in the founding of the National Park Service in 1916.

In the 1930's another major federal conservation push was initiated under President Franklin D. Roosevelt. Acceptance of resources planning for the future was developed through the efforts of his Natural Resources Committee. Roosevelt instituted the Civilian Conservation Corps, creating hundreds of projects such as planting trees and cutting fire roads and trails to provide jobs for men hit by the depression. The establishment of the Soil Conservation Service under Roosevelt's administration provided vitally needed education and advice to farmers about the abuses that created the dust storms of 1934–35, which stripped as much as a foot of topsoil from millions of acres of farms (8). (The lesson was temporary, however, because cultivation of drought-vulnerable lands in 1954–57 led to renewed dust storms that damaged 10–15 million acres of farms.)

The history of wildlife conservation followed the same trend as land and resource preservation. Some efforts were made as early as colonial times, when hunting restrictions attempted to protect deer, woodland game birds, and migrating waterfowl. Not until 1880 did all the states have some form of game laws (9). The early protection laws were poorly enforced until game wardens came on the scene in 1878. However, even this protection was too late for the bison, wiped out in 1894, and the passenger pigeon, whose last survivor died in the Cincinnati Zoo on September 1, 1914 (8).

Federal legislation protecting wildlife and establishing refuges was first passed at the turn of the century. The Wildlife Restoration Act of 1937 gave impetus to efforts to acquire and manage land for wildlife habitat. The tendency, however, has been to manage for "sport" species except for symbolic or endangered species, such as the bald eagle and the Florida key deer.

Now, with growing educational or recreational value attached to seeing almost any wild animal or wild area, conservationists are turning their attention to non-game species and to maintaining representative ecosystems. Unfortunately, hunting restrictions cannot save a bird whose breeding marsh is drained and filled for a trailer park, nor can habitat management prevent the accumulation of pesticides that destroy its reproductive ability. We are reaching a new realization that the total decrease of all man's impacts on the environment is needed to save individual species.

By the beginning of World War II the conservation and management tradition had become firmly rooted in our national conscience and was the basis for virtually all federal and state programs affecting the environment. But while conservation sprang from observations of the adverse impacts of man's actions, little thought was given to the identification and disclosure of those impacts and there was little consideration of impacts in the decision-making process. Instead, those concerned about the growing problems of pollution and environmental degradation demanded expanded protection. What was needed, they argued, was not just the preservation of resources, but the protection of all resources by regulation of pollution.

Regulation and Pollution Control

The history of recent environmental law begins with the Rivers and Harbors Act of 1899, also called the "1899 Refuse Act," sometimes considered the first "environmental" law. It required, among other things, a permit from the Army Engineers to deposit any refuse or polluting substance in navigable waters (10). However, it was not enforced except by occasional judicial action. A single agency authorized to control water pollution was finally created in 1956, but was given little power. In 1965, a water quality act was passed providing money to the states for water pollution treatment and control, but still no tough regulatory body was mandated.

Although the Refuse Act had been used sporadically to prosecute polluters since its passage, those frustrated with the slow progress of water cleanup in the late 60's began using the Act's provision for citizen reporting of violations to the United States Attorney. Environmental groups circulated flyers with instructions for collecting and providing the necessary information. Many United States attorneys reported that their offices were swamped with complaints and evidence. This led to the passage in 1972 of a new Federal Water Pollution Control Act, which established a federal-state permit program under the Environmental Protection Agency (EPA) and provided billions of dollars to state and local agencies to treat wastes and clean up rivers and streams.

While the injection of large amounts of state and federal money did result in measurable increases in water quality nationwide, budget restraints and ecological complexity prevented money from becoming the major element of federal environmental protection programs, or even a good across-the-board prescription for environmental ills. Regulation became the cornerstone of federal and state reaction to environmental problems, with preservation running a poor second.

Other regulation attempts include the first Insecticide Act, passed in 1910 to protect purchasers from misbranded products. Later, in 1947, the Federal Insecticide, Fungicide and Rodenticide Act expanded the statute's coverage to protect the public from hazards associated with the use of these poisons, and required registration of products with the Secretary of Agriculture. The present Act, passed in 1972, provides for labelling pesticides with cautions and warnings, as well as directions for use. The power is granted the EPA administrator to deny registration if a pesticide is injurious to humans, other vertebrates, or useful plants, even if used as directed (*10*). But there is no prohibition against misuse of a registered pesticide, and the Act does not apply to products distributed entirely within a single state. No attempt is made to determine the total effects of pesticide use.

Another example of federal regulation is the passage in 1970 of amendments to the earlier Clean Air Acts calling for air quality criteria and state plans for implementation and enforcement. But the difficulties of controlling pollutants from an enormous number of industrial and commercial sources and automobiles continue to hamstring the program. Disputes over measurement techniques, the nature of air pollution, and the costs of cleanup have slowed enforcement to a standstill even in the most polluted areas.

Other recent environmental laws have expanded government control and added dozens of new concerns. Laws, procedures, and court decisions cover parks, recreation and wilderness areas, wetlands, deserts and other sensitive locations, endangered species, wild rivers, marine mammals, noise, solid waste, historic preservation, nuclear power, oil pollution, strip mining, oil shale leasing, and more. The states have also begun to create their own procedures for preservation and regulation. But state regulation has suffered the same political and scientific setbacks plaguing federal attempts to halt environmental degradation.

Histories of attempts and failures of environmental law could be recited for each of the issues raised in recent times and for the programs created to solve them. Each issue has its chronicle of efforts to create regulatory law and bureaucracy. In some cases, studies were mandated to assess the impacts and amount of damages, particularly when human health was clearly involved. EPA's research and monitoring function is concerned with establishing an index of current environmental quality and studying the effects of environmental insults. The Council on Environmental Quality is also empowered to conduct investigations into environmental quality and define and interpret changes in the environment and their causes. Research on water quality standards includes consideration of the impacts of pollution levels on fish and wildlife. The toxicity of pesticides must be considered in registering a product, but if their application is unknown and uncontrolled, we have no way of quantifying the real impacts of their use.

Air and water pollution provide the typical case. Both sets of laws are aimed at controlling pollutants from a variety of sources, or the specific impact of pollution from a single source. Missing from this effort is a requirement for considering more than one kind of impact from a single cause, and more importantly, the consideration of alternatives to the pollution source before it becomes a reality.

Environmental impact assessment appeared in some provisions of environmental laws of the 1960's, but carefully confined and restrained. It was still not part of the decision-making process. The old values of exploitation regardless of the effects had been brought under control and eliminated from a few of the nation's more precious areas, but those values were still unchallenged in the millions of permit decisions taking place every year in federal and state agency offices and local government councils. And significantly, the public still had no real voice in that process.

Project Evaluation Law

Several of the elements that are now considered important features of impact assessment came together in the 1960's as part of a trend in government decision-making quite separate from conservation and pollution control. We will look at Senate Document 97 (SD 97 (*11*)), promulgated in 1962, which followed in the tradition of a long line of project evaluation laws, beginning with the Treasury Report on Roads and Canals in 1808 and continued by the Reclamation Act of 1902, which required such things as "examinations and surveys," and reports to Congress on cost estimates and facts relative to the practicability of projects. Other precursors of NEPA's requirements—the 1935 Federal Power Act, the "Scenic Hudson" case, and the important Section 4(f) of the 1966 Department of Transportation Act—have been discussed elsewhere (*12*).

SD 97 was specific to plans for water resources projects, and was developed by the Secretaries of the Army, the Interior, Agriculture, and Health, Education and Welfare for application to their programs. It updated and put into a planning framework earlier requirements stemming from the Flood Control Act of 1936 and Bureau of the Budget Circular A-47 of 1952 that projects proposed shall show benefits greater than their costs.

Although that sounds like an obvious requirement, in practice a benefit/cost analysis is more difficult than it might seem. One problem is the measurement of costs and benefits that cannot be quantified in dollars and cents, or can be quantified by a variety of methods lending different weights to the disputed side of a benefit/cost equation, depending on whether the project is favored or not. A second problem is the difficulty of projecting values into the future, and agreeing on the number of years in a project's lifetime over which to compute these values. Environmental benefits such as the creation of aquatic habitats are among the disputed estimates, usually quantified by such methods as adding the market value of commercial aspects of fish and wildlife to a market simulation of the value of sport fishing and hunting, which can be derived in a number of ways. Environmental costs are among the unquantifiables that rarely get into the equations—neither immediate impacts, such as destruction of wildlife habitats or the loss of wild rivers and scenic canyons, nor future impacts, such as the opening up of wilderness areas to growth or the promotion of agriculture in locations where soils could be easily abused.

SD 97 did not solve these problems, but brought them into the light and improved the situation somewhat by requiring a "comprehensive public viewpoint . . . in the evaluation of project effects. Such a viewpoint includes consideration of all effects, beneficial and adverse, short range and long range, tangible and intangible, that may be expected to accrue to all persons and groups within the zone of influence of the proposed resource use of development" (*11*, p. 5). The methods used to compute the values of secondary benefits must be included in planning reports. The definition of costs includes "induced costs: all uncompensated adverse effects caused by the construction and operation of a program or project, whether tangible or intangible . . ." (*11*, p. 11). But specific guidance as to the inclusion of environmental costs is left out, even though preservation of the environment is listed as one of the basic planning objectives along with economic development and the well-being of people.

The language of SD 97 is echoed in the National Environmental Policy Act written seven years later, with its talk of adverse and short- and long-range effects, and the problem of quantification. Greater similarity, however, lies in the arrangement for coordination between federal agencies and with regional, state, and local agencies. The project report must be furnished to interested agencies, and statements from them must be accepted for inclusion in the report within a specified period of time. The sponsoring federal agency shall consult with other agencies whose interests and responsibilities might be affected by the project. These requirements anticipate important aspects of the preparation and review of environmental impact statements.

SD 97 can be regarded as a predecessor of NEPA in another important aspect—the comparison of alternatives to the proposed project. In fact, in placing consideration of alternatives in a comprehensive river basin planning framework, SD 97 avoided one of NEPA's drawbacks. The consideration of alternatives at the project proposal stage, as is usually done under NEPA, is much more constraining than the formulation of programs and projects as part of a comprehensive plan which is supposed to balance development, environmental protection, and human well-being objectives. For example, planners could evaluate water conservation or a recycling project as alternatives to a water supply project, but environmental impact statement drafters at the project stage usually consider alternatives only in the design, size, and location of the supply facilities. Although based on the stated assumption of an expanding economy and therefore aimed at resource exploitation, SD 97 does establish a policy that requires consideration of all relevant means, including nonstructural as well as structural, which reflect different basic choice patterns for providing water and related land resource uses.

SD 97 and other recent project evaluation laws set the stage for introducing environmental impact assessment into the decision-making process. It remains for the National Environmental Policy Act to bring the intangibles into the spotlight, to introduce environment as an important concern of all agencies, and to create a procedure which allows citizens to open the government doors, both to get a look at the process of approving projects, and to walk in and have their say. The environmental impact statement (EIS) provided the handle for these doors. We can now turn to NEPA itself and examine the requirements which are intended to open them.

Creating the Process

In passing the National Environmental Policy Act of 1969 the Congress of the United States set the stage for the entire EIS process. Each state which decided to adopt an analogous law likewise set the stage within that state, as similar to or different from NEPA as that state's legislators chose to have it. As the initiators, members of Congress and state legislators played a vital role, both to give legal authority to the process and to outline the contents and procedures that must be followed. But from the moment of the initial concept, a law can undergo metamorphoses during its legislative adoption and in actual practice, until the reality that is created bears little resemblance to the original legislative intent. The original bills did not start out to create an entire new set of governmental procedures, but NEPA as finally signed created new responsibilities allowing for a great variety of interpretation.

The legislative history of NEPA is briefly reviewed in the following paragraphs. You may want to delve into the references for a more complete idea of what happened, particularly if you agree with Kenneth Boulding that "it is only as we learn the real processes of society that we can mold the future toward our present ideals" (*13*).

NEPA began as H.R. 6750, introduced by Representative John D. Dingell of Michigan, and S. 1075, supported by Senator Henry M. Jackson of Washington. H.R. 6750 called for the formation of a Council on Environmental Quality (CEQ), and required an annual report on the state of the environment. Jackson's bill was the result of work done by the Senate Interior and Insular Affairs Committee (*14*). The bill was modelled after the Employment Act of 1946, which created a council to advise the President and required an annual report on the economy (*15*).

During the initial work on the bill, there was no "action-forcing" provision, but at the public hearing in April, 1969, the committee discussed the idea of an impact statement requirement with Professor Lynton K. Caldwell of the University of Indiana. Supporters of the law considered that some specific action should be required of federal agencies in order that the bill be more than just environmental "motherhood" legislation. Committee witnesses referred to the 1969 Santa Barbara oil spill from offshore wells operating under Department of the Interior leases and other events to make the point that governmental policies and activities have contributed to environmental degradation.

The first version of Section 102 of NEPA (see Chapter 8, Part 2) was drafted by Jackson's committee staff and counsel. Few members of Congress recognized the potential effects of the environmental impact statement (EIS) provision, Section 102(2)(C), although Senator Edmund S. Muskie of Maine, who was sponsoring a bill similar to Jackson's, was concerned that the section might be used by agencies to write justifications for environmentally damaging projects, and might hinder those agencies engaged in environmental improvement such as pollution control. Both concerns were reflected in changes in the wording of the bill, but are still subject to debate (*16*).

The Nixon administration did not object to Section 102, although it did oppose the creation of the Council on Environmental Quality. In July of 1969 the Senate unanimously approved the bill including Section 102. The House bill was passed in September without Section 102 as a result of the actions of Representative Wayne N. Aspinall of Colorado, who was the bill's chief opponent. The House-Senate conference committee agreed on a final form of NEPA which included the EIS provision, and reported the bill out in late December. The conference report was adopted by both houses by voice vote shortly before Christmas and Public Law 91-190 was signed by the President on New Year's Day, 1970. Only a few of the legislators appeared to have appreciated the potential of the law (*17*).

Although without the legislators there would have been no law, in terms of the results the legislators played a minor role compared with the executive and judicial branches of government. This would come as no surprise to those who attempt to make changes through government action, even those who most exhaust themselves trying to get laws passed. They know that legislation is only the first step—those concerned must also watch the way it is put into action by the executive branch, from the President, who issues executive orders, to the clerk who fills out the forms. Each decision made in the often complex sequences translating a law from print to action can affect how well the intent of a law is carried out. It is appropriate to note here that three states, Michigan, New Jersey, and Texas, have EIS requirements which arose not from the legislatures, but from within their administrative branches—the first two by executive order, the last through an interagency council policy (*18*).

Therefore we can speak of the EIS process as created to a large degree by the administration of NEPA and the state requirements. Each level of administration plays its own role, emphasizing the aspects important to those administrators, filling in the gaps left in the instructions in the law, or otherwise interpreting the original requirements in order to carry out their responsibilities. For example, after NEPA was passed, the President promulgated Executive Order 11514 (*19*) in furtherance of NEPA's purpose and policy. This order assigned the responsibility for issuing guidelines for Section 102(2)(C) to the Council on Environmental Quality along with its other responsibilities as interpreted by the President's office as chief administrator. The CEQ, in writing the guidelines for federal agencies to follow, set many precedents of interpretation (such as the concept of controversiality as a criterion for deciding whether an EIS is needed), some of which were also followed by the states in writing and interpreting their own laws. But the CEQ's role has been largely advisory (*20*), leaving most of the actual interpretation to the individual agencies. This has led not only to differences in procedural matters, such as the timing of public disclosure, but also to differences in more basic conceptions of the law's meaning, including agencies' interpretations of their own missions and their definitions of significant environmental impact (*21*).

How the law is interpreted is ultimately the task of the courts. Although they must depend on individual cases brought before them, the judiciary can expand or constrain a law, often creating meanings or procedures beyond those envisioned by many of the legislators. A case in point is *Friends of Mammoth v. Mono County* in California, which expanded the California Environmental Quality Act to cover private projects requiring local permits. NEPA has been generally strengthened by the courts. For example, two views could be held about the meaning of "to the fullest extent possible" as it applies to an agency's compliance with Section 102. The phrase was originally assumed to be a compromise between Senator Jackson's desire to force action from the agencies and Congressman Aspinall's insistence that agency mandates should not be changed (*16*). It could be taken to mean either that the NEPA duties were somehow limited by an agency's original responsibilities or that NEPA was to be complied with fully unless an existing law expressly forbid full compliance or made it impossible. The courts have chosen to follow the latter, stricter interpretation of compliance.

Chapter 5 discusses the evolution of NEPA in the courts. For those readers who wish to "learn the real processes of society," legislative committee hearing reports, law review journals, publications of institutes for governmental study, environmental newsletters, or other sources can provide histories of the evolution of the state laws with which you will be involved.

As a final element in creating the framework for the EIS process, we should note the role played by the concerned public. In presenting testimony at earlier committee hearings and in supporting their representatives, the public enabled NEPA's conference committee to overcome opposition to many of the important provisions of the bills and put them into the law. Likewise, in watchdogging the administrative agencies and bringing key cases to court, citizens and their organizations played a critical role in the definition and implementation of the Act, and will probably continue to do so as long as they feel this process is necessary.

The NEPA Revolution

The National Environmental Policy Act has as its major action-forcing provision the requirement, in Section 102(2)(C), that every federal agency include in every recommendation on a planned major action a detailed statement on the environmental impact of the proposed action (see Chapter 5 for a detailed explanation). The section goes on to require that prior to making such a statement, the agency shall obtain comments of other agencies with jurisdiction or expertise on environmental impacts. Copies of the statement and comments must be made available to the public, and shall accompany the proposal through the existing review processes.

Two other sections contain notable provisions requiring agencies to do things in an unaccustomed way and to get serious about intangible values. Section 102(2)(A) directs all agencies to "utilize a systematic interdisciplinary approach which will insure the integrated use of the natural and social sciences and the environmental design arts in planning and in decision-making which may have an impact on man's environment." Section 102(2)(B) directs them to "identify and develop methods and procedures . . . which will insure that presently unquantified environmental amenities and values may be given appropriate consideration in decision-making along with economic and technical considerations." Title II of the NEPA creates the Council on Environmental Quality, which is to aid the agencies in these tasks.

What makes the Section 102 requirement—the environmental impact statement (EIS) or Section 102 statement, as it is sometimes called—so different from the provisions of other laws we have considered? At first glance it would appear not to have much effect at all, and indeed, many congressmen appeared to have thought that it would be simply a "good intentions" provision. It does not preserve anything. It does not set standards or provide for enforcement of regulations. It does not give anyone the power to stop an action if it is found environmentally damaging. It does not authorize appropriations or funds to improve projects with adverse environmental effects. It does call for evaluating the effects of government actions, but so have other laws. And yet, it has been one of the most interesting and controversial pieces of federal legislation.

Let us look for a moment at what the law requires. Chapter 5 goes into more detail, but for our purposes, we can describe Section 102's requirement as a statement, prepared by any federal agency, about the consequences of any action it intends which will have a significant effect upon the environment. The statement is to be included in any recommendation or report proposing such an action. It is intended as a tool to aid decision-makers in the normal agency review process, by giving them more information about the proposal.

The law appears to call for a three-part consideration: 1) identification of impacts and irretrievable commitments, 2) prediction of their effects, and 3) evaluation of those effects in terms of short-term gains vs. long-term losses, and the trade-offs between alternatives.

As an effort to design better fences rather than rounding up the cows already out, the EIS requirement has more in common with benefit/cost analysis than with pollution control laws. But it departs radically from project evaluation laws in the broadness of its applicability. It amplifies the concepts of SD 97 with respect to the environment and applies them to much more than just water resource projects. Along with apple pie and the American flag, everyone was concerned about the environment in the late 1960's. Congress in its enthusiasm created a mandate that fell upon every federal agency, a mandate that was added to whatever responsibilities that agency already had. It was as if the original legislation setting up each agency and assigning its duties had been taken out and amended to read: "You shall also consider your effects upon the environment in whatever we have authorized you to do."

The broad extent of the applicability of NEPA is matched by the extent of consideration that the agencies are required to give to their actions. One of the staff members of the Senate Interior Committee who helped draft Section 102 of NEPA said he had expected federal EIS's to be brief, general statements averaging about two pages in length (*17*, p. 340). But the guidelines issued by the Council on Environmental Quality and the court cases under NEPA have made it clear that the EIS as a "detailed" statement must fully explore all known consequences and alternatives—including consideration of effects and options outside the agency's actual control.

In May of 1972, after a number of key cases had been decided, the CEQ issued a memo to agencies on procedures for improving EIS's (*23*). The memo discussed four substantive issues, interpreted by the CEQ as duties of the agencies:

(*1*) duty to disclose full ranges of impacts
(*2*) duty to "balance" advantages and disadvantages of the proposed action
(*3*) duty to consider opposing views
(*4*) duty to discuss all reasonable "alternatives" to the proposed action.

In later sections we consider how broadly the word "environment" was meant to be interpreted. The court decisions, summarized in these four duties, in themselves establish NEPA as a full disclosure document. Not only must all costs and benefits be considered, including those which cannot be quantified, but all reasonable alternatives and their impacts should be included and opposing views taken into account.

Full disclosure of impacts and alternatives also meant more complete substantiation of why an agency took the action it did. Although the Council on Environmental Quality holds that the primary purpose of the 102 statement is the assessment of the environmental effects of proposed actions, the requirement to consider alternatives, particularly if they present less environmentally damaging choices, would lead one to expect some justification of the proposed project. Senator Jackson, one of the bill's sponsors, explaining the bill on the Senate floor in October of 1969, said that he expected any adverse effects which could not be avoided would be justified by some other *stated* consideration of national policy (*23*, p. 3).

The emphasis on consideration of alternatives is another revolutionary feature of NEPA, particularly as broadened by some courts to include all alternatives reasonably available to the government as a whole—even if outside the control of the agency preparing the statement. No previous law had given such a sweeping obligation even to agencies most limited in purpose. It would appear, for example, that the Department of the Interior, in writing an EIS for an offshore oil lease, should consider not only energy supply alternatives, but conservation alternatives. For example, the EIS could suggest that the Department of Defense might cut back on energy-consumptive military programs, or the Department of Housing and Urban Development might raise insulation standards for all federally-funded housing construction.

In the contemplation of alternatives to be included, the standard to be used is "reasonableness." Detailed discussion is not required of alternatives that are deemed only remote and speculative possibilities. But the requirement that they should be mentioned at all, even if they might mean basic changes in statutes or policies of other agencies, means that decision-makers can be reminded of other courses of action, perhaps often enough to begin exploring their realization.

Another value of the requirement to discuss alternatives is the potential for introducing mitigating measures into the actual project design and operation. While a bad project may not be stopped, the environmental impact study might suggest ways of heading off some of the impacts, such as by more aesthetic structural design, restoration of adjacent wildlife habitats, sediment control measures, accident prevention procedures, noise barriers, or other suggestions that can be made part of the plans or required as a condition for granting a permit. Improvements whose costs are not justified by monetary benefits are more readily eliminated from a project's budget, either in an effort to reduce overall expenditures or to make the cost-benefit equation come out more favorably. NEPA and its state equivalents have made it easier for agencies to negotiate modifications with permit applicants, and have provided a justification for environmentally aware staff to introduce such measures into their agencies' own project designs.

This attention to unquantifiable impacts as well as more measurable effects, and to broad alternatives as well as specific mitigation measures, calls into question the relationship of the EIS requirement to an agency's policies and planning in general. We treat this more thoroughly a little later in this chapter, but here the point should be made that NEPA and the state laws created planning tools for those decisions which did not already have a planning framework such as the river basin comprehensive plan mentioned above for water resource projects. The EIS can be used to examine the policies and objectives of the agency with respect to a proposal. The document can lead to the exploration of plans and programs of other agencies as well as the physical and social environment, and to the design of alternatives and their evaluation in order to formulate the best approach. In essence, all of these actions are the planning process itself, particularly when all alternatives are given equal value from the beginning (as the Army Corps of Engineers sometimes does, (*32*)) and a particular project is decided upon only after the evaluation is complete. When the EIS is used in this way, the results might be that projects arising from special interests, or conceived narrowly to solve a specific problem, would have to be put in a larger perspective related to the agency's own objectives, and compared with the plans and objectives of other authorities. Other options would have to be compared with any one proposal, and their environmental aspects assessed in a document made available for the public to scrutinize.

The environmental impact document can serve not only the function of planning, but that of educating the agencies themselves, and of creating cooperative arrangements for comparison of goals and programs. Staff members who already feel that their functions take the environment into sufficient account, and who fight in many cases to avoid what they see as merely additional work, are missing the implications of the EIS process for improving decisions. But many employees feel frustrated by their lack of ability to translate their environmental concerns into action within their responsibilities and welcome the opportunity to learn more about the environmental effects of what they do and about how they can bring those considerations into their work. In-house training courses, professional or university extension programs, and other means have enabled them to bring a more comprehensive understanding to their jobs. The requirement for an interdisciplinary approach has often led to the hiring of personnel with more diverse backgrounds, providing a much richer experience within the agency. The consultation provisions bring staff members of different agencies into contact, allowing for sharing of information and for better appreciation of the diverse responsibilities and levels of expertise of federal, state, and local governments and their agencies.

Of course, not all this planning, education, and cooperation actually takes place. The Sierra Club, for example, has accused the Forest Service of making commitments on its timber sales but postponing a complete evaluation of the environmental impact of a sale (*24*), thus preventing the environmental study from aiding the Service in its land-planning. Depending on the attitudes and the backgrounds of staff and administrators, the new concepts may be readily incorporated, or they may be ignored for as long as the agency can avoid being detected. For example, many federal agencies have been ignoring the section of NEPA requiring EIS's on recommendations for legislation. The Environmental Protection Agency, for one, was accused by the National Resources Defense Council of violating NEPA by not completing EIS's on two suggested amendments to the Federal Water Pollution Control Act which were sent to

Congress in October of 1974. EPA decided to resubmit the proposals and stated the intentions of complying with NEPA *(25)*.

Cooperation among agencies on related issues is hindered by the single-issue focus of government problem-solving, which has allowed departments to evolve their own separate ideologies, methodologies, and programs. Resistance to coordination also occurs within a given agency, both from a lack of desire to change the status quo and from a territorial defensiveness reflecting the bureaucratic survival instinct *(26)*. On a more pragmatic level, planning, consultation, and coordination are not always fully implemented due to lack of time, money, or personnel.

But the final revolutionary aspect of NEPA is one that works against any bureaucratic lack of enthusiasm—the encouragement the Act gives to public participation and the creation of an instrument of citizen challenge to government decisions. Although citizen participation requirements were strengthened during the 1960's in the Bureau of Land Management, Forest Service, Army Corps of Engineers, Housing and Urban Development, and other agencies, NEPA wrote into the law the requirement that an environmental impact statement and comments upon it shall be made available to the public, removing any bureaucratic discretion regarding this public access. The guidelines to NEPA say that their procedures "are designed to encourage public participation in the impact statement process at the earliest possible time" *(22,* Section 1500.9(d)). Agencies should facilitate the comment of public and private organizations by announcing the availability of draft EIS's* and making copies available to those who request an opportunity to comment. Methods should be devised for publicizing the existence of statements, by newspaper notices, for example, or by the maintenance of a list of interested groups. Only actual reproduction costs can be charged to citizens requesting copies of a document. Sufficient review periods are to be established for draft and Final EIS's *(22,* Section 1500.11(b)). All substantive comments including those of citizens as well as other agencies should be attached to the final statement *(22,* Section 1500.10(a)).

An increased role for the public was created also in an indirect sense. Besides participation in the document preparation or review, NEPA gave the public a way for going into court and challenging a project on the grounds of an inadequate EIS, or lack of any environmental review. The courts have traditionally been hesitant to rule on agency decisions made in the course of the

---

* A draft EIS refers to the first working draft of the report, or part of it, not necessarily ready for circulation in public hearings. A Draft EIS with a capital "D" refers to the document released for circulation, comment, and public hearings. A Final EIS is capitalized because it is always ready for such release.

agency's lawful administrative responsibilities, unless an abuse of discretion or arbitrary or capricious behavior can be shown. This attitude still has force in deciding whether an agency acted correctly in approving a project despite adverse impacts revealed in an EIS, as long as all procedures were followed. But the EIS requirement allows citizens to raise legal questions before the final decision—to challenge whether an EIS should have been prepared in cases where the law appears to have been ignored, and to question the scope of what has been taken into account by challenging the adequacy of the statement. The role of the citizen and that of the courts is discussed further in Chapter 5. Although citizen participation can be time-consuming and costly, the new public roles created by NEPA have allowed many more individuals and groups to watchdog government actions, and help make the process more balanced.

In summary, the effects of NEPA cannot be fully evaluated for several more years. Although the law was passed in a short time, the revolution requires changes in people's attitudes as well as in their legal responsibilities, and such changes do not come about quickly. We can summarize by saying that the full realization of NEPA as an aid to the decision-making process will lead us toward:

(*1*) environmental consideration as part of *all* governmental actions

(*2*) full disclosure of all impacts of a proposal

(*3*) methods of taking into account non-quantifiable costs and benefits in our decisions

(*4*) attention to a wide range of alternatives to any one action

(*5*) encouragement of mitigation measures as part of a project's design

(*6*) better substantiation of an agency's decisions

(*7*) systematic and interdisciplinary approaches to problem-solving

(*8*) more attention to planning and closer scrutiny of agencies' planning processes

(*9*) education of agencies and their personnel with regard to environmental concerns

(*10*) more interagency cooperation

(*11*) better avenues for public participation and more awareness by decision-makers of the public interest

The Value of NEPA

Before turning to the operation of impact assessment, it would seem appropriate to present the reader with an example of a situation where the values of NEPA that we have been recounting are rather clearly illustrated. In this case, an early EIS would have prevented a series of faulty decisions causing a major waste of time and money, and the possibility of abandoning an already completed facility.

In western Marin County, California, the small community of Pt. Reyes Station sits at the south end of Tomales Bay, a unique long narrow estuary lying in a depression created by the San Andreas earthquake fault (see map, Fig. 1-1). The United States Coast Guard has established two radio communication centers in the area, a transmitting station on nearby Pt. Reyes National Seashore and a receiving station on the coast 17 miles south. In search of an equidistant housing site for the personnel assigned to the facilities, the Coast Guard selected a parcel just south of the town of Pt. Reyes Station. The housing site they chose is adjacent to Lagunitas Creek, which flows west and north, joining Olema Creek to form the major fresh water supply for the south end of Tomales Bay. The flood plains of these creeks, measured at the 100-year flood level, extend fairly far back from their banks, and flooding of the property along the creeks is not an uncommon occurrence.

The project was to house forty-one single men and thirty-six families (170 new residents, or half again the town's population) in dormitory and multiple family type housing. The access road led directly to Pt. Reyes Station's "downtown"—the stretch of Coastal Highway One that serves as the main street for local shopping and weekend visitor needs. The Coast Guard entered into negotiations with the North Marin County Water District (NMCWD), which serves the town for water supply and sewage treatment. Sketches of the housing project's design were published in the local paper in August of 1971. The design was later downgraded because of budget shortages, but the final plans were not given local publicity.

In January of 1972, unknown to the citizens concerned, the Coast Guard had produced a negative declaration saying there would be no adverse impacts, based on what they called a draft environmental impact statement for the housing project. The totally inadequate four-page "statement" ignored potential impacts on the community such as weekend traffic problems, or impacts that might be projected because the 100-year flood line crossed the housing construction site. The effects of sediment run-off (particularly from construction) or potential pollutants from the project were not mentioned, despite the fact that eutrophication or pollution could affect the creek's sport-fish breeding productivity and the valuable wildlife habitat (under consideration at the time and now preserved as a state refuge) formed by the marshlands and mudflats at the south end of Tomales Bay. Fish and wildlife impacts were not mentioned at all. But most important was the assumption that the Coast Guard could proceed with the housing construction with no study of a sewage disposal facility.

With only unorganized citizens and county staff expressing concern, the Coast Guard broke ground on the project in July of 1972, after signing a contract with NMCWD for a sewage treatment plant to be completed by December of that year. One member of the water district board voted against the contract, citing a lack of study of the impacts of placing a sewage treatment plant within a flood plain and an earthquake fault zone. In addition, the facility was to be sized to handle potential growth in the area, and plans included the possibility of making a deal with a developer to locate the plant on his property in exchange for treatment capacity to handle a controversial second-home development. Indeed, some townspeople wanted additional capacity. Many of their homes were operating on faulty septic systems polluting the Bay, and hookup to the plant was seen as one way out of the problem.

Pressure was building within the community and among county-wide conservation groups for a closer look at the entire project. The freshly completed Tomales Bay Environmental Study (27) gave the citizens and county staff a great deal of knowledge about their area with which to raise questions. The water district was aware that it had a problem on its hands, as evidenced by correspondence with the County Public Works Department in August of 1972. The Department recommended that the sewage treatment plant not be located where proposed, because construction of levees for the treatment plant would increase the level and extent of flooding in the surrounding area, and any breach in the levees, from flood or earthquake, would create a health hazard by dumping sewage into the creek and onto surrounding properties.

The Coast Guard's negative declaration came to light in August. By September a coalition of Pt. Reyes Station residents, conservation groups, and the maverick NMCWD director had determined to file suit to force either the Coast Guard or the water district to prepare an EIS on the sewage treatment plant. No statement had been prepared prior to the contract signature. This could be seen as a violation of the California requirements on the part of the water district, or of the federal requirements on the part of the Coast Guard. Each agency said the statement was the responsibility of the other.

The water district, being more responsive to local concerns, finally agreed to prepare an environmental impact report under the California law, and hired a consulting firm. Meanwhile the housing project was completed and occupied, with sewage being trucked out. During the construction it took vigilance and pressure from the citizens, their lawyer, the county environmental planner, and the local Fish and Game warden to move earth piles left next to the creek after construction and to get the exposed soil mulched before the winter rains began—a mitigation measure that could have been built into the project from the start had adequate environmental review been done on the housing project.

The environmental impact report showed that the site chosen for the sewage treatment plant was under water at times during the year. Alternative locations sought by the water district staff to meet their contract requirements were ruled out by geologic or soil constraints, and were often so far from the housing location that extensive and expensive piping would have to be laid. The Coast Guard was trucking sewage by this time at a cost of $750 a week to the nearest treatment plant. It was becoming increasingly clear that there was no local site for the plant as designed, and that the contract should never have been signed by NMCWD.

The water district and its consultants attempted to redesign the project to fit the conditions. To add to their burden, the voters of California had in 1972 created the Coastal Zone Conservation Commission, whose regional board had jurisdiction over most of the area in which this project was proposed, and who objected to the visual impact of the high levees needed to prevent infiltration of flood waters. The Commission rejected the project in September, 1974.

A project that was at first estimated to cost $125,000 spent over $130,000 for studies alone. Total cost for the project was estimated three years later as $687,000. The Coast Guard continues its trucking, and may be forced to abandon the housing unless it can join in a new sewage treatment effort between the water district and the town, or find another solution. NMCWD now has tough environmental impact reporting regulations.

The observance of NEPA would have brought to the Coast Guard's decision-making process the benefits of better planning and more thorough consideration that we set forth in the preceding section of this chapter. The first step in environmental impact assessment is a description of the proposed action and the affected environment sufficient to permit an assessment of potential impacts (*22*, Section 1500.8(a)(1)). If the Coast Guard had made that attempt as part of the planning process, a better definition of the project would have emerged early in the work as "housing plus sewage treatment facility." Full disclosure of the environmental setting would have revealed the fault zone and flood plain limitations, and would have shown the relation of wildlife habitat and the community and its facilities to any proposals. Sites could then have been surveyed keeping the dual aspect of the project and the local constraints in mind. Freed from the necessity of having the treatment plant close enough for pipeline connection to an already committed settlement, a far greater range of alternative locations could have been considered. In fact, with a clear description of the plant's requirements and knowledge of the surroundings, a screening procedure would have eliminated the impossible locations, and property choices then could have been made within the remaining area based on housing site requirements. Mitigation measures, such as sediment control, could have been specified in the project design and not left up to the perseverance of local authorities—consultation with those authorities before the project's approval would have occurred had NEPA been followed.

And lastly, participation by the affected citizens, in more than just design review, might have turned up some of the problems and allayed some of the fears that divided the townspeople's opinions on the project, and drove the conservationists to seek legal aid. Citizen knowledge could have been used to help in the total project-planning and the financial and personal embarrassment of the Coast Guard and NMCWD would have been avoided.

Having made the point of the present and potential value of NEPA and the resulting state laws, and some of their revolutionary aspects as seen from the perspective of past environmental regulation, we can turn now to a consideration of how impact assessment operates.

EIS and Decision-making

The National Environmental Policy Act and similar laws passed by a number of states have required the impact assessment process to be embodied in the form of an environmental impact statement (EIS) or environmental impact report (EIR). Here we use the abbreviation "EIS" to refer to environmental impact statements in general. We will use "EIR" when discussing those states that require environmental impact reports. An EIS typically contains:

(*1*) description of the proposed action, including its objectives

(*2*) description of the setting—the environment as it exists prior to the proposed change

(*3*) identification and prediction of the impacts that might occur as a result of the action

(*4*) description of alternatives to the proposed action

(*5*) evaluation of the impacts in terms of adverse effects, irreversible commitments, or other discussions as required by law

(*6*) comments of other agencies on the proposal

Chapter 8, Part 5, contains a sample table of contents for an EIS prepared under NEPA. Chapter 5 contains a discussion of the requirements of the law, both federal and state.

The federal and state laws also mandate the kinds of actions that must be assessed. Fulfilling the legal requirements is generally a prerequisite to gaining necessary approval or funding for a project that comes under the law. EIS's might be required for only a government's construction projects, such as roads or dams, or for programs such as pest control or park management plans. Private actions which need federal government sanction, such as offshore oil drilling which requires a federal lease, are covered by NEPA. Some states extend their requirement for impact assessment of private actions to the local government level, requiring an EIS on, for example, a private housing development which needs a city or county permit.

For each kind of action covered by law, a government employee or an appointed or elected official must make a decision about whether or not the action should take place. The next section describes some of the government decision procedures and the role the EIS plays. Impact assessment is intended to aid the decision-maker by giving him or her a more complete idea of the effects of a choice—looking not only at the intended benefits which are the reason the action was proposed, but also at any other effects, intended or not, that will occur on the surroundings and on other plans and proposals. Chapters 2 and 3 go into the two broad areas in which information on impacts might be given to the decision-makers: the natural environment and the socio-economic environment.

The government agency responsible for approving the proposal may do the impact assessment or may contract it out to consultants. Private developers may be allowed to submit an EIS, but the public agency is generally held responsible for the contents of the document. In addition to EIS's done to satisfy legal requirements, developers or their employees, architects, planners, engineers, and others who propose or design projects may do some form of impact assessment to aid their design decisions. Private citizens or environmental groups sometimes do their own studies when they question a government agency's conclusions. Most often, an EIS is not completely done by one person because it requires the input of people from a variety of backgrounds to cover all the possible significant impacts. In addition to a generalist who might direct or pull together the entire study, contributors could include a geologist, soil scientist, hydrologist, biologist, sound engineer, landscape architect, sociologist, or economist. Chapter 6 considers who actually does an EIS and how it is done.

Impact assessment is usually done as a one-time procedure in response to a specific proposal. But as a part of the decision-making process, it can also be seen as one aspect of planning—that is, as a procedure that can occur before a specific project is selected for focus. Impact assessment is a step in problem-solving: it provides the study of side effects and how they should influence decisions. When you want to solve a problem or achieve a goal, the desired results are usually in mind. But resources may be wasted if the action you choose doesn't have the desired effect. And every action has effects other than those wanted—sometimes trivial, such as displacing a few air molecules, sometimes major, such as destroying a regional ecosystem. If the latter were the case, you might want to compare the effects of that action with alternative ways of reaching your goal, or to evaluate the importance of the goal by considering whether the side effects are serious enough to cancel the project. Impact assessment, therefore, in its most systematic form, raises a set of questions:

(*1*) What is the need and what are the goals?

(*2*) How well will a given action or each of several alternative actions meet the desired goals?

(*3*) What effects other than the desired ones will occur as a result of each potential choice?

(*4*) Will these other effects be desirable or not, and how should they count in making the decision to carry out a specific action?

We first referred to impact assessment as a process. A process is a sequence of behavior that constitutes a system and has a goal-producing function (a system is a set of interrelated elements) (*28*). Impact assessment is a process in several senses. The goals can be considered as: a) a product—a document which reports the findings of the study; b) an action—the decision made on the basis of answering the questions posed above; and c) an improved process—the environmental decision-making process, whose many individual goals aim toward the long-term objective of improving the relationship between humans and their environment.

We now turn to decision-making itself and consider governmental authority over public and private activities which employ the EIS as a tool.

Government Actions

The reader should have a good idea of where impact assessment is used in the decision-making processes of American government in order to prepare useful documents. Of necessity, this section will have to be expressed in examples and generalities. The separate states in their historical development have evolved a variety of structures of local authority. State governments themselves group their functions into a variety of departmental organizations. Since this is not a text in comparative government, we attempt only to give the reader a general picture of the kinds of decisions made at different levels of government which can require impact assessment. You are urged to become acquainted with the specific agencies of the state, local, or federal government that you will be dealing with, and to use this section as a guide to explore the decisions that your involvement with impact assessment will affect.

The two primary questions to ask in sorting out government activities with respect to the EIS process and the decision procedures to be followed are:

(*1*) Which body of government is carrying out or approving the action?

(*2*) Who will be funding the activity?

The answer to the first can be a federal or state agency, a local general-purpose government (i.e., a county or city) or its agencies, or any of an assortment of possible special governmental bodies. Examples of special agencies are a multi-state agency such as the Tahoe Regional Planning Agency (created by a California-Nevada compact consented to by Congress (*29*)), a regional government or special-purpose agency within a state such as a council of governments or a regional transit district, a state-authorized district such as a water or utility district, or a local special-purpose authority such as a school board. We are here using "agency" very generally to cover agencies, bureaus, departments, boards, commissions, or other subunits of governmental authority.

All the state laws, like NEPA, require impact assessment for projects or major actions carried out directly by their state agencies, although a law may be limited to specific agencies. Texas' law, for example, applies only to the agencies which are members of the Interagency Council for Natural Resources and the Environment. The Virginia law is limited to construction projects proposed by the executive branch of the state which costs over $100,000, but this law excludes highway and road projects (*7*). The majority of the states have applied their requirements to all their state agencies, but only a few, for example California, Massachusetts, and Washington, have extended the law to local governments as well.

The second question above can be answered by considering whether the activity is publicly or privately financed. If it is publicly financed, one agency may be carrying out the project but another level of government may be involved in the funding, in which case the funding agency's regulations may apply. For example, a state without its own EIS requirement may still have to prepare an impact assessment for a highway project funded in part by the federal government. Those states whose EIS requirements are not applied to local agencies do require an impact statement for state-assisted government projects. Privately financed projects requiring EIS's are those not carried out by a government but which require some form of government approval: lease, permit, license, etc. Those states which extend the EIS requirement to the local government level also require EIS's on private activities approved by local bodies. A number of states mandate EIS's on private activities which require state agency approval. If a privately funded activity requires an EIS before approval, usually a sequence of decision procedures prevails which is somewhat different from those applicable to the approving agency's own actions. It is not always clear from the state laws or executive orders to what extent EIS requirements do in fact apply to local governments or private actions. Texas, Virginia, and Indiana laws definitely do not apply to private actions; other states may have ambiguous requirements which will have to be settled in the courts, as California did in *Friends of Mammoth*, noted previously.

The variety of decision procedures that we are discussing arises from the activity breakdown which is illustrated for the states in Fig. 1-2. You are encouraged to identify which situations require EIS's in your state, and to review the way in which the appropriate agencies make their decisions. It should be noted that there are a few local authorities which have passed EIS-type requirements on their own, notably New York City.

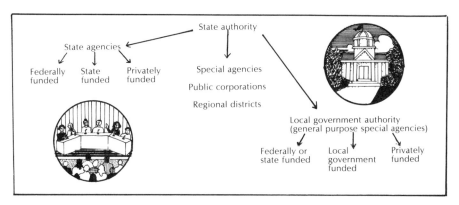

Fig. 1–2 Activities which may require EIS under state or local authority.

Before turning to agency procedures, a last point should be made about types of government and the activity of planning. In referring to a city, county, or similar local government we speak of a general-purpose government since it has the responsibility of a variety of functions. Within it may be several departments with more single-purpose functions, such as a health department or public works department. Somewhat equivalent to the general-purpose government is the multi-purpose state and federal agency which has the task of balancing a number of objectives, such as the United States Forest Service which must provide for recreation, watershed protection, and grazing as well as timber production. General-purpose governments and multi-purpose agencies usually prepare plans (and in the case of local governments, zoning ordinances which correspond to the plans) which are not projects in the strict sense, but describe the over-all goals for an area and how they should be met. In some cases the adoption of a plan or zoning ordinance is thought of as a separate government activity which, if carried out, could have environmental impacts which ought to be assessed before making a final decision. Therefore, EIS's have been required, for example, on Forest Service plans for a national forest and on local general plans and the enactment or amendment of zoning ordinances in California. In summary, public projects, private project approval, planning, and zoning are the basic types of decision processes in which EIS may play a part.

Agency Procedures

Agencies differ not only in the kinds of decisions that they make but also in the degree of complexity of their procedures from initiation to documentation to final decision. We will look at two examples, a federal agency's projects and local government private project approval, and deduce from them some general aspects of procedures to look for in studying any one agency.

Federal Agency Projects—Army Corps of Engineers

The Army Corps of Engineers makes major changes in the environment, but most are preceded by years of pre- and post-authorization procedural requirements. Nonmilitary water resource projects are usually initiated at the local level by a group of citizens who call a problem such as flooding or shoreline erosion to the attention of one of their congressional representatives. The representative consults with the Senate or House Public Works Committee and a resolution is introduced in Congress asking that part of the Corps' budget be applied to pre-authorization planning for this problem. The appropriate district office of the Corps would then typically spend several years, depending on the size of the project, preparing a pre-authorization study or survey report which goes up the Corps hierarchy for approval and eventually to Congress with a request for project authorization. The trip through Congress may take one or two years; if the project is large it must wait for the omnibus rivers and harbors or flood control bill which is introduced every two years.

After Congress has authorized the project, the Corps' district office goes through two phases of post-authorization study. Phase One reviews and updates the survey report, since enough years may have elapsed for new conditions to exist, both in terms of the definition of the problem and in terms of the response of the public to the proposed solution. Assuming that Phase One leaves the initial project intact, Phase Two calls for the detailed engineering plans and specifications necessary to go to contract. Projects can take from five to seventeen years from initiation to construction, depending upon their complexity and size. Shorter procedures apply to smaller projects, particularly those sponsored by local public agencies under the Chief of Engineers' small-projects authority, which may take from three to five years.

Where in all this does the Section 102 requirement come into play? The established procedures for survey report EIS's are outlined in Fig. 1-3. The local Corps of Engineers District Engineer's office is normally responsible for the decisions about compliance with EIS requirements. An environmental assessment is done by environmental planners in the District Engineer's office based on an environmental inventory and an assessment of economic, social, and environmental effects as required by the 1970 Rivers and Harbors Act (*30*). The District Engineer's office circulates a working paper and also directs the public meetings which obtain input for a Draft EIS. After the Draft EIS is circulated to government agencies and the public, it goes with the survey report (the Corps' basic decision-making document) to the Division Engineer's office, which is the next step up in the Corps' hierarchy for both civil and military engineering projects. Copies of the Draft EIS also go to the CEQ at this stage, to begin the discussion period.

The Draft EIS and the survey report are reviewed last by the Corps' Board of Engineers for Rivers and Harbors and the office of the Chief of Engineers. The Chief's Office works with the local District Engineer to prepare a revised Draft EIS, circulate it again for review (including to the CEQ), and prepare the Final EIS. This is submitted to the office of the Secretary of the Army and then to the federal Office of Management and Budget with the Chief's report on the project. After receipt of any comments from the Office of Management and Budget, the Secretary's office sends the Final EIS to the CEQ and to the Congress with the final report on the project. The District Engineer's office takes care of public distribution of the Final EIS.

The Corps' EIS process occurs during the initial planning stages before authorization, is updated during Phase One, if necessary, and is considered done by the time detailed plans are being drawn up for the project. However, in the past, well documented cases (*31*) show that the Corps has had to modify its plans due to insufficient initial study, in many cases returning to Congress for money beyond the amount specified in the benefit/cost estimate—all of which implies a need for on-going study. In the Warm Springs Dam case (see Chapter 4), where an EIS was prepared for a project authorized before NEPA was passed, serious environmental questions were raised, indicating that the Corps' present use of the impact assessment process could help correct the deficiencies of pre-NEPA studies, at least for non-engineering issues. However, the lawsuit on the inadequacies of the Warm Springs EIS showed that the Corps, like any agency, is open to challenge on the thoroughness and extent of its considerations, and that its procedures can be delayed even years if the adequacy of the EIS is questioned.

The decision procedures of the Corps have evolved in the last decade. For example, in 1967 the Corps' west coast district engineers began to make a point of meeting with conservation groups, recreation clubs, and others at the beginning of a project study. In part this was to identify and head off potential controversies, but it also served to broaden the perspective of the agency on its narrowly defined projects which respond to the concerns of specific interests. In 1969 these meetings became a mandatory liaison program. Efforts to develop new methodologies have been undertaken to try to improve the EIS process and meet NEPA Sections 102(2)(A) and (B). For example, the Corps has investigated a technique of surveying and presenting citizen and agency opinions in a "pro/con" format for evaluating alternatives, such as for small-boat harbors in Elliot Bay, Washington (*32*).

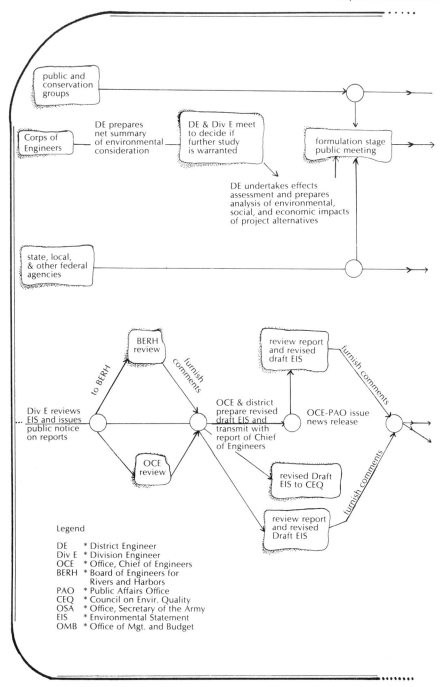

Fig. 1–3 Army Corps of Engineers' "Flow Chart for Environmental Impact Statement" with "Survey Report."

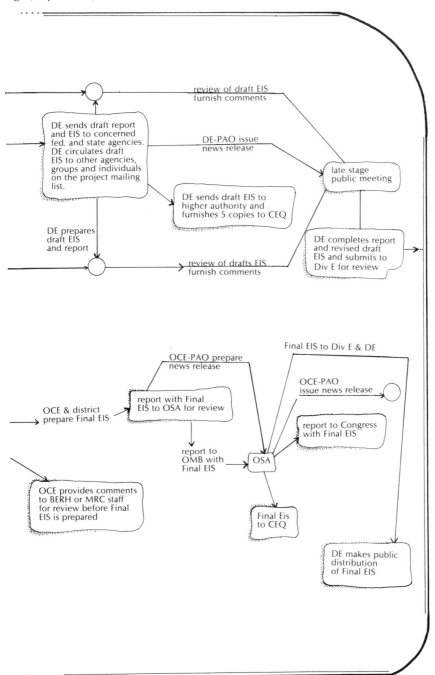

review of draft EIS
furnish comments

DE sends draft report and EIS to concerned fed. and state agencies. DE circulates draft EIS to other agencies, groups and individuals on the project mailing list.

DE-PAO issue news release

late stage public meeting

DE sends draft EIS to higher authority and furnishes 5 copies to CEQ

DE prepares draft EIS and report

DE completes report and revised draft EIS and submits to Div E for review

review of drafts EIS furnish comments

Final EIS to Div E & DE

OCE-PAO prepare news release

OCE-PAO issue news release

OCE & district prepare Final EIS

report with Final EIS to OSA for review

report to Congress with Final EIS

report to OMB with Final EIS

OSA

OCE provides comments to BERH or MRC staff for review before Final EIS is prepared

Final Eis to CEQ

DE makes public distribution of Final EIS

We note that the Corps solicits the views of interested citizens and holds hearings for input. Unfortunately the Corps often relies upon interest groups for environmental information, which places the burden of proof on those concerned. Although this gives them the opportunity for involvement, it is rare that a citizen group can find the time, money, and information to compete with detailed engineering studies. Expert friends or members of such groups could easily be hesitant about committing their professional reputations without the ability to do the necessary studies.

Private Projects—Local General-Purpose Government

The above comments on the Corps of Engineers are presented not as a thorough critique of its EIS and decision-making processes, but to illustrate some of the aspects of those processes of which you should be aware (*33*). A second example of the use of impact assessment quite different from that of the Corps shows that there are common considerations despite the variety of projects or agencies. We take the case of a private action approval under a general-purpose government such as a city or county, and put it in the most general terms to indicate some of the possible variations.

Private projects frequently undergo a three-stage approval process. There is usually an initial review by the staff of departments within that government, such as a planning department (zoning conformance), public health office (sanitation, water supply), public works (access requirements), building inspection (structural codes), or various combinations and permutations of these functions if such requirements (or others) have been adopted. Small communities may have a single official in charge of one or many of these duties. The staff usually notifies the applicant of other agencies whose permission may be required (water district, air pollution district, coastal zone commission, etc.). Some permits may be required before the local government gives its approval; others may require the local government go-ahead first.

In addition to staff, there may be an appointed board which reviews the project, such as a planning commission, a board of zoning adjustments, or an architectural review commission. After hearing recommendations from the staff, this board decides whether to recommend approval or denial to the elected officials who have final authority, such as a board of supervisors or city council. The lower board may have been delegated some authority to make the decisions, with the question being passed to the higher board only if there is an appeal of the first decision. Or there may be a staff person, such as a zoning administrator, who handles minor matters with appeal to the appointed or elected boards. The variations are multiple.

Environmental considerations may begin before the government ever sees a piece of paper, if the applicant has done some study of the proposed site and the project's effects. This may be done for the practical purposes of better design, a more saleable product, or greater ease in getting through the permit process, but there are a growing number of environmentally-conscious developers who do look beyond their immediate profit.

The local government usually begins environmental considerations the moment the application is handed in. The staff or the applicant may be required to answer "yes" or "no" to a short list of questions or to fill out an elaborate information form. This step, and each of the others to follow, are set forth in the government's procedures, which might be an adopted ordinance, resolution, or set of regulations which the offices must follow.

The initial determination of whether this application is an activity covered by the law, whether it is exempt on any grounds, and whether there is significant impact calling for an environmental statement, can be made by an official of the department that first receives the application, or a questionnaire may be circulated among several departments, or there may be a special office set up within that government to handle the environmental statement procedures at various stages. For example, the department which receives the application may be responsible for deciding whether the project is exempt, and if it is not, the application may go to an office of environmental quality or an environmental administrator for a decision on the need for an EIS. If the project is considered not to have significant impact, a "negative declaration" may be required; if such a declaration is challenged, a hearing might be held by the planning commission, or an environmental hearing officer, or under some other arrangement to give the public the opportunity to show that an EIS is needed.

Similar variations in arrangements exist for the duties of deciding who will do the EIS, who will carry out the public notice procedures (and how they will be carried out), what the EIS will cost, how it will be reviewed, who will hold hearings for public comment (or whether hearings will be held), when a draft statement is ready to be called a "Final," and other procedures. Each local authority also sets the time periods for various stages of the process, with the exception of any state requirements. Specific lengths of time may be set for the initial determination, the public notification and hearing procedures, the review of the Draft EIS, the appeals process, and other stages. The reader should be sensitive to whether the timing is designed for adequate public comment or to speed the process for the developer's sake, and whether there is flexibility, depending upon the nature of the project (whether extensions can be granted, by whom and under what circumstances).

An example of a flow chart which outlines some of these arrangements is given as Fig. 1-4. The Final EIS is certified or adopted prior to approval by the appropriate body. We should point out that projects often change during the course of approval procedures, as a result of the EIS work or traditional concerns

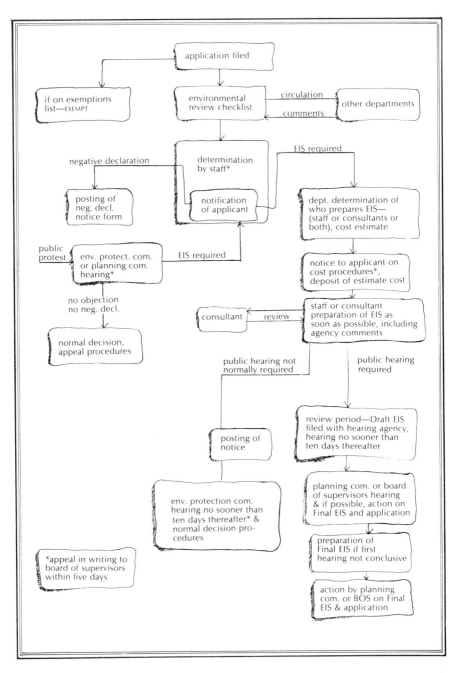

Fig. 1–4 Example of local government flow chart for private project EIS procedures.

(such as density, slope, transportation) raised by staff or the decision-making boards.

What do local general-purpose government procedures for private project approval have in common with Army Corps of Engineers procedures for water resource project authorization? We can use these examples to outline the following questions that will enable you to understand how any agency makes use of the EIS process:

(*1*) How are the following actions handled—who is responsible, what are the procedures, what time periods are involved?

    (*a*) initiation of the activity (who decides the need for the activity?)

    (*b*) initial screening for EIS requirement

        1) applicability of the law

        2) exemptions under the law

        3) significance of impact

    (*c*) decision that EIS or other study is required

    (*d*) preparing the draft document

        1) responsibility for contents

        2) actual preparation

    (*e*) public contact

        1) notices

        2) hearings

        3) availability of documents

        4) format for public input

    (*f*) in-house review

    (*g*) coordination with other agencies

    (*h*) preparing the final document(s)

    (*i*) approval of the EIS or report (at various stages)

    (*j*) approval of the activity (at various stages)

(*2*) What documentation is required?

    (*a*) nature of documentation

        1) EIS, EIR, environmental assessment

        2) staff reports

        3) other reports

    (*b*) sources of information (thoroughness, objectivity)

    (*c*) funding the studies

    (*d*) expertise of those doing the work

    (*e*) the real client of the study (the public, the decision-makers, the CEQ . . . ?)

    (*f*) when are the stages of the studies (working papers, drafts, final versions) done in relation to the stages of planning and decision-making?

(*3*) What are the monitoring and feedback arrangements? Are there any standards against which to measure the activity, or any long-term follow-up on the performance?

Question (3) above deserves elaboration as the final point of this section. In order for the decision-making systems to work for the betterment of society, there must be some way to find out whether or not the choices made actually have the effects predicted. The final step of monitoring and feedback is a weak link in our social processes because little time and money are allotted for post-decision data-gathering and evaluation, unless something goes drastically wrong. Feedback often comes as a result of irate citizens' challenging the decision in court, or suing for damages. Local governments have zoning enforcement which usually sends officials to a building site or finished project only if a complaint has been lodged. Citizens are relied on to make sure that permit conditions are being followed. Waiting for complaints or suits is a poor way to find out the results of a continual stream of decisions from governmental agencies. Many people will not complain because of lack of information, time, or desire to "get involved." Citizen action often takes money and organizational ability, and sometimes specialized knowledge of how to measure effects.

Regular public action is a nice goal for citizenship, but the day is still far in the future when any citizen has the skills and resources to rally his or her neighbors to mount effective protest against an activity which is harming them or their environment. The goal of impact assessment is to avoid after-the-decision protest, but unless we monitor the results of present decisions, we will not get a true picture of our ability to predict effects.

You have now been introduced to the EIS and to some of the decision processes which incorporate the requirements of NEPA and state laws affecting the environment. We have discussed why all this work is necessary, how the concept of impact assessment evolved, and what makes it an unusual and important process to incorporate into our already complex decision-making procedures. It is time to turn to some of the questions that these new laws have raised, and the potential for change both in the laws themselves and in the processes that they affect.

The Impact Statement in Flux

This book began as a description of what an environmental impact statement is and what should go into it. We have determined to give the reader a broader perspective, because the concept of impact assessment and impact statements is constantly evolving. Chapter 8 is included to alert you to the sources and kinds of changes that might occur. Some of these changes will go beyond the EIS itself, to affect our decision-making processes. We will discuss here two of the most far-reaching questions raised by NEPA, which illustrate the scope and potential of impact assessment to change our government's processes:

(*1*) What is the definition of environment? What kinds of impacts should be evaluated? Should we just look at the natural environment—plants and animals, soils and rocks—the biological and physical surroundings of people? Or should we go further to encompass the social and economic environment, to assess the impact of taxes and growth, of neighborhood destruction and family relocation, of the loss of relationships and the transformation of communities?

(*2*) What is the relationship of EIS to planning? Why should the assessment report be completed after the project design has been chosen? Shouldn't consideration of impacts be used to help decide the *kind* of project in the initial planning stages? Shouldn't different levels of impacts, such as regional air pollution and local traffic impact, be evaluated at different stages in a comprehensive planning process?

Definition of Environment

California's Governor Reagan vetoed in 1974 a bill which would have added an optional "economic impact statement" to the environmental impact report required under the California Environmental Quality Act, although many jurisdictions in that state had already been considering such impacts as part of their EIS's. Connecticut, Michigan, Minnesota, Montana, and Wisconsin have economic impact requirements. Others point out that economic values have always been the criteria for decision-making. The federal government has long required economic assessment in the form of benefit/cost analysis for all public works projects. NEPA requires that methods be developed to add consideration of "unquantified environmental amenities and values" to decision-making "*along with* economic and technical considerations" (Section 102(2)(B), emphasis added). Such language, it is argued, illustrates that these considerations have been the traditional basis for decisions, and therefore the EIS should focus on those environmental elements that have been ignored in the past. The federal guidelines require that an EIS deal with "changed patterns of social and economic activities" in discussing secondary impacts (*22*, Section 1500.8(a)(3)(ii)).

But courts have been more expansive. Part of the EIS's consideration, for example, can include whether the benefit/cost analysis has been correctly calculated. A court decision in Alabama disallowed a project on the basis of a NEPA case in which a recalculation, using current interest rates and a more realistic project lifetime, showed that the project would return less value than its cost (*34*). The Fifth Circuit Court in this case relied on the wording of NEPA's

Section 102(2)(B), quoted in part on page 243, and the general policy statements of Section 101 (see Chapter 8, Part 2).

Chapter 3 goes into more depth on the mandate of NEPA and its guidelines to include economic and social impacts, but for our look at the EIS in flux, let us turn for a moment to the arguments raised over the extent to which social impacts are legitimate territory for the EIS.

There are those who feel that if the word "environment" is used to include the social and economic environment, it becomes synonymous with the "good life," and loses its meaning (35). But in a sense, all natural environmental impacts are social in that they must be translated and evaluated in terms of human needs and desires. It is hard to draw the distinction between talking about nature and talking about people when your goals, according to the policy declaration of NEPA, are to "assure for all Americans safe, healthful, productive, and aesthetically and culturally pleasing surroundings" and to "maintain, wherever possible, an environment which supports diversity and variety of individual choices" (Section 101(b(2) and (4)). Indeed, the EIS requirement in Section 102 is aimed at actions "significantly affecting the quality of the *human* environment" (emphasis added).

Montana, Washington, and Wisconsin use much the same language as NEPA in their policy statements, and also include in their guidelines requirements for discussion of social impacts. For example, Wisconsin includes consideration of population distribution or concentration and effects upon public services. Wisconsin's Department of Natural Resources Guidelines for the Environmental Policy Act define environment as "the totality of conditions and influences, both natural and man-made, which surround and affect all organisms, including man" (36).

Montana construes "human environment" to include *not only* social, economic, cultural, and aesthetic factors, but also the biophysical properties of natural ecosystems (37). Montana thus reverses the emphasis of those who would limit environmental consideration to only the biophysical environment. Florida's Environmental Land and Water Management Act requires a report including impacts on the economy, public facilities, public transportation, and housing, as well as on the environment and natural resources of the region.

In California the question of social versus natural environment took a peculiar turn illustrating the confusion that can arise. The original California Environmental Quality Act of 1970 (CEQA) did not contain a definition of the environment. An early interim set of guidelines defined environment as the "totality of man's surroundings; both social and physical, both natural and man-made." But in the legislative bargaining that took place during the passage of the major CEQA-amending legislation in 1972, a much narrower definition of environment was included in the Act: "the physical conditions which exist within the area which will be affected by a proposed project" including noise and objects of historic or aesthetic significance (CEQA, Section 21060.5). However, the Secretary for Resources wrote in his cover letter accompanying California's CEQA Guidelines that a strict limitation of environmental impact to physical conditions "did not appear to be the intent of the Legislature" as reflected by the insertion of sections speaking of adverse effects on human beings and growth-inducing impacts (*38*).

As a result, those who consider themselves social planners in California look to the impact assessment requirements as one way of getting their foot in the door. It appears that what we are logically moving toward is a total impact assessment process, creating a more equitable and holistic decision-making process.

The Relation between EIS and Planning

The continuing interpretation of the meaning and intent of NEPA and the various state EIS laws are one source of change in the EIS process. Another is its relationship to planning. Planners are beginning to question the validity of the work EIS generates in relation to the over-all project-planning and decision process of which it is a part.

The paperwork, expense, and bad feeling generated by criticisms raised in an EIS after a project design is completed create a difficult atmosphere for working out changes, and limit their possibilities. A built-in project bias is almost assured, for it is unlikely that an agency would find fault with an action that presumably it had studied thoroughly. This is less true for those projects proposed by a private developer seeking approval from an agency that must certify an EIS before granting the permit. But if a developer has put time and money into the proposal, and there is no alert citizenry to raise questions, the EIS tends to be a routine report rarely examining the initial assumptions and decisions that went into the design.

NEPA and a number of the state laws, in recognition of these problems, have urged that consideration of environmental impacts begin early in the planning process. Some agencies have adopted this notion in the form of a preliminary document, an "environmental assessment," often covering several alternatives, which is completed before the decision is made as to which alternative will be the actual project on which the EIS is written. But this is not necessarily required, and the NEPA goals of full disclosure and public participation are not always met in these procedures. Although the extra work that such a document entails usually means time saved later in the EIS preparation, agencies that are not sympathetic to the goals of these laws in the first place can easily wait until after the critical project go-ahead decisions are made. At that point EIS's can be prepared which do little to question any basic problems that such decisions might inspire, as we saw in the Coast Guard housing project case.

The ideal relationship between impact assessment and planning has yet to be developed. We will raise a number of issues that will have to be resolved before a workable process is designed. It may be that no one solution will be found, but that individual procedures will depend upon the agencies involved, the kinds of projects under consideration, the state-of-the-art in environmental assessment, and other factors.

Air pollution, major traffic conditions, ground water supply or pollution, loss of wildlife habitat for certain species, and other broad-scale questions will have to be answered at a jurisdiction-wide or regional level. Questions of cumulative effect of a number of small projects cannot be adequately decided on an individual project EIS basis, although they certainly should be mentioned to alert the decision-makers. (The planners in one California county, for example, repeatedly mention in minor subdivision EIR's that each approval is adding to the gradual loss of prime agricultural land in that jurisdiction. They are hoping that the supervisors will eventually take on the question as a county planning issue and decide whether they want to preserve any such land before it is entirely paved.)

But all impacts cannot be assessed at the jurisdiction or regional level. Some are project-specific, such as the visual impact of the structural design or loss of vegetation on the site. Others require, before the regional impacts can be assessed, some idea of the nature of the projects to be built. Infiltration and run-off, for example, can vary widely depending on whether a watershed is developed with a preponderance of single-family one-acre homesites, or with more urban density multiple-unit projects which include parking lots and other impervious surfacing.

In addition, the size of the project under consideration will affect whether it should be treated in terms of jurisdiction-wide planning or local impact decision-making. A housing development of 2,000 units might require regional-level traffic impact assessment, whereas one of 20 units might have its traffic impact readily evaluated in an EIS or declared insignificant in a preliminary survey.

In multi-phase projects with several approvals required, it may be that the agency which would normally be designated the lead agency would do a report covering the broad concerns, and additional responsible agencies would add supplementary materials on specific impacts. A three-stage evaluation of this sort was ruled to be the solution in a geothermal power development case in Sonoma County, California. The county would do a "leasehold environmental assessment," covering the entire area within which geothermal leases would be granted. The State Public Utilities Commission would do an EIR on an individual power plant application and its wells as a single project. This EIR would contain less detail on the wells than on the plant because specific information about the wells would be developed at a later date by the driller and the county. When the drilling permits were submitted to the county, it would prepare a supplement to the P.U.C. EIR, containing additional information about the wells. The leasehold evaluation would consider the environmental sensitivity of the whole area and indicate the least vulnerable places for development to take place. Presumably the P.U.C.'s EIR would consider the questions of whether the power plant was needed and should be in the proposed location, whether the wells could be safely sited in the vicinity of the power plant, and what the over-all impact of well-drilling would be at this location. The county's supplement would then focus on the siting of individual wells, with the assumption that the state had considered the broader impacts in deciding to approve the project (39).

Another complication enters into our inquiry as to the relation of planning and the EIS, illustrating the complexities of decision-making. Assuming we have the basic information about an area to estimate environmental problems, in many cases we have a choice of technology or planning constraints which can change the nature of the decision. For example, stream channelization is an alternative to flood plain zoning or watershed management. A jurisdiction may rather pass the cost of channelization as a public works project on to the community as a whole than deny development in the flood plain or do the research necessary to create the standards for run-off or impervious surfacing that watershed management requires. The decision then becomes one of visual impact on the neighborhoods that the channel would cut through, the possible loss of the stream's recreational value, and the loss of stream habitats for wildlife and vegetation. The effects are shifted from future residents and those who would benefit from new development on the flood plain or in the watershed to the existing residents and the stream environment.

Clearly, what we need is a method of environmental planning that can pull all of these issues together. We will need to combine planning decisions, knowledge of carrying and recovery capacities of the environment, and project impact assessment. If this kind of environmental planning were done properly, the local jurisdictions could handle the major environmental issues at the general plan level, or perhaps at the regional level in cooperation with a regional agency. The local government could then, as a possible methodology, derive performance standards based on estimated environmental impacts at the site level and use these standards to dictate kind and intensity of development in the final permits.

California originally attempted to forgo the EIR requirement for local permits once a local jurisdiction had a "conservation element" in its general plan, but quickly realized that such elements were too general to substitute for most of the considerations covered by EIR's. Furthermore, these plans, with zoning as their major enforcement tool (and zoning for preservation, such as for open space, still subject to legal attack), lacked the kind of implementation that conservationists desired. EIS's are not direct implementation tools, but they at least allow the public to participate in individual decisions, and perhaps prevent the worst projects from taking place or insure that mitigation measures are required.

Despite all the complications we have mentioned, environmental planning does exist. Policies on environmental quality are being added to the usual statements on land use, transportation, housing, etc. Data about environmental conditions can be evaluated with respect to policies, and programs formulated to meet environmental criteria and prevent degradation, as was done in Fairfax County, Virginia (40). In the Green Spring and Worthington Valleys of Maryland, environmental constraints were used to formulate basic planning alternatives (41). In Nevada and California, the Tahoe Regional Planning Area used the basic goal of keeping Lake Tahoe blue to establish criteria for development based on erosion potential and other factors (42). Numerous other examples could be given of jurisdictions which are beginning to accumulate the basic data and establish criteria for making environmental decisions at the planning level instead of project by project.

Impact assessment is implicit in all environmental planning. To merge EIS requirements with planning more explicitly, it is suggested that different levels of impact assessment be assigned to different stages in the planning process—state, regional, local jurisdiction, site planning (43). No scheme yet proposed deals with all the problems mentioned above. The American Institute of Planners, the national professional planning organization, has begun to look into the problem as of this writing, and some proposals will undoubtedly be forthcoming.

It is beyond the scope of this book to go into environmental planning methods in detail, or to elaborate a proposal for changing the EIS. It is our role to alert you to the problems and to the potentials for change in the EIS process that efforts to solve them might bring.

Aims of This Book

The variations in meaning of "environment" and the relation of the impact statement to planning show that it would be shortsighted to focus only on the current requirements in federal and state laws. Therefore we have aimed this book to cover both the impact statement as a product you might be asked to produce and impact assessment as a process, as a contribution to the methodology of planning.

Regardless of the changes in the law, impact assessment as a procedure and a way of evaluating the effects of our actions promises to be around for a long time. We intend to prepare the reader with an appreciation of its values and pitfalls, in order that you may be able to understand its contribution wherever it may end up in the decision-making process.

Impact assessment has already produced its own terminology (see NEPA, Chapter 8, Part 2). Necessarily, and for the education of our readers, it appears in this book.

The astute reader will notice that each contributor to this book voices his or her opinion on the value and role of the impact statement process and its future. We have made no attempt to eliminate contradictions, in the belief that the assortment of ideas and attitudes expressed reflects the diversity of thinking on a new concept. No one viewpoint is necessarily correct, but by their very existence different views will influence the direction that the future of the process will take.

Notes and References

1. Anonymous. "Fish, Wildlife and Pesticides," U.S. Department of Interior, 1966. See also Woodwell, George M. "Toxic Substances and Ecological Cycles," *Scientific American*, March 1967, in *Man and the Ecosphere*, W. H. Freeman and Co., San Francisco, pp. 128–135.
2. Plass, Gilbert N. "Carbon Dioxide and Climate," *Scientific American*, July 1959, in *Man and the Ecosphere, op. cit.*, pp. 173–179.
3. Martin, Paul S. "Prehistoric Overkill," in Detwyler, Thomas (ed.), *Man's Impact on Environment*, McGraw-Hill, New York, 1971, pp. 612–624.
4. Deevey, Edward S., Jr. "The Human Population," *Scientific American*, Vol. 203, No. 3, September 1960, pp. 195–204.
5. Braidwood, Robert J. "The Agricultural Revolution," *Scientific American*, September 1960, in *Man and the Ecosphere, op. cit.*, pp. 17–25.
6. Jacobsen, Thorkild, and Robert M. Adams. "Salt and Silt in Ancient Mesopotamian Agriculture," *Science*, Vol. 128, November 21, 1958, pp. 1251–1258.
7. Marsh, George P. *Man and Nature; or, Physical Geography as Modified by Human Action*, Charles Scribner and Co., New York, 1864, revised edition, 1871.
8. Owen, Oliver S. *Natural Resource Conservation*, Macmillan Co., New York, 1971.

9. Reitze, Arnold W., Jr. *Environmental Planning: Law of Land and Resources*, North American International, Washington, D.C., 1974, pp. 10–12.

10. Gray, Oscar S. *Cases and Materials on Environmental Law*, Second Edition, Bureau of National Affairs, Washington, D.C., 1973, pp. 784–785, 988.

11. 87th Congress, Second Session. "Policies, Standards, and Procedures in the Formulation, Evaluation, and Review of Plans for Use and Development of Water and Related Land Resources," Senate Document 97, May 1972.

12. Council on Environmental Quality. *Environmental Quality—Fifth Annual Report*, Washington, D.C., December 1974, pp. 223–224.

13. Boulding, Kenneth E. *A Primer on Social Dynamics*, The Free Press, N.Y., 1970, p. 18.

14. Senate Committee on Interior and Insular Affairs and House Committee on Science and Astronautics. *Congressional White Paper on a National Policy for the Environment*, Serial T (Committee Print), Washington, D.C., October 1968.

15. Council on Environmental Quality. *Environmental Quality—Third Annual Report*, Washington, D.C., August 1972, p. 222.

16. Anderson, Frederick R. *N. E. P. A. in the Courts*, Resources for the Future, Washington, D.C., pp. 8, 9. This reference contains a good discussion of the legislative history of NEPA, especially of the policy section (Section 101) and the evolution of Section 102's provisions.

17. For a critical history, see Barfield, Claude E., and Richard Corrigan. "Environment Report/White House seeks to restrict scope of environment law," *National Journal*, Washington, D.C., February 1972, pp. 336–349.

18. Council on Environmental Quality. *Environmental Quality—Fifth Annual Report*, Washington, D.C., December 1974, pp. 401, 405.

19. Nixon, Richard. Executive Order 11514, "Protection and Enhancement of Environmental Quality," The White House, March 5, 1970.

20. The CEQ's role may be in the process of changing, however. In the case of *Warm Springs Task Force v. Lt. Gen. William C. Gribble, Jr.* (Army Corps of Engineers), Supreme Court Justice William Douglas granted a stay of construction pending appeal largely on the grounds of the CEQ's objections to the adequacy of the EIS (June 17, 1974).

21. Andrews, Richard N. L. "Environmental Policy and Administrative Change: The National Environmental Policy Act of 1969—1970–71," unpublished doctoral dissertation, Department of City and Regional Planning, University of North Carolina, 1972.

22. Council on Environmental Quality. "Preparation of Environmental Impact Statements: Guidelines," *Federal Register*, Vol. 38, No. 147, August 1, 1973, pp. 20550–20562. Everyone who works with EIS's should obtain a copy of the latest "Guidelines." The CEQ is located at 722 Jackson Place, N.W.,

Washington, D.C. 20006. The *Federal Register* can be found in most metropolitan libraries.

23. Council on Environmental Quality. "Memorandum to Federal Agencies on Procedures for Improving Environmental Impact Statements," Washington, D.C., May 16, 1972.

24. Bennett, Joel, and Gordon Robinson. "Afognak—Unique and Threatened," *Sierra Club Bulletin*, Vol. 59, No. 10, November–December 1974, p. 27.

25. National Wildlife Federation. *Conservation Report*, No. 37, November 29, 1974, p. 499. For a good discussion of how bureaucracies can distort the law in environmental issues, see: Moorman, James. "Bureaucracy v. the Law," *Sierra Club Bulletin*, Vol. 59, No. 9, October 1974, pp. 7 ff.

26. Henning, Daniel H. *Environmental Policy and Administration*, American Elsevier Publishing Co., Inc., New York, 1974, Chapter 3, "The Environmental Administrative Process."

27. *Tomales Bay Environmental Study—A Compendium of Reports*, prepared by Ruthann Corwin for the Conservation Foundation and others, published by Audubon Canyon Ranch, Marin County, California, 1972.

28. Ackoff, Russell L. "Towards a System of Systems Concepts," *Management Science*, Vol. 17, No. 11, July 1971, pp. 662 and 666. See also Chapter 2.

29. 91st Congress. "Tahoe Regional Planning Compact," Public Law 91–148, December 18, 1969.

30. Department of the Army, Office of Chief of Engineers. "Preparation and Coordination of Environmental Statements," Regulation No. 1105-2-507, Washington, D.C., April 15, 1974.

31. Morgan, Arthur. *Dams and other Disasters—A Century of the Army Corps of Engineers in Civil Works*, Porter Sargent Publications, Boston, 1971, especially pp. 34–36.

32. U.S. Army Corps of Engineers. "Public Brochure: Alternatives and their Pros and Cons, Small-Boat Harbors, Seattle Harbor, Elliot Bay, Seattle, Washington," Seattle District Corps of Engineers, April 1971.

33. Several studies of NEPA and the federal agency decision-making process are cited in the CEQ's *Fifth Annual Report*, cited above, pp. 386–387.

34. *Montgomery v. Ellis*, 364 Fed. Sup. 517.

35. Hagman, Donald G. "NEPA-like State Laws—A Description and a Critique," University of California, Los Angeles Law School, Los Angeles, 1973, p. 53.

36. Department of Natural Resources. "Guidelines for the Environmental Policy Act," Wisconsin, 1973.

37. Montana Environmental Quality Council. "Revised Guidelines to Implement the Montana Environmental Policy Act," 1973.

38. Livermore, Norman. Cover letter accompanying "Guidelines for Implementa-

tion of the California Environmental Quality Act of 1970," Resources Agency, Sacramento, February 5, 1973.

39. *The California EIR Monitor*, Vol. 1, No. 23, October 21, 1974, Resources Agency, Sacramento, pp. 1–2, discusses this example but neglects the leasehold EIR which Sonoma County had prepared.

40. Office of Comprehensive Planning. *Growth, Change and the Environment: The Environmental Planning Process*, Fairfax County Planning Dept., Virginia, 1974.

41. McHarg, Ian. *Design with Nature*, Doubleday/Natural History Press, Garden City, New York, 1969, Chapter 8, "A Response to Values."

42. Tahoe Regional Planning Agency. *The Plan for Lake Tahoe*, Advisory Planning Commission's Subcommittee Plan, South Lake Tahoe, California, August 1971.

43. Sedway, Paul H. "The Environmental Impact Report—Time for an Overhaul," *Cry California*, California Tomorrow, San Francisco, Summer 1974. Twiss, Robert H. "Linking the EIS to the Planning Process," in Dickert, Thomas, and Katherine Domeny (eds.), *Environmental Impact Assessment: Guidelines and Commentary*, University Extension, University of California, Berkeley, 1974. Corwin, Ruthann. "Environment, Planning, and Psychology," unpublished doctoral dissertation, Graduate Division, University of California, Berkeley, 1975.

2 · Environmental Science
Perspectives and Methods

Part 1. A Retrospective Introduction

Most of the chapters in this book necessarily contain a certain amount of jargon. As environmental sciences and the body of environmental law have grown, a somewhat specialized vocabulary has developed. In this chapter we will try to keep the number of such words to a minimum and to note new words or specialized definitions applied to common words as we use them in the text. Keep in mind, however, that the job of writing an environmental impact statement, or any environmental document, is an assignment in clear, concise communication. Technological and specialized words should be used for precision only. Your major effort should be to make the document as understandable to the general public as possible.

Before examining the application of environmental science to decision-making within the framework of law, you should understand the basic reasons why we are confronted with the present environmental dilemmas and the responses to them in the form of the new methods of forecasting environmental and other impacts. Because the forecasting of impacts relies heavily upon the natural and social sciences, you should also examine these sciences as they relate to what we now call "environmental science."

For untold generations we of *homo sapiens* have modified the earth for our

D. B. Tyler, born in 1928, is a principal of Impact Consulting, and has served as an environmental consultant to United Nations agencies in Asia, as well as writing and reviewing environmental impact documents in California. For the past five years, he has organized and taught environmental courses at the University of California, Berkeley, and is at present working in an *ad hoc* interdisciplinary program, Macrosystems Ecology, at the same institution. His history includes considerable experience in engineering and scientific applications of electronic instrumentation in the fields of biomedical and oceanographic research.

own purposes, and until recently we have done so with very little thought to the consequences. It has been only in the last two decades that we have come to understand that we live in a closed global system, finite in its materials, and so integrated that every action has an impact on all components of the entire global system. We realized this when we found that fallout from any one nuclear explosion settled over the entire earth, or that pesticides and lead applied to agricultural and transportation systems in the northern hemisphere accumulated in the bodies of Antarctic animals. Few people in the technological Western world had a clear understanding only a decade ago that mankind's present and future survival are inextricably bound to the well-being of earth's agricultural systems. Even today, in the face of massive and well publicized food shortages, too few realize that those same systems are in turn dependent on other intricate living systems to sustain them.

If you choose to reduce environmental problems to simple terms, you may say that the "environmental crunch" arises from the way in which very large numbers of people use resources. By "resources" we mean here all the known materials of the earth, organic and inorganic, that are depended upon by mankind. Miners and drillers for oil and gas use the term "reserves"; that usage covers only resources that are of proven economic value and that are as deposits non-renewable. Our use of "resources" includes those reserves and all other materials occurring in Nature, whether now of economic value or recyclable, whether organic or inorganic, before they are grown or extracted or processed into the stuff of civilization. Some materials may not be commonly classed as "resources," or for that matter even recognized as resources, because people are no longer encultured in their use. Wild edible plants in North America have lost their "resource" identity because we no longer eat them, but instead call them weeds. The environmental crunch stems from the fact of increasing population on a world-wide basis, and the manner of extracting, using, and disposing of the resources we have selected to support technological civilizations. The threats that we perceive to the continued well-being of the earth's ecosystems concern most of us because they manifest either direct or indirect menace to the human populations of the globe. Human interest in environmental quality is basically self-interest.

We will be dependent on the earth's own living systems to sustain whatever modes of living we shall have in the future. That future, therefore, depends on the continued viability of our natural systems.

We must determine whether or not any proposed activity among these systems will produce an "impact," and if so, to what extent it will be adverse. Both the law and prudence dictate that when we evaluate potential impacts we consider short-term and long-term effects as reflected in present environmental quality and future survival.

Because it is the major focus of our concerns, the word "environment" itself should be defined. Merriam Webster's *New Collegiate Dictionary* states:

> *2 a:* the complex of climatic, edaphic, and biotic factors that act upon an organism or an ecological community and ultimately determine its form and survival *b;* the aggregate of social and cultural conditions that influence the life of an individual or community . . .

When we speak of the "natural environment" or "natural systems" we are referring primarily to definition "a." Human communities fall under the rubric of both "a" and "b." As you may have suspected, because environmental science is a new field, there are almost as many definitions of "environment" as there are writers in the field. The same, regrettably, applies to many of the other environmental terms. For example, most writers in this field express a concern for "the environment"; we will see that systems-scientists use that term for the portion of a problem that they are *not* immediately concerned with. Because definitions garnered from reading the popular press are more confusing than enlightening, we will define some of the principal terms used in this chapter:

Ecology: The study of the interrelationships of an organism or a biotic community and its environment.

Ecosystem: An open system, with respect to material and energy flow, comprised of non-living (abiotic) and living (biotic) components in a geographic locale, whose interrelationships are such as to form a dynamic self-perpetuating complex. All ecosystems are bounded by—have interfaces with—other ecosystems. Consequently, each has inputs from and outputs to other ecosystems. In practice, the boundaries of ecosystems are established arbitrarily, depending on the purpose of the worker.

Biome: A major habitat type, identified by either its geomorphic form, such as "rocky shoreline," or by a major plant community in the case of terrestrial systems, like "Arctic tundra" or "tropical rain forest." Biomes are large ecosystems. Examples of any one type are found in many places on the globe separated from similar biomes by differing biomes.

Ecosphere: The entirety of the earth's biomes. That portion of the earth inhabited by and influenced by living organisms, and therefore capable of supporting life indefinitely. It is not a "pure" ecosystem because for all practical purposes it is closed to material flow. Energy enters and leaves this system primarily by electromagnetic radiation.

Ecologist: One with formal training in the science of ecology who pursues either theoretical or applied ecology as a profession. Should be distinguished from

Environmentalist: One with a keen interest in environmental quality who may or may not be professionally qualified.

Environmental professional: One who is engaged in the preparation, evaluation, or review of environmental impact documents, or is engaged in research or teaching directly related thereto on a professional basis.

Environmental worker: A person working on some aspect of the preparation, evaluation, or review of environmental documents, but who may not have responsibilities encompassing an overview of an entire project. May be, but need not always be, an "environmental professional."

Environmental scientists: One who is trained in one of the natural or social sciences and is engaged in theoretical or applied research work in that science as it pertains to environmental matters.

Environmental science: Really not a "science." Only so in the same sense that medicine is a "science." An art employing many sciences and technologies in matters pertaining to maintaining or enhancing environmental quality. Again as in medicine, where "medical scientists" are not normally practitioners of the art, but rather on medical school faculties or pharmaceutical company staffs, environmental science is not practiced by "environmental scientists" *per se,* but rather by

Environmental practitioners: Those who are charged with the responsibility of preparing, evaluating, reviewing, or making decisions, based upon environmental impact documents and the functional equivalent of such documents. Note that according to this scheme an environmental practitioner would be an environmental professional or in some cases an environmental worker, and either of these persons *could* also be an environmental scientist. But an environmental scientist is not, *ipso facto,* an environmental practitioner.

Environmental decision-maker: A person charged with the responsibility under law to render decisions affecting environmental quality. Environmental decision-makers are usually elected officials at the city and county levels, or are civil servants, or are appointed at state and federal levels. Their decisions are required by law to be made with due regard for the expert opinion provided by those we call environmental practitioners.

Science: Usually considered to be divided into two major areas of study. These are: *natural sciences,* bodies of knowledge about how physical entities behave according to laws and theories that are discoverable through a process of observation and experiment, hypothesis formation and testing, all in accord with accepted "scientific method"; *social sciences,* bodies of knowledge concerning interpersonal relationships in human societies discovered by means emulating the application of "scientific method" in the natural sciences. In practice, the natural sciences tend to rely very heavily on experimentation and the social sciences on observation.

Technology: The application of the sciences, chiefly the natural sciences, in the fabrication of machines and functional structures, usually in production of goods, commerce, and communication. Technology is the product of engineering and allied arts to a very considerable extent. It is the misapplication of technology that has been responsible for declines in

Environmental quality: The state of the environment, especially with respect to rational use of resources to sustain and enhance human quality of life, survival of rare and endangered species, and long-term prospects for maintaining the earth's life-support systems of myriad ecosystems in diverse biomes throughout the ecosphere.

These stipulative definitions are, of course, not the *only* possible definitions. We do ask, however, that you accept these definitions as what *we mean* by these terms as used in this chapter.

Since the publication of Rachel Carson's *Silent Spring* in 1962, a growing awareness of the multidimensional nature of our threats to the earth's life-support systems has gradually been coalescing. We are not just endangering ourselves and the rest of the world with biocidal chemicals; we are also depleting prime agricultural land at an alarming rate in the face of what may well prove to be climatic changes portending reduced yields from remaining lands. We are using energy resources in enormous quantities, and in the process creating incredibly complex industrial societies with constantly growing demands for even more energy. These societies produce wastes unmatched in all history. On a world-wide basis, there is good reason to believe that we are increasing our numbers to, or perhaps have already reached, a point where the earth cannot support us all at even approximately the level of aspirations that has been created around the globe. For example, citizens of the United States constitute about 6% of the world's population, and if it is true that we utilize about 35% of all the world's production of energy resources, then it would require an increase in production and consumption at a rate about 480% greater than the present to give the world's population an "American" standard of living. And that is so only at *present levels* of population. The world's population is expected to double near the turn of the century.

In earlier times such problems on a global scale were non-existent or very nearly so, even though it is true that human populations have a very long history of abusing agricultural lands. In almost every instance such abuses have pushed the offending civilization into a headlong plunge from world power to poverty. But, in the last century or so, we have tremendously multiplied our power to produce physical change, for good or ill. The capacity to effect such changes was wrought by the wizardry of the industrial revolution. But, as with all revolutions, it was not an unmixed blessing. The industrial revolution was nurtured by, and in turn reinforced, an intellectual and scientific revolution producing an array of technologies of astounding effectiveness. From the 19th century onward these technologies were applied to the industrialization of production, the medical arts, transportation, and communication. New technologies were then applied to the sciences, which gave rise to new bodies of scientific information from which arose even more sophisticated technologies. Thus greater bodies of scientific information were accumulated and these gave rise to newer, more sophisticated technologies, which in turn were applied to the sciences to produce still more information. A process that is still very much in progress, though it may be that at present we have entered a period of diminishing returns requiring huge technological investments for minimal scientific returns.

During this long process, profound changes occurred in the life-style of the peoples in the new Technological World. Mechanical systems fired by energy from fossil fuels replaced human and animal labor. Health care was greatly improved. The vast majority of the population was separated from any direct connection with food production. These "advances" were seen as benefits derived from the application of technology, the handmaiden of science, to the industrial revolution. But we should be wary of any such conclusions, until we have had a chance to examine some of the basic "laws" concerning how large systems function.

Even if we had had the foresight to know the benefits to be derived from undergoing an industrial revolution, all the urging in the world would not have produced the changes we have seen. The changes were not set into motion by altruism. The essential ingredient was the prospect and realization of gain—not just by the wealthy few, but by vast numbers of people. Admittedly the distribution was, in most cases, extremely uneven. But the gain to large segments of the population was appreciable. It encouraged the growth of large business, with profits to investors and management, and with more jobs for more people. Consequently, population growth was by no means discouraged. More people meant more houses, more goods sold, and more jobs. Local realtors, chambers of commerce, and home or land owners pushed for growth because it meant gain.

An important point is that the system worked well enough for a sufficient number of people that it could perpetuate itself under the aegis of democratic forms of government. Almost all of this was accomplished under the laws of the land which, notwithstanding the role of special interests in formulating and administering such laws, seemed to operate mostly for the common good.

Momentous turnings in human affairs do not happen *in vacuo*. The intellectual torrent which gave rise to the scientific revolution and hence to the technological age swept away the philosophical and moral underpinnings of earlier times. The industrial revolution could not have gone forward in any appreciable way until we had donned the blinders of the single-valued ethos, economic gain. This value was and is given general expression in the accumulation of material possessions in blissful ignorance of the ways in which complicated systems operate. It appeared for quite a time as if we had created a way of making everyone richer with no end in sight. To be sure, there were wars, depressions, and injustices, but given time the architects of the system would correct these flaws. Most of us did not perceive that we had created a complex system of positive feedback loops without the appropriate counterbalances of negative feedback. Indeed, this state of affairs could not be seen until a systems science had evolved. Such an evolution began tentatively before the second world war and in earnest during the post-war years.

A science of "general systems" which is truly applicable to *all systems* has not as yet been universally recognized in the scientific community. Nonetheless, sufficient is known about systems behavior that some general principles have emerged and gained very wide acceptance. For the moment, it is enough to say that it is now well known that systems having only positive feedback are ultimately self-destructive.

Another salient feature of our present condition must be mentioned. Almost without exception, our problems stemming from the interaction of predominantly positive feedback loops in the complex systems and created from the industrial revolution onward are multiplying at an accelerating rate. Changes both swift and profound are upon us before we have time to assimilate what has occurred in the immediate past. These changes are not to be understood in the context of a single discipline. They are systematic changes. Small wonder that most economists are bewildered by the appearance of "impossible" combinations such as recession *and* inflation. Professional "tunnel vision" is by no means confined to economists, however. Several of the leading spokesmen among "environmentalists" have proclaimed publicly that the world's problems are the result of population growth to the exclusion of almost all other concerns. Other "environmentalists" have argued with considerable heat that those same problems are due almost exclusively to technology. Neither position can be justified from a holistic view of the matter when perceived in terms of whole systems interactions. There is no *one problem* and there can be no one solution. Indeed, when dealing with systems it is wiser to search for appropriate directions and goals toward which to move, rather than single "solutions."

"Solutions" in environmental matters have a long history of creating problems as bad as or worse than the original problem for which the "solution" was the supposed answer. Examples are legion, such as the discovery of the acid rain produced by air-pollution control devices installed on autos and smokestacks. What was lacking in this case and the hundreds of others that occur every year is a holistic view or systems approach to the problem.

Unfortunately, taking a compartmentalized view of problems is deeply inculcated in each of us by our present educational system. Indeed, the more "educated" we are, the more likely it is that we will be able to analyze problems only in terms of the discipline we have chosen to study. A striking example of how single disciplinary thinking permeates the thought patterns of most experts is betrayed in the widely used term "side-effects." This term was produced by the same variety of professional tunnel vision that has given rise to most of the world's environmental problems. To most people "side-effects" carries the connotation of a totally unpredictable and unimportant result popping up in some unexpected place, an unfortunate occurrence that could not have been foreseen. That connotation is usually sheer bunkum. What are described as "side-effects" are responses of the system in question, whether it is a human body or an ecosystem, to the application of whatever manipulation had been directed at some component of the system. Side-effects are really *systems*-effects. As such they are predictable in the majority of cases. However, to predict systems-effects, you must know a great deal about the whole system involved, through both experimentation and pragmatic experience. Calling unanticipated adverse effects of manipulations of natural or human systems "side-effects" is an admission of gross ignorance of the system involved and of its behavior. "Side-effects" have no place in environmental literature.

During the industrial revolution the natural sciences, and the social sciences that later emerged from them, were busy constructing their own very special kind of blinders. It would not be accurate or fair to say that the scientific community shared the single-valued ethic of the majority at that time. In fact, they were caricatured as being dedicated and unworldly. Even today it is fairer to say that scientists, though perhaps more worldly now, are nonetheless still dedicated to the advancement and the application of knowledge. But dedication to a particular discipline has been exacting an ever-increasing price in isolation from other scientific disciplines. In the words of an old cliché it has become necessary to "know more and more about less and less."

Scientists in their various disciplines have become, as it were, entrenched in a mine shaft which branches off, continuously "sprouting" new trenches or tunnels for each new discipline and sub-discipline. From such trenches the workers can see where they have come from, and in general the direction they are heading. And they can see in detail the exposed face of the discipline they are mining. But they cannot see even the adjoining trenches, much less the branches far removed from them. Others attempt to hurl bits of relevant information between trenches to their comrades in allied fields. Rare individuals have the temerity to be "generalists." Generalists spend very little time in the trenches, but they have a comparatively excellent view of the mine with its numerous branches. They are in a position to see the interrelationships and how things fit together. However, they do not have a clear view of the veins of knowledge being uncovered in the trenches. Moreover, when the going gets rough, they cannot seek the shelter and comparative anonymity of a trench without abandoning the only position from which they can make a meaningful contribution. Environmental practitioners engaged in environmental impact forecasting are, perforce, generalists.

As generalists, environmental professionals face no simple task. The great systems that comprise the world do not operate as physical systems, or chemical, biological, geological systems. Nor are they organic or inorganic complexes. They are all of these things at once and are further complicated by the admixture of complex human variables. As such they must be viewed as wholes for they behave as whole systems. Among these systems any one action not only affects the system wherein it takes place but may well be reflected in other systems thousands of miles removed from the obvious and intended results.

Part 2. The Role of Environmental Professionals

The role that environmental professionals play in society is very much in the formative stages. Without knowing exactly all the dimensions that the profession will ultimately encompass, we can be certain that the profession cannot endure, much less flourish, without strong public support and confidence. Such public support demands unswerving integrity as the hallmark of environmental professionals. Regardless of who any particular employer may be, the profession carries with it an inherent public trust that the facts developed and presented by environmental professionals will be untainted by special interest or bias. In a professional capacity, an environmental analyst must not be a "preservationist," "conservationist," or "developer," but should strive to set out the facts in as objective a manner as possible. Subjective viewpoints, of course, have an important place in environmental decision-making, but they should be clearly identified as such.

All this sounds easy. It is not. We are all human and we are all biased and it is probably impossible for us to be consciously aware of all our own biases. The "realities" of client relationships, especially for those in the private sector, represent another pitfall in the practice of environmental science. At best, future contracts for environmental work may depend on the "treatment" given a client's project in an environmental impact document. At worst, environmental professionals or their employer may have a considerable financial stake in the decision of the decision-making body before which the document is presented. For example, it is not uncommon for a firm of civil engineers to have an "environmental" group in-house to prepare impact documents for clients for whom they will later do considerable construction contracting. While not impossible, it seems highly unlikely that one's employer under such circumstances would really want a thoroughly objective and unbiased disclosure of all the facts. This would be an especially sensitive matter if the project were controversial and the potential follow-on work substantial. You can readily see that such moral dilemmas are not confined to private enterprise. The pressures on professionals are the same if the employer is a government agency with a large share of its prestige and budget committed to a particular project, or if it is subjected to pervasive political influences.

In the political arena and in most of our public lives the course of events is determined by a complex process involving opposing parties. Yet in this system environmental professionals must not be advocates in their professional stance. If an environmental profession is to exist it can only do so by always presenting the interested public with unvarnished facts.

It follows that, in order to present "unvarnished facts," we must be able to face them unflinchingly. Some unpleasant facts do not concern particular projects; rather, they concern the environmental profession itself. Consider the question of who is a thoroughly competent and qualified environmental professional. If by "professionals" we mean those whom the public can confidently expect to have demonstrable competence and sound judgment in their professed field, and if we require the level of performance to be, say, that of a physician or attorney, then the answer must be "no one." Ask yourself how many environmental professionals know the intimate functions and interrelationships of an "environment" as well as a physician knows, however imperfectly, the human body. We do not expect physicians to be infallible. But the difference in scope of knowledge and quality of performance between the medical profession and the environmental profession is awesome.

Another unpleasant fact is that the relative youth of environmental science is by no means the only reason for the difference. Whether or not those now engaged as environmental professionals were well qualified in the disciplines from which they came into the profession, very few have had any formal training in environmental sciences, *per se,* and an even smaller number have had any exposure to methods of whole systems investigations. Inasmuch as "environments" behave as whole systems, this is a rather fundamental lack. Imagine the furor that would be raised if an expert in organic chemistry decided to hang out a shingle professing to be a physician and surgeon although totally ignorant of such medical skills as human anatomy and physiology. In the days immediately following the enactment of national and state environmental legislation, scores of people entered the environmental field armed with no more qualifications than a talent for writing brochures, a glib tongue, and lots of *chutzpah.* Many others, with training in one or another related environmental science, took a quickie course in environmental impact assessment, or did some cursory reading in basic ecology texts, and thus "prepared" launched themselves on their new careers.

At the present state of our art, the only thing that can be said with certainty is that we don't know with certainty what the detailed behavior of ecosystems will be, although advancement of knowledge regarding ecosystems behavior is proceeding on many fronts. Thanks largely to the International Biological Programme, much new data is being published and new insights gained in the realm of functional relationships of a wide diversity of ecosystems.

We are at present confronted by the pressing necessity of developing the art of environmental science. As with any new discipline, we must develop appropriate methodology, terminology, and philosophy. In doing so, we must, of course, draw upon the older disciplines. At the same time we must be aware of the limitations of each, especially since environmental science is charged with developing comprehensive overviews of complex subject areas. To do so, we must view problems as wholes—*holistically*—adding the complex variables of human activities to the intricacies of "natural" ecosystems behavior, to predict the subsequent behavior of the entire system. We cannot hope to be *entirely* successful in this, but we must be substantially so. Environmental impact "assessment" should probably be more accurately termed *forecasting*. We are after all attempting to predict the course of future events under differing sets of circumstances—the project and its alternatives.

From a systems point of view, we have a very critical omission in our present procedures. Once a project has been through the environmental impact review proceedings, there is no provision for determining the degree of accuracy obtained in the forecast of environmental impacts. No follow-up studies are done, on anything like a routine basis, if at all. Thus environmental practitioners are deprived of essential feedback with which to improve the process. It is as if a doctor never saw patients again after prescribing treatments, and thus was completely ignorant of the fate of his patients.

Another matter that we must pay close attention to is the emerging new terminology of this profession. Public support requires that we be understood. New terminology should be kept to an absolute minimum. Large segments of the public view "jargon" as a device for concealing the facts from the uninitiated. In too many instances, they are quite right. For this reason, where special terminology is unavoidable, forthright intelligible "translations" should be provided for the interested public. For example, why do we use the term "environmental impact *assessment*" instead of *forecast*? Those who are familiar with the environmental impact process, and also with the dictionary definition*

---

* Merriam Webster's *New Collegiate Dictionary* defines the words as follows: *Assess . . . 1:* to determine the rate or amount of (as a tax); *2 a:* to impose (as a tax) according to an

of those two words, should be able to agree that it is the environmental setting as it exists in the project site and region that is *assessed*. The most crucial part of the process is *forecasting* what will ensue from the project or any of its alternatives. Forecasting is the major responsibility and thrust of the entire effort. Are we attempting to obscure something from public view by employing the word "assessment" in a special and apparently unnecessary sense, when we have a perfectly good descriptive word at our disposal? Or does the word "forecast" carry too heavy a burden of implied follow-up studies and uncertainty? "Forecast" seems to convey a far more precise sense of what the process really is, and what our responsibilities are in that process. "Assessment," on the other hand, in the sense that most of the public have encountered the word, seems to carry a flavor of a governmental process which is carried on by inaccessible public officials in a manner on occasion unfair but regularized and certain. Can we honestly describe the environmental impact process so? Should we wish to?

Why all this fuss over the choice of a single word? If we cannot be honest even with ourselves in selecting our new terminology, how can we ever expect to merit the confidence of the public? We need clarity and public trust far more than we do a shiny new jargon.

Public support is increasingly important because the first flush of enthusiasm for environmental matters on the part of the public is past. As world economy slows, the pressures for developing remaining land and resources can only increase. Many difficult decisions lie ahead affecting the quality of life, the legacy we leave to future generations, in the face of increasing polarization between opposing environmental and economic interests.

With due allowance for the exceptions to any sweeping generalizations, this polarization may be characterized as a situation in which (i) businessmen, developers, and to some extent labor leaders view environmentalists as impractical, as fools or worse, and (ii) environmentalists tend to see businessmen, developers, and some of organized labor as unprincipled, grasping villains. At the risk of receiving brick-bats from both sides, we say that neither view is totally wrong or substantially correct. That *some* environmentalists are

---

established rate; *b:* to subject to a tax, charge or levy; *3:* to make an official valuation of (property) for the purpose of taxation; *4:* to determine the importance, size, or value of *syn* see ESTIMATE . . .

Assessment . . . *1:* the act or an instance of assessing: APPRAISAL; *2:* the amount assessed

Forecast . . . *1 a:* to calculate or predict (some future event or condition) usu. as a result of rational study and analysis of available pertinent data; *esp.:* to predict (weather conditions) on the basis of correlated meteorological observations; *b:* to indicate as likely to occur; *2:* to serve as a forecast of: PRESAGE < such events may — peace > — *vi:* to calculate the future *syn* see FORETELL — forecaster *n.*

impractical is as undoubted as that *some* representatives of economic interests are unprincipled—but in neither case do they represent anything approaching a majority. As for the "truth" between this polarization, it is obscured by differences in perception and time frames.

The number of people whose self-image is that of a villain must be remarkably small. It is not unprincipled to be concerned for your economic well-being and that of the people who look to you to provide for them. This can be so whether those others are members of your family or employees and stockholders in your company. That self-interest is involved does not change the fact that the economic well-being of others is also deeply involved. It isn't a difficult step to rationalize that "what's good for General Bullmoose is good for the country." And from the perspective of economics that may be demonstrably true. The perspectives of the economic sector are, by and large, encompassed within periods of investment amortization. Viewed over longer time frames the situation may not appear as beneficial as at first blush. Herein lies the crux of the difference between the two opposing perspectives. Environmentalists tend to take a much longer view of resource transactions than is customary in commerce or government. Consequently, environmentalists frequently charge the others with being short-sighted. They also have a much broader view of "place" than is customarily economically relevant. For example, environmentalists are concerned about where chemicals such as pesticides go *after* they are applied to the "target" species, an externality with which conventional economics is not concerned.

Thus, environmentalists may be considered to be eagle-eyed along the corridors of time and across space. Yet, disconcertingly, they often display appalling myopia when gazing at the breadth of the socio-economic structure in which they live. They are portrayed repeatedly in the popular press as not considering the livelihood of workers employed in industries whose operations they seek to curtail, and as having no appreciation for how such cutbacks would ripple through the economy. Be that as it may, the environmental movement has exhibited very little grasp of the systems-effects of the actions they espouse. An example from the redwood district of California can illustrate this. If conservationists are successful in saving a major stand of redwoods, it does not diminish the demand for redwood lumber. In fact, it increases the demand by shortening the supply, which will tend to increase cutting rates on the remaining unprotected stands. If preservationists are successful in protecting the entire species, the demand for wood products will be transferred to other forest species, resulting in increased loss of those species. If the demand cannot be met from forest products it will shift to other, possibly non-renewable resources such as plastics made from petroleum products. Moreover, all of these shifts will take place in a socio-economic milieu wherein the prevailing spirit is devil-take-the-hindmost. This is hardly conducive to the cooperation that will be necessary from all sectors to insure long-term environmental quality.

In the redwood example, environmentalists and others answered the prospect of substantial losses and unemployment in the lumber industry by saying that such losses would be compensated by corresponding increases in tourist trade in "the redwood empire" over the years. They apparently did not recognize that even if the tourist trade more than replaced the dollar volume of the timber cut and sold, very few, if any, loggers and saw-mill workers would ever be in a position to move into that industry—to most of them it simply meant unemployment. For that matter, tourist dollars, in any amount, would not diminish demand on the remaining trees. On the contrary, they could only increase it. This is an example of what might well be called the "externalities" of the environmental movement. Such externalities are leading to an erosion of public support for the environmental movement. It is an irony that just such disregard for externalities, on the part of industry and government, gave rise to the environmental movement. Externalities result from failing to treat a problem as a whole.

For environmental professionals there must be no externalities. In the past, almost everyone acted with his or her own special concerns in mind. Relatively few of us ever took the holistic view. A corporate executive had a duty to make a profit. A governmental official was responsible to see that projects were built. And so on for almost all of us.

Heretofore, no person, corporation, or agency had the responsibility to see the impact of any action on the whole, across the gamut of human activities imbedded in the complexities of "natural" ecosystems—to take the holistic view. It is now the duty of those forecasting environmental impact to do so. In the process, we are challenged to act in such a way as to maintain and build confidence and support among all sectors of the population.

This is no mean task. The dynamics of the situation are such that it will be impossible to satisfy everyone or every interest that bears upon any particular environmental problem. Almost all enduring environmental decisions must be trade-offs. For the time being, extemporized compromises between human economic needs and desires contrasted with their ecological costs (present benefits versus long-term productivity) must be made. Aesthetic experience and expectations enter as serious considerations. However, we should avoid being diverted from the major problems into trivia and cosmetic solutions. Public concern, aided by organizational "image" building, frequently misdirects our efforts. Anti-litter campaigns and highway beautification, *per se,* contribute remarkably little to over-all environmental quality. But our efforts may be misdirected even in matters of considerable immediate importance, such as air pollution.

As an example, not too many years ago, jet planes emitted a plume of dense black smoke during take-offs and landings. Most of this smoke was unburned hydrocarbons and particulate matter. It was decidedly unsightly, but it settled to the ground rather quickly and was not as serious a component in smog as other materials, such as the oxides of nitrogen. A public aroused to the steady deterioration of air quality in our metropolitan centers had its attention captured by the jet's highly visible smoke trails. With the acquiescence and participation of the federal government, the airline industry converted the jet engines to operate at a higher temperature. The result is that the jet engine emissions are all but invisible, because now they contain far fewer "smoke" particles. Unfortunately, they now contain much larger amounts of oxides of nitrogen—a vastly more polluting substance than the smoke trails formerly emitted. A single jumbo jet, taking off and landing once, now produces as many oxides of nitrogen as are produced by about 2,500 take-off and landing cycles of small, private, propeller-driven aircraft. Efforts to "clean up" jet engines produced a cosmetic solution that actually *increases* the contribution to photochemical smog by transport aircraft. We can well do without any more such "solutions." Neither the elasticity of the earth's living systems nor the forbearance of the public are inexhaustible.

Environmental professionals cannot be perfect in dealing with colleagues in other sciences, governmental bodies, private clients, or with the public, but must maintain a level of performance in ethical and professional matters commensurate with the responsibilities with which we are entrusted. Much remains to be hammered out on the forge of experience, before definitive statements about many of the areas that concern us deeply can be made. Nonetheless, the need to act is thrust upon us now—and a beginning has been made.

In the face of our own individual shortcomings and imperfections, the challenge to live up to our code of ethics (see Appendix below), and to perform our professional duties in a manner meriting implicit, as well as explicit, public trust in this profession is one to test the character, dedication, and intellectual competence of any person to be found on this earth. To take part in the development of environmental science, as a discipline and as an applied art, may well be the most exciting human undertaking in history. If we are not equal to the task, it also may well be the last.

Appendix

CODE OF ETHICAL PRACTICE
Preparation and Processing of Environmental Documents
Association of Environmental Professionals

1. Whereas, the goal of my endeavor is to provide a full-disclosure environmental document in which decision makers and the public can place full confidence,

2. Therefore, I will subscribe to this Code of Ethical Practice:

3. I *will* examine all relationships or actions which could be legitimately interpreted as a conflict of interest by clients, officials, the public, or my peers; and I will fully disclose my financial or personal interests in the project and each alternative, including the no-build or null alternative.

4. I *will* encourage, by every reasonable means, that environmental planning begin in the earliest stages of project conceptualization.

5. I *will* refuse to create an environmental document as a justification of a project or as a platform for opposition or advocacy.

6. I *will* abstain from attempting to improperly delay the outcome of an action or project through the environmental document process.

7. I *will* produce an objective environmental document; I will not allow any of my relationships with clients, employers, or others to interfere with my duty to provide a full-disclosure environmental document.

8. *If preparing a document pursuant to the environmental document process, I will:*

9. define a level of investigation appropriate to the nature and scope of the proposed project or action, and its probable impacts;

10. select and use qualified persons of pertinent disciplines in the conduct of the study;

11. incorporate the best principles of the design and environmental planning arts in recommending measures for mitigation of environmental harm and enhancement of environmental quality;

12. rely upon the independent judgment of an interdisciplinary team to determine impacts, define and evaluate all reasonable alternatives to the proposed action, and assess short-term versus long-term productivity with and without the project or action;

13. encourage public participation from the beginning in an open, frank and productive atmosphere to stimulate democratic consensus;

14. write in a clear and accurate manner, to achieve objectivity and remove all possible bias;

15. list all study participants, their qualifications and affiliations;

16. cite all sources, written and oral;

17. strive to create a complete, scientifically accurate, objective environmental document that can be defended professionally.

18. *If reviewing an environmental document, I will:*

19. insist upon review of original techical reports or findings upon which conclusions or recommendations summarized in the environmental document are based, to ensure they are in conformity with applicable laws and guidelines;

20. assure that the assessment *(sic)* reflects my own best judgment where I am

qualified to judge, and that of independent persons expert in areas beyond my capability to assess *(sic)* effects deemed "significant";

21. determine that the document is consistent with all pertinent laws, ordinances, guidelines, plans and policies to the best of my knowledge and ability;

22. certify acceptability of the environmental document only if I am satisfied that it has been prepared and reviewed in conformance with all of the above.

This code appears as adopted by the Association of Environmental Professionals in plenary session at the second annual conference and membership meeting on the 29th of March, 1975, at Stanford University. Your attention has been called to the use of the terms "assessment" and "assess" for reasons we have already discussed; "forecast" is a better term.

Part 3. Concepts and Constraints

As with all new disciplines, environmental science is compelled to face the twin problems of building its own methodology and defining its own vocabulary. For the most part our new methodologies will call upon already existing tools fashioned by others in the various related arts and sciences. The number and diversity of possible tools is enormous. Many are now employed by workers in established fields such as geology and civil engineering, and can be applied to environmental problems, *ad hoc*. Other tools must be fashioned anew, drawing upon an amalgam synthesized from different disciplines.

Because most, if not all, of our tools come to us by way of the sciences, we should acquaint ourselves with some of the basic strengths and weaknesses of science. Even though mathematics has often been described as the "language of science," it is not required that all environmental practitioners be masters of that subject. Still, an acquaintance with *some* mathematical notions is absolutely essential. Also, various kinds of models and modeling methods will probably be increasingly used in environmental matters. Therefore, in the following discussion we examine briefly mathematical notions and consider some aspects of modeling.

It is implicit in much of the federal and state environmental procedures that science has much to contribute in the resolution of environmental problems. We must recognize the reasons why science has considerable validity in environmental applications, *and* also those instances in which science cannot be effectively employed. These distinctions follow from the ways in which scientific facts are accumulated. Aside from the question of scientists unconsciously injecting their own personal biases into their choice of studies and their reporting of the results, differing methods of acquiring "facts" result in some scientific opinions being as reliable as next morning's sunrise while other opinions, based upon other methods, may be pure eyewash. It is well to be acquainted with a basis for making such distinctions.

At this point you should take special note of the fact that we did not say "the basis for making such distinctions." We are proposing *a* basis, a *single perspective* from among many possible perspectives. Therefore, what we say here is not to be construed as if scribed in stone tablets. We merely offer it for your consideration, in the hope that you may find it useful and may be prompted to explore on your own what can and what cannot be successfully attempted by science, at its present state. Several excellent starting places appear in the references at the conclusion of this chapter.

Some classes of questions are quite amenable to the classic techniques of scientific inquiry. Others are not. Those questions which science is best able to respond to could be termed *high yield* questions. Those which will produce little or no reliable result could be termed *low yield* questions.

High yield. These questions are concerned with repetitious events among explicitly delimited entities which have explicitly delimitable and measureable properties. These events, all other things being equal, can be confidently expected to recur within an exactitude consistent with the limits of accuracy and precision of earlier measurements. Typically, high yield questions concern a small number of entities that may be individually analyzed and that behave in a deterministic way. By "deterministic" we mean that there are a manageable number of variables (dimensions) in the system, and that if we can *completely* specify the state of the system with respect to those variables, at one time, the state of the system can be completely determined for the next interval of time. If these conditions do not obtain, then the number of entities must be sufficiently large so that, even though individual behavior may be random, their average behavior may be derived statistically, and treated *as if* it were deterministic. Examples of the first situation are relatively simple mechanical systems and ensembles of similar systems. Examples of the statistical sort are to be found in the behavior characteristics of large populations of all sorts of chemicals, gases, measurements of things, people, etc. Problems involving medium numbers of entities in populations are still largely intractable.

Because science deals with predicting future events from the study of past events, it follows that science is concerned only with repetitive events. It cannot deal with events which are *necessarily unique*. In other words, when dealing with events that are one of a kind, we can only address those portions that *are* "of a kind," and consequently are shared with past, and presumably future, events. Consider an event really unique in *all its particulars*. To qualify as such it must never have occurred before and will never recur. We would find such an event as impossible to accurately describe as it would be to investigate. Even the simplest act of referring to something outside ourselves—pointing—requires a culturally shared meaning to the physical gesture and an implicit assumption of a recognizably shared coordinate system by which the referent may be located. Shared attributes are the *sine qua non* for any description and subsequent discourse and investigation.

Traditionally, science has been divided into two major categories, "natural" sciences and "social" sciences. Many natural scientists go a step further, and refer to natural sciences as the "hard" sciences and social sciences as the "soft" sciences. Such a distinction is intended to convey a difference in rigor of application of scientific method, and the resulting difference in reliability of the results. Physics, chemistry, astronomy, much of geology, biology, and oceanography are generally considered to be "hard" sciences. Psychology, sociology, and much of anthropology are usually lumped together as "soft" sciences. Ecology, geology, oceanography, meteorology, some of anthropology, and many others, under this kind of scheme, are probably best considered mixtures of "hard" and "soft." In actual practice it usually boils down to hard sciences dealing with deterministic or quasi-deterministic systems with a manageable number of variables. As a practical matter, "hard" sciences can tell us what *will (or did)* happen, with a very high degree of reliability. "Soft" sciences can tell us what is *likely,* within varying degrees of confidence, to happen (or to have happened). The so-called "soft" sciences then, have the enormously more difficult task of contending with a bewildering array of complex random variables. Accordingly, they are compelled to rely upon statistically derived probabilities to predict events in stochastic processes.

Thus, high yield questions produce two major kinds of results. The first are high reliability deterministic answers, and the second are answers based upon probable outcomes and are not so reliable. The applications of natural science, predominantly in fields of engineering, give rise to most of the immediate effects of a given project on the natural and human ecosystems in which the project is located. Second order effects almost invariably result from ramifications extending into the realm of the "soft" sciences, and therefore, instead of being certain, are more or less probable outcomes of the given project. The lack of certainty associated with second order effects frequently leads to widely differing estimates by qualified experts. Differing situations will have differing levels of certainty associated with various projected outcomes. This is one of the fundamental reasons why environmental impact forecasting must remain ultimately judgmental in character. This is especially so because many questions cannot even be answered with stated probabilities between possible outcomes. We have termed these *low yield* questions.

Low yield. Questions in this category are not amenable to scientific inquiry. They frequently will produce acrimonious debate among both laymen and scientists, however. The reason for this is that many low yield questions have the appearance of being proper scientific questions, but, because of practical considerations, no definitive experiments can be designed and carried out to test them. Questions about low-level dosages of biotoxins such as radiation, pesticides, smog, and industrial pollutants are examples. The practical problems arise because, in order to get statistically significant data, either the necessary number of experimental animals or the amount of time or money becomes wholly unrealizable. Perhaps the best we can do in these situations is trust the judgment of experts familiar with the behavior of those biological systems. But of course experts often disagree and once more we find ourselves with a question that resolves into a judgmental matter. It should be obvious that the most prudent course is to take the most conservative estimate and thereby minimize the hazard. However, many times the most conservative stance will foreclose what appears to be a reasonable trade-off between some hypothetical absolute public protection and some highly desired public benefit. The use of energy from oil and coal equated with acceptable pollution of air is an example of such a trade-off.

A similar situation occurs if we are required to "prove" that something, such as an earthquake fault, does *not exist* in a particular locale. Positive proof is readily obtained if we discover a fault by exploratory methods such as trenching. Negative "proof" is another matter. If we present evidence that no fault was found by trenching, it can be countered by saying the trench was not deep enough, or wide enough, or long enough . . . and so forth, *ad infinitum.*

Low yield questions of these kinds are inescapably judgmental, then, but our judgment should be conditioned by extrapolation from what is known to occur to what can be considered likely to occur. Therefore this class of questions can be termed *extrapolatory,* as distinguished from other judgmental matters.

For practical purposes, then, science can provide us with assistance on a descending scale of certainty. *Deterministic* systems can, if competently treated, produce answers which may be considered, for all intents and purposes, as facts. Systems characterized by random behavior must be treated as *probabilistic,* with varying degrees of confidence in the results, depending upon specific circumstances and investigative methods. *Extrapolatory* questions are beyond the reach of statistical methods, and we must rely on educated guesses and our own judgment.

We should all be aware that no individual scientist or group of scientists holds a patent on "ultimate truth." Scientific "truths" convey no absolute certitude. Each law, theory, or hypothesis is provisional, and subject to revision should contrary facts be established.

During the course of your work as an environmental professional, you will be repeatedly confronted with figures purporting to demonstrate (*i*) growing demand for services, (*ii*) projected population levels, (*iii*) rates at which some resources are being used, and all manner of other projections relating to rates of increase or decrease in matters that come before you for evaluation. Such figures should not simply be taken at face value. They should be scrutinized to see if they really make sense over the lifetime of the proposed action. One frequently occurring example is projection of future air-pollution levels. One EIR projected an emission level derived from projections of the automobile population as it was assumed it would be twenty years later. When the official projections for human population increase were compared with the projected increase in automobiles, it was found that the automobile population was forecast to continue to grow at a rate about *double* that of the human population. Your professional judgment is required to decide if this disparate growth rate for autos is reasonable in the context in which it is used, and how these figures influence other aspects of the proposal and the estimates of other services.

Projected increases in the cost of motor fuels and sharply rising costs for new vehicles together with mounting pressure for mass transit systems would make suspect projected increases if used to validate a claim for new highway construction. However, if used for a projected air pollution study, they would be quite conservative because they very probably overestimate the number of future emission sources—thus producing a projected worst-case situation.

Some mathematical skill is required to learn how to handle the relatively simple equation upon which almost all of the projections of future populations are based. This equation is used whether the "populations" involved are people, money, cars, kilowatt-hours, or what have you. The equation is derived from the compound interest formula, and in the notation familiar to most ecologists is:

$$N_t = N_0 e^{rt} \qquad (1)$$

N_t means the number in some future population at a time, t, specified. It doesn't matter if the time (t) is in seconds, hours, months, years, or any other unit so long as we stick with whichever unit we have selected as appropriate for the problem. Bacterial populations can double in minutes—elephants may take decades.

N_0 is whatever population number we started with at the beginning of the interval of time under consideration. The convention is to call such a starting time "time zero" (t_0). The original population, N_0, is multiplied by the base of the natural logarithm, e, raised to the "rt" power. In other words "rt" is the exponent by which e is raised. The term "rt" merely means some value, r, multiplied by another value, t; and "r" is the rate of increase expressed as a decimal. The factor "t" is the time period specified to have elapsed to arrive at the new population number, N_t. The rate of increase, r, is in percentage expressed as a decimal. For example, if a population were increasing at a rate of 5% per year, to find the size of the population when t = 8 years, rt becomes .05 × 8 = 0.40. Thus, the base of the natural logarithm, e, is raised to the 0.40 power. When that operation is done, we see that e^{rt} (that is, $e^{0.40}$) is equal to about 1.4918. Therefore, multiplying the original population by 1.4918 will give a very close approximation to the size of the new population, which we can see (because 1.4918 is very close to 1.5) will be very close to one and a half times the original population number after eight years have elapsed. That basically is how it works. For populations that are *decreasing* the only change is that a negative sign is placed in front of the exponent, rt. Thus a population diminishing at a rate of 5% per year would have this fact represented by making r = −0.05; then, for a time of 8 years, −0.05 × 8 = −0.40 would be the value for rt.

Still this method requires that we have either a table of powers of e^x, wherein we make x equal to rt, and then look up the number to use as a multiplier for N_0, or an electronic calculator with the appropriate keys to perform that operation. These useful tools are not always available. But we can transpose the equation and solve it in such a fashion that a useful formula can be obtained that does not require either a table or a calculator. The solution of the original equation, $N_t = N_0 e^{rt}$, in terms of rt is:

$$rt = \text{Log}_e N_t - \text{Log}_e N_0 \qquad (2)$$

Since $\text{Log}_e N_t - \text{Log}_e N_0$ represents a subtraction, we can simplify this further by making a symbol to stand for this difference. We'll use "Log_e Diff." Therefore:

$$rt = \text{Log}_e \text{ Diff.} \qquad (3)$$

With this simplified version, if we know any two of the quantities we can always get the other one. By transposition:

$$r = \frac{\text{Log}_e \text{ Diff.}}{t}; \text{ and } t = \frac{\text{Log}_e \text{ Diff.}}{r} \qquad (4);(5)$$

Armed with this equation and its variations just given, we can find the years it will take a population to double, given the rate of increase. Or we can find the rate necessary to produce a doubling or two-fold increase within a given period of time. We can also find out the same information for a three-fold, ten-fold, or any number of multiplications of the original population. But all of this is providing that we know what to "plug in" as a value for Log_e Diff. This value can sometimes be calculated from the data itself. For instance, if it is claimed that a population, or a demand for some product or services, is growing at a rate of (again) 5%, and therefore demand will double in 13.86 years, we know that since Log$_e$ Diff. is equal to the product of rt, then it must be very nearly .05 × 13.86, which is 0.693. For more precise calculations, the following table of values for Log$_e$ Diff. is provided:

x = Fold				Log$_e$ Diff.				Approximation
2 times	.	.	.	0.6931471806	.	.	.	70
3 times	.	.	.	1.098612289	.	.	.	110
4 times	.	.	.	1.386294361	.	.	.	139
5 times	.	.	.	1.609437912	.	.	.	161
10 times	.	.	.	2.302585093	.	.	.	230
20 times	.	.	.	2.995732274	.	.	.	300
50 times	.	.	.	3.912023005	.	.	.	390
100 times	.	.	.	4.605170186	.	.	.	460
1000 times	.	.	.	6.907755279	.	.	.	690

Notice that for crude approximations, some short-cuts are possible. For example, a quick-and-dirty doubling time can be had by merely dividing 70 by the growth rate as a *percentage* (not as a decimal). Thus: 70/5 = 14. That's pretty close to 13.86. Likewise, a three-fold increase estimate can be had by dividing 110 by the percentage: 110/5 = 22; that is very close to 21.9722. Similarly for all of the values just given; ten-fold would be 230/5 = 46, the actual value is 46.0517 + . All of these approximations are quite close enough to be useful in spot-checking data and claims, and ferreting out some of the underlying assumptions. One word of caution: note carefully that because the relationships here are logarithmic, the value for Log$_e$ Diff. for a twenty-fold increase is *not* just ten times a two-fold increase. You should also see that if the same approximations are divided by the time, the answer will be the rate of increase as a percentage; thus: 70/10 = 7%. This indicates that a population of anything that doubles in about ten years is increasing at a rate of 7% per year, for example. In short, to find the rate divide by the time, and to find the time divide by the rate.

There are two extremely crucial facts of life which are imbedded in these formulas. The first is that populations growing logarithmically take shorter and shorter times to double (triple, etc.) the original numbers in that population. In the example just explored, it took about 14 years to double a population growing at 5% per year. But a ten-fold increase, starting from the same time, took only 40 years. Note well that 46 is not 10 times 14. It is only about 3.3 times the interval (14) that it took to accomplish the first doubling. This is so because new members added also add their contributions to the population increments.

As an illustration, suppose that we knew that the entire world's supply of a non-renewable resource was not more than 100 *billion* units of eventually recoverable material, and at the outset our demand for this resource was a quite modest 10,000 units per year; then, at a steady rate, the material would last for 10 *million* years. If we measured our human generations at about 23 years, we would have enough material to last us slightly more than 434,294 *generations*— for all practical purposes, an indefinitely long supply. But now suppose instead that, after discovery, our demand for this material increased at a rate of 10% per year. At that rate of demand, the entire world supply would be gone in *less than 7 generations*—the resource entirely consumed in just over 150 years. Such is the power of exponential growth.

Do smaller growth rates help? Yes, but not as much as you might think. In the resource example above, changing the rate to 1% increases the time by a factor of 10, or 70 generations—still a far cry from nearly one-half million generations. Starting with a pair of humans at about the time that Homer's *Iliad* was composed in ancient Greece, *ca.* 700 B.C., if that tiny population of two had grown at but one percent per year up to the present time, their descendants would number over *one million million, alive today.* To give you a feel for how large that number really is, it would require 250 people for every person now on earth to equal it.

Clearly, the second crucial fact to be derived from these formulas is that exponential growth cannot continue indefinitely. We shall return to this basic idea when we discuss systems. Before we leave this topic we should briefly consider the dynamics that apply when population and demand for resources per capita are *both* growing. Using a minor variation of the formula already presented, we can discover what the new demand will be at any future year, providing the *rates* of increase are constant for both. Likewise, given the same conditions we can determine when the supply of a known quantity of a resource will be exhausted. The demand placed upon a resource by increasing per capita demand and an increasing population is determined by *adding* the two percentages, each expressed as a decimal, and substituting that sum for "r" in equation (1), the "growth" formula previously introduced:

$$\text{Demand}_t = \text{Demands}_0 e^{(r_1 + r_2)t} \tag{6}$$

Once r_1 and r_2 have been added together, this formula is handled just the same as equation (1). For example, if a population were growing at 2% per year and per capita consumption of a resource growing at 5% per year, the total demand for that resource would be growing at a rate of 7% per year. As in the previous example, the demand for this resource would double in about 10 years (remember, the crude approximation for doubling is 70 ÷ percent change per unit time, i.e., $70/7 = 10$, in this case).

The new per capita demand (or consumption) for some future population can be obtained quite readily from the formula just given. Formula (6) can merely be divided by the number in the new population:

$$\text{New per capita Demand} = \frac{\text{Demand}_t}{N_t} \tag{7}$$

N_t has the same meaning as before, the number in some future population.

It is important to notice that in the case just seen, *any* combination of growth rates for population, and per capita resource demand, whose sum is .07 will produce exactly the same result. Likewise, in the earlier example of demand growing at 10% (.10), any combination that equals .10, produces precisely the same outcome as that example.

Are formulas such as these really accurate predictors of things to come? The answer must be ambivalent—yes and no. If the starting population of things has been accurately enumerated, if the growth *rate*, as predicted, remains constant over the period of time considered, if there are no other factors operating to reduce or expand the population of things over the time considered, then the conclusion is as inescapable as $2 + 2 = 4$. If all these conditions do not obtain, then the results will differ accordingly.

Much has been said in recent years concerning modeling social and economic systems and ecosystems. Some ambitious models have been attempted for the *entire world*. Albeit far more modest, the formulas we have just explored are also models. In fact, models are an inseparable part of environmental impact forecasting. Indeed, models are inseparable from descriptive and experimental science.

Model. A representation of a set of objects, attributes of objects, and the relationships and interrelationships existing between and among such objects and attributes, to a level of resolution, accuracy, and precision assignable by the modeler. All models are bounded, conditional abstractions.

In mathematical terms, when one system exactly duplicates another, the one is said to be *isomorphic* to the other. Isomorphy is defined thus: If for each element in system A there is an exactly corresponding element in system B, and for each relationship in system A there is an exactly corresponding relationship in system B, then the two systems are isomorphic (equal + form) with respect to each other. To be consistent with what we have said about the abstract nature of models, we can merely claim *relative isomorphy* for models, because models cannot correspond to "reality" in all its particulars. As a simple example, a road map is only relatively isomorphic to the actual highways and the land upon which they are laid. This important proscription applies only to the degree of isomorphy that can exist between a model and the actual world of objects and events. It does not apply between models. A mechanical model could theoretically be duplicated by other models that would be isomorphic to it, but none of them could be *completely* isomorphic to the actual world.

Models may be thought of as having five properties, all interrelated. The first three are intrinsic to the model. The last two are associated with the specific purposes of the modeler. These properties are: Generality, Precision, Reality, Utility, and Wholeness.

Generality, as the name implies, means the number of different situations to which a model may be applied. *Precision* in a model means: producing exact repeatable results consistent with the level of resolution chosen by the modeler; strictly accurate. (*Precision* in the instrumental sense means repeatability of results without regard to accuracy, not useful here. A model that produces precisely the *same wrong* results each time it "ran" would be of no use to us.) *Reality* means the degree of relative isomorphy existing between the model and that which is modeled. *Utility* should be understood to mean how well the model serves the modeler's purposes. *Wholeness* is the degree to which a model is holistic, and therefore models all those variables responsible for creating the significant dynamics of the actual ecosystem. The last two properties depend on the intentions of the modeler. A large group of modelers might agree on the degree of *generality, precision,* and *reality* obtained in a particular model, but the model would have entirely different *utility* for each modeler, depending on her purpose, and different *wholeness* depending on the size of the ecosystem each desired to model.

It has been widely held in the literature on ecosystem modeling that with respect to the first three properties, a sort of exclusionary principle applies. One of the properties must be sacrificed to achieve the other two. Thus a model that is *general* and *real* cannot be *precise,* and so forth. We can derive three kinds of models from this "exclusionary principle":

1. General and real, therefore not precise—an inferential model;
2. General and precise, therefore not real—a theoretical model;
3. Precise and real, therefore not general—a unique model.

In the last example, (*3*), "unique" means that the model applies only to a very specific ecosystem, *i.e.,* only the one for which the model was created. Results from such a unique model cannot be applied to other ecosystems with equal validity. Usually, environmental professionals will be dealing with unique models of specific ecosystems in forecasting impacts of various activities. An inferential model (*1*) can produce trends that actual systems are likely to follow. In the principles we have discussed, extrapolatory questions can be modeled inferentially. Theoretical models are great for number-crunching in computers, but the results may be widely at variance with what happens in "the real world," because the model lacks some of the variables that obtain in actuality. An example of a theoretical model, on a modest scale, is the formula for population growth given earlier.

Many ecosystem modelers, particularly those with backgrounds in the physical sciences and engineering, strongly disagree that such an "exclusionary principle" exists. In dealing with modelers, you should be aware of this schism in theoretical point of view. The differing theoretical postures most likely result from members of each school having their major experience with considerably different kinds of systems. Physicists and engineers can point to a vast array of diverse systems wherein the number-crunching certitude of the hard natural sciences can be effectively employed. In general, such experts tend to be much more adept at mathematical techniques than is typical of practitioners of the soft sciences. The latter have less confidence in mathematical formulations, *per se.* Moreover, many ecologists and social scientists have had the experience of being "sold" a highly touted mathematical model, only to discover that the model was, indeed, quite unrealistic when they attempted to apply it to the extremely complex systems with which they must deal.

Again, without recourse to a lengthy theoretical discourse, the "truth" probably lies somewhere in the middle. Some systems behave as though such an "exclusion" did not exist; typically these are systems with few variables. Systems with enormous numbers of variables behave as though something quite like an exclusionary principle were at work. An operational formulation of this problem suggests itself to resolve this impasse. Consider what we would have if it were possible to achieve utmost generality and utmost precision in a model of an ecosystem. Utmost generality would mean that it would apply to *all* ecosystems. Utmost precision at all levels of resolution would be *complete* isomorphy with the "real" system. Since we have utmost generality the isomorphy would be to *all* ecosystems. We would have, in effect, recreated reality in so far as we are capable of perceiving it. In terms of model properties, we would have created the utmost model reality thereby. The relationships can be depicted thus:

$$G \,\&\, P \rightarrow R \; . \; . \; . \; . \; \text{where } G = \text{Generality}$$
$$P = \text{Precision}$$
$$R = \text{Reality}$$

(The arrow symbol should be read as "approaches.")

This is strongly suggestive of a very simple algebraic expression:

$$GP = R \, ;$$

which transposes to:

$$G = \frac{R}{P} \, ; \text{ and } P = \frac{R}{G}$$

These two expressions themselves strongly suggest that the relationships observed in very complex systems may not be exclusionary at all. Operationally, at least, they can be considered to be reciprocal relationships. As precision increases, generality goes down, if we maintain the same reality in the model—*i.e.*, the model becomes more and more specific to one particular system. The converse is also valid. Increasing generality decreases precision accordingly. Strictly speaking, we are not allowed to use an "equals" sign, because we are at a loss to know what numbers to plug into these formulas. We do have very good reason to believe that the relationships vary as we have indicated, so we can use another symbol which means "varies as," $\propto$, without the obligation to plug numbers in. Thus for the three possible types of models we have introduced:

$$R \propto GP, P \propto GR, \text{ and } G \propto PR$$

This suggests that achieving the utmost for any two model properties yields a model with all three maximized, or as we have said recreates reality as the modeler perceives it. If it were possible to do this, all three kinds of models would merge into one "super" model. This can never be done. Therefore, we have a situation in which all three kinds of models have one property that is a function of the other two, and it is a different property for each.

Model	*Properties*
Inferential	= G,R
Theoretical	= G,P
Unique	= P,R

The practical implications of these relationships are important for environmental practitioners. For example, a unique model for one ecosystem cannot be used for some other ecosystem; a theoretical model will produce unrealistic results—just how unrealistic will depend on the kind of trade-offs made in designing that model; an inferential model cannot be used to produce reliable "numbers" in projections—it *can* be used to project trends, and to gain insight into ecological and other processes that we do not as yet understand well enough to assign specific values to.

One more theoretical point: Many believe that an hypothesis cannot be refuted or substantiated with a model. However, if what we have said about models is true in the broad sense, there can be no other way to test an hypothesis than with a model (or models). Moreover, the way to test a model, any model, is with *another* model, *not the same* model. The same model can only produce what we have built into it, whether it is right or wrong. Another model based on the same observed phenomena, but with different data acquisition and processing modes, which confirms the output of the first model gives us some reason for confidence. A third model different yet still confirming the original results increases the likelihood of our first model being reliable. It is important to realize that comparing a model's data output with "real world" data is just a case of comparing one model with another, since our "real world" data are necessarily a model of events in the "real world."

The advent of computer-implemented models in recent years has given us an enormously powerful, though not infallible, tool for analyzing the past, present, and future behavior of incredibly complex systems. But are such computer-generated analyses and predictions reliable? That depends.

Since computers are basically high speed processors for logical and mathematical formulas, our answer must be that, given all the restrictions we earlier applied to projections based upon formulas, and given that all the assumptions both explicit and implicit used to fashion the model are a close match to the "real world" system being modeled, then the outcome projected by the computer is highly reliable. Such a model would have a high degree of relative isomorphy with respect to the system modeled. But its forecasts would by no means be infallible.

Social and ecologic systems have far too many variables to model them all. And sometimes a very tiny change can produce stupendous transformations. On a world-wide scale of modeling, individual humans are far too insignificant to bother with—the modeling too coarse to "see" them. Yet, we all know that the intellect and persuasion of a single human have repeatedly altered the course of history and transformed societies in all parts of the globe. Moreover, they have done so in ways that probably no modeler could have foretold, ways that can only be modeled after the fact.

Nevertheless, the electronic age has granted us the power to conjure an oracle whose prescience is not unlike Dickens' "Ghost of Christmas Present." We cannot see the future with crystal clarity with this new tool—we see only the shadows of things to come. If we take alarm at the predictions our new oracle brings forth from its studied isomorphies and ask if these projections *must* be so, the only answer we can get is the same reply Dickens' spirit gave: "If these shadows remain unaltered by the Future . . . ," it will be so.

More than just the distant future is shadowed from our view, however. Each resource transaction seems to have, in addition to the economic costs and benefits we have become accustomed to calculating, a *penumbral* debt, not only in terms of economic externalities, but in terms of degradation of environmental quality. The term "penumbral" was selected because it means partially shadowed. If we look closely enough, most if not all of a particular resource transaction's penumbral costs will be disclosed to us. A great many of our present environmental problems stem from not bothering to look at all.

Penumbral costs, then, include economic externalities, and more importantly, ecological and social costs.

Human societies, particularly technological ones, accumulate penumbral debts because the breadth and scope of project planning is not sufficiently broad; again we are back to the fact that most human enterprises are not considered holistically. To avoid or reduce penumbral costs we must learn to think anew. Proposed products or projects should be viewed as imbedded in complex interactive social and natural systems.

Barry Commoner in his recent book, *The Closing Circle*, has given us an aid to use in learning to think this way. The "Four Laws of Ecology" he enunciated are presented below, although we have taken the liberty of altering them to more accurately reflect practical considerations:

   1. *Everything is connected to something else.*
Put in another way, *you cannot do just one thing.* The natural world and the social systems existing in it are interconnected in complex ways. Therefore it is minimally prudent to find out how a new action is likely to fit into this complex scheme *before* doing it, rather than learn too late that we really did not understand. What old connections must be broken and what new ones established, and how will these new connections cause the rearranged systems to behave?

   2. *Everything must go somewhere.*
It is axiomatic in dealing with ecosystems that materials cycle. Therefore, you cannot really throw something away. You merely move it from one place to another, or transform it from one thing to another. What is it going to do when it is moved or transformed? This also can be restated as "There is no 'away.'"

   3. *You do not get something for nothing.*
This points to the fact that all actions, whether presumed beneficial or not, have costs—if not direct costs, then penumbral costs. Look for them.

   4. *Nature knows best.*
Millions of years have been invested by Nature in evolving ecosystems and their components, and the interactions among and between them that create and sustain this earth's life-support systems. We know that random mutations in germ plasm (DNA) are almost invariably fatal. Random tinkering with ecosystems is not very likely to be beneficial. Therefore, we need to have done our homework very carefully before tinkering is attempted. Whatever we decide to do, Nature will respond to. In this sense this dictum has been phrased, "Nature bats last." We had better be sure Nature's responses are not far more than we thought we had bargained for.

Before we take up the topic of how to apply all this to "real world" situations, we must call your attention to one more item in your intellectual equipment. Even if you thoroughly disagree with the author's conclusions, the reasoning which underlies the dynamics of a "commons" should be at your disposal. Garrett Hardin in *The Tragedy of the Commons* argues persuasively that if each person has equal access to a commons, such as a commonly owned and shared grazing pasture, and each seeks to maximize his own personal gain, the result will inevitably be tragedy for all. A notorious example of a tragedy in a commons still being acted out is the world-wide decimation of the populations of great whales.

The established disciplines in the sciences must be relied upon to provide the tools for looking at the pieces of ecosystems and the social systems associated with them. This reductionist view is indispensable for examining the details of any specific situation. We have attempted to provide a perspective for integrating all the pieces into a comprehensive whole. To that end we introduce one more conceptual term. It is tiresome and repetitive to have to keep saying "ecosystems and social systems," or "ecosystems in which man is a part," and other lumping phrases of the sort, to indicate a concept that can be conveyed with one word. Therefore, the term *macrosystem* will be used to mean ecosystems in which man is either directly involved or in which the effects of human activities are detectable. Macrosystems should also be considered to be large enough to merit our consideration in environmental impact forecasting. The discussion of methods which follows applies to macrosystems.

Part 4. Methods

There is a report, from workers attempting to measure the "I.Q." of Australian aborigines, to the effect that one group absolutely refused to answer questions individually, but after all members of this group conferred together, they gave mutually agreed upon answers that were correct in every instance. As a group they achieved extraordinarily high scores, far beyond any scores that would have been achieved by any *one* of any ethnic background whatsoever.

Macrosystems are so complex that no one person can hope to comprehend them in detail at the levels of resolution required for environmental impact forecasting. The moral is: *Do not work alone.* Work in a team. How to select teams will be taken up a bit later. Now we are concerned with how to conceptualize macrosystems.

Let's start with a very simple question. (a) How much does a common grocery item, a can of beans, cost? (b) What are its penumbral costs? Make a list of such penumbral costs—not just one in your head; write it down. After the list is "completed," get a little help from your friends. Make a new list including all their suggestions for penumbral costs. Can you agree upon the list? Is the new list longer than the one you made by yourself? You can expand this little game to get a better insight into how "team thinking" works. Instead of having everyone help you make a combined list, have them each make a separate list, as you did. Then discuss all the lists, and make a new composite list. You have probably already guessed that none of the individual lists is likely to be isomorphic to any other, and that the composite list will be longer (and more valid?) than any single list. Naturally, there is no *one* answer. There are many possible answers, depending on the purposes of knowing the penumbral costs in the first place.

If your first response was: "Cost in terms of what? Money? Materials? Energy?—you are off to an excellent beginning. In any case, let's examine this can of beans and carry our examination far beyond what would normally be considered in an environmental impact forecast (EIF). Penumbral ecological costs might include contamination of run-off water by pesticides, herbicides, and other chemical additives used in the fields where the beans were grown; pollutants emitted by farm machinery, processing, and transportation to the retail store, and by the shopper if the trip to the store was by motor vehicle; decline in long-term productivity of the soil due to improper farming techniques; resources committed to the whole process; contributions to solid and liquid waste disposal problems at every step along the way; total energetic cost all through the process.*

Are migratory farm workers involved? If so, what kind of community services do they receive? Were the beans produced by "modern" agribusiness? If so, what of the farm workers displaced by machines? How about penumbral economic costs—the externalities? Were you through making cash outlays for that can of beans when you plunked down your cash at the market? Not by a long sight. Disregarding the costs which appear in your taxes to dispose of tin cans, consider the costs that have escalated taxes time after time as successive waves of displaced farm workers have moved to the cities. In this country the response of the middle class to this influx of relatively poorly educated and unskilled (with respect to industrial requirements) workers has been to flee in droves to ever-expanding suburbias, thus reducing the cities' tax base. The cities are left with a necessity for higher tax rates to pay for ever-increasing social services of all kinds; this in turn has been reflected in higher state and federal taxes to somehow fill the breach. At this writing, New York City, the symbol if not the center of our economic system, is teetering on the brink of bankruptcy from just such a situation. All from the penumbral costs of a can of beans? No, not really, but the penumbral costs of that can are a part of the picture.

---

* It is disturbing to think that if any other animal had the same energetic expenditure to gather food as we do, it would starve to death. According to experts, we expend 5 to 10 kilocalories for every single kilocalorie we get from our food in the United States.

You have probably seen that it is possible to start with something as humble as a can of beans and weave incredibly complex scenarios of macrosystems connections and interactions. But you may recall that we said we can only make models, *and* that models must be bounded, as well as being conditional abstractions. Setting bounds according to our purposes, in identifying penumbral costs, limits our inquiries to a manageable level. The practice of setting boundaries, in fact, is the paramount activity of thinking holistically—that is, of systems thinking.

In actual practice, defining those boundaries can get very complex. However, the fundamental process is one of defining boundaries to the macrosystems of concern so that all recognizable significant "side-effects" are transformed to systems-effects contained within the system boundary. With that critical proviso, boundary setting is arbitrary.

Because boundary setting is arbitrary, it contains a trap for the unwary, a trap both theoretical and practical. On the practical side, no project has unlimited time or money with which to include, and therefore investigate, every conceivable connection and effect that might be associated with all possible activities. The study must be confined to a scope and level of resolution that can actually be accomplished within a reasonable budget. The theoretical trap can lead people not to get started at all, because they are bewildered and paralyzed by the complexity of the whole system. This malady is termed "holistic paralysis." Before prevention of this distressing ailment can be discussed we need to know a little something about systems and how they behave. "Real" systems out there in the "real world" do not stand out distinctly from their environments, and "standing out" is the characteristic our senses have been evolved and trained to notice. We must, therefore, resort to models of systems that interest us in order to make them stand out.

The simplest model of a system is the so-called "black box." In our representation here it is just a rectangle with an arrow indicating an input and another arrow indicating an output. The convention is, when we think of something as a black box, that the box is never opened to look inside and see what makes it work. Whatever is inside the black box acts in some way to alter the input so that the output is in some way different from the input. Probably the easiest way to conceptualize how a black box works is with numbers. If we put a 2 into the input and got a 4 at the output, we could assume that something was operating inside the box to increase the 2 to a 4. But we would not know exactly what occurs "inside." Among the possibilities are multiplication and addition. If next we insert a 5 at the input, the output will allow us to know a bit more about whatever operation is occurring inside. A number 10 appearing at the output will strongly suggest that the internal operation is to multiply by 2. On the other hand, a 7 appearing would make us suspect that the operation is to add 2 to whatever is put into the box. Another possibility, had we gotten 25 after putting in 5, is that the box squares every quantity put into it. In short, we can infer quite a bit from observing the input and output, without opening the box at all.

In terms of systems, the thing to be transformed (whatever it is—in the example above, the 2, 5, or 7) is called the *operand*. The mechanism, device, ecosystem, or whatever that does the transforming is called the *operator*. Whatever emerges from the transforming process is termed the *transform*. In the instance above, the transforms are 4, 7, 10, and 25.

In everyday life we use black boxes all the time, but usually without thinking of them as such. To the vast majority of us, the telephone is a black box. We have not the slightest idea what is inside it, how the dialing mechanism works, or any of the other intricacies of reliable telephonic communication. Still we regularly rely on it to perform whatever operations are required to enable us to communicate.

Time required for transformations to take place is not a consideration in the examples just given. However, time may elapse between input and output without affecting the basic principle at all. If one considered a species population of animals at some time to be an input to a black box in which the operator is an ecosystem, and some time later there is a greater number of animals of the same species population in the ecosystem, the new number of animals is the transform produced by the ecosystem as operator. Notice that what has transpired in the ecosystem can be *represented* by assuming the operator to be the equation for compound growth (equation (1) introduced earlier in this chapter), with "t" set to the elapsed time and "r" set to represent a rate of increase that produces the observed result, in the appropriate time span. Of course that equation *does not cause* population to increase, it merely represents it. We do not really know all that has transpired in the real ecosystem. But we do know that with respect to that species population the effect upon population growth can be represented (that is, modeled) reasonably closely by that equation. We also are almost justified in assuming that *if the ecosystem continues to behave with respect to that species population as it has done in the observed elapsed time*, we can project future population levels while such conditions remain. If conditions change, our projections are no longer valid.

That is the crux of the validity of mathematical modeling of ecosystems. It is also the focus of much of the controversy surrounding many such models. Notice that we said "almost justified." There are many *implicit* assumptions in what we have just done that need to be revealed: (*i*) We have assumed that "r" has been constant over the entire period. That may not be the case at all. The growth rate could have been relatively small at the outset, and only recently greatly increased, but with the result that we count the same number of total animals at the end of the time. Or the exact opposite could be occurring—a large rate of increase followed by a catastrophic recent decline in reproduction. Both instances could yield the same absolute numbers of animals, so that we would not be able to distinguish between them if we only look at numbers at the beginning and end of the period. (*ii*) We have assumed no migration, into or out of the population to other ecosystems. (*iii*) We have assumed we can accurately count the population twice, once at the onset and again at the end of the time. And so forth. If any of our assumptions are patently unwarranted, the next period of time will produce results drastically different from what we are expecting. The mathematics only *represent* what has occurred, but do not *mimic the actual processes*. Ecosystems do not have mathematical operators. They have unique ecosystemic operators.

Now let's consider what happens when we peer into a black box to see what's inside. What we'll find is a bunch of smaller boxes connected together in such a fashion as to produce the results we have been observing at the output. At this point we are looking at what in systems terms is called the next "level of resolution," in this case "downward" or "inward." Each of the little boxes is a part or "sub-system" of the whole. Each of these little boxes, were it to be opened, would reveal that it also is composed of interconnected sub-systems, at the next lower level of resolution. Thus the physical world can be considered composed of myriad systems each made of hierarchically ordered sub-systems, each of which is composed of its own sub-systems, and so on down to the limits of our knowledge of the universe composed of matter. At *some* level, any system is a collection of black boxes into which no one can see.

Fortunately, in everyday affairs, including environmental work, it is not necessary to know *everything* about the systems with which we are concerned. Almost any system is comprehensible, if we choose a level of resolution one step above the level where we would be forced to call the parts black boxes. Naturally that level varies from individual to individual and from subject to subject.

The idea of sub-systems complexed together to form whole systems is one of the basic ideas of systems thinking and holism. Computers do computing, but only people can do the kind of whole-systems integration of concepts and foresight indispensable to holistic approaches, or systems thinking. A major postulate of holism is that *the whole is more than the sum of its parts*. That means that when the sub-systems are combined, new system properties not attributable to any individual parts emerge at the next higher level of resolution, at the system level. Such new properties are referred to as "emergent" properties. This view is perhaps hard to justify in terms of strictly mechanical systems, but not with living systems (macrosystems), and levels of resolution wherein mechanical systems interact with macrosystems. For example, living populations have properties that no individual has: birth rate, death rate, age structure, migration rate, sex ratio, and so forth. A telephone system, viewed as interacting with human social attributes, has profound social emergent properties not inherent in just the mechanical structure. When the telephone system is considered solely as an engineering accomplishment, with these social interactions severed, divorced from its macrosystem, the emergent social properties vanish. Thus, one of the most important features of systems is how they are interconnected.

Eons ago, Nature came to a conclusion that quite a few humans are reluctant to acknowledge: Living systems must be connected together in such a fashion as to produce a state of dynamic equilibrium, if the systems are to endure. If a system always has a net gain in growth, we wind up with such absurdities as a universe wall-to-wall with elephants. If the system always has a net loss, eventually it disappears. Living systems remain living by transforming resources. By extension we accept operationally that human populations and enterprises that rely on resource transformation are subject to the same ultimate natural constraints. Systems contained in macrosystems should also be interconnected to produce dynamic stability. Ecologists call such stability *homeostasis*.

A home furnace controlled by a thermostat is an example of a dynamically stable, *homeostatic* system. It transforms resources (changes fossil fuel into heat) to achieve a desired level of temperature. That level is called the "set-point." When the system is working properly, it oscillates around a temperature value which has been set on the thermostat. If the temperature drops below the set-point, the furnace fuel supply and ignition turn on. When the temperature meets or exceeds the set-point level, the furnace is turned off. To accomplish this, information about the temperature state of the system must be "communicated" to the device that controls the furnace. To do this a temperature-sensitive switch is used. "Information" that the temperature is below the set-point closes the switch that turns the furnace on. Similarly, sensing that the temperature is at or above the set-point opens the switch, thus turning the furnace off. The process of "communicating" this information to the furnace is termed *feedback*. A system for maintaining temperature—the furnace and associated parts—has information about the state of the home temperature, relative to the set-point, fed back to it. The output of the furnace system is "heat." That output changes the state of the larger system, the home, and that change in temperature is coupled back to the furnace system, thus changing the output of the furnace.

In general, when any portion of a system output is applied (fed back) to the input of that system, either directly or indirectly, that process is called feedback. Unfortunately, usage in terminology relating to feedback varies. Some system-scientists use terminology relative to a set-point. Thus "deviation amplifying" feedback is used to describe feedback "loops" (from output to input) that drive the system further and further away from the set-point value, either above it or below it. In that usage, deviation amplifying feedback is also called "positive" feedback. Feedback tending to drive the system back to the set-point is called "deviation correcting" or "negative" feedback. Radio engineers, who invented the term in the first place, follow a different usage. According to electronic engineering usage, positive or regenerative feedback is that which tends to increase the amplitude (size, amount, etc.) of the output of the system into which the feedback is applied as an input. Negative or degenerative feedback tends to reduce the output. Used in this sense, both positive and negative feedback are terms which may be used without reference to some arbitrary set-point. When you are discussing systems feedback with others, be sure you are agreed on which kind you are all talking about. A system operating *below* some set-point requires "positive" (regenerative) feedback in one person's parlance, and "negative" (deviation correcting) in another's. Avoid talking at cross-purposes.

Suppose we took the simple black box we mentioned earlier with an operator inside it such that the input is multiplied by two. Thus, a 4 appears as an 8 at the output, and so on. Now we connect the output back to the input so that the total output is fed back. The 8 that just appeared becomes 16 on the next cycle, and 32 on the next cycle, and so forth, growing exponentially. If this system were capable of going through 100 such cycles the final number produced would be too big to name, something like 1,268 followed by 27 zeros. We get this stupendous result from the relatively simple device of connecting the output to the input, creating a regenerative (+) feedback loop. Living populations and other populations relying on transforming resources for their growth, with no insufficient or degenerative (−) feedback to counteract them, grow in this fashion. Only the time per cycle would vary from population to population depending on species' biology. For living populations, death is one form of degenerative feedback. In fact the "r" in equation (1) is derived from the birth rate minus the death rate, $r = b - d$. Obviously, if "b" is greater than "d" the population grows, and if "d" is the greater, the population gets smaller. Depletion of resources essential for a particular population leads to an increase in degenerative feedback through either reduction in birth rate or increase in death rate.

Living populations must rely on transforming a sufficient supply of appropriate resources peculiar to each species. Most populations of organisms vary around some average population number for any given ecosystem. The variation is almost always within the resource availability constraints of each ecosystem. Ecosystems are, among other things, a mixture of a vast array of resources. Indeed, the living populations are, of course, themselves resources for other living populations. Ecologists call the ability of an ecosystem to support a particular species population its *carrying capacity*, with respect to that species.

Carrying capacity is frequently abbreviated as "K" in ecological mathematics and modeling. It is the number of organisms in that species that can be continuously supported by the available resources in the ecosystem. Resource availability is one of the homeostatic mechanisms which act to produce either regenerative feedback, when resources are plentiful, or degenerative feedback, when demand exceeds supply. Populations that oscillate around some set-point value, such as carrying capacity (K), are said to be homeostatic. We said earlier that exponential growth could not continue indefinitely. Suitable resources for a population to transform are finite (Q.E.D.).

Populations and other features of ecosystems may be considered sub-systems of ecosystems. They are connected together so as to create homeostasis within the ecosystem. In such dynamic equilibrium ecosystems do change, but they do so on evolutionary time scales. Connections between sub-systems may be thought of as providing either regenerative or degenerative feedback to the component sub-systems. A rough approximation of whether the result of a series of such connections on the last sub-system to be considered is positive or negative may be had by adding the signs along the connecting path. Then just follow the standard mathematical rule for signs—*i.e.*, an odd number of negative signs yields a negative result; an even number, a positive result. The weakness of this method is that it takes no account of the magnitude of each connection. Weak interactions are not equivalent, despite their "signs," to strong ones.

Ecosystems are themselves interconnected to produce the major biomes of the earth. Biomes are likewise interconnected. Over long ages Nature created a complex hierarchical system of homeostasis encompassing the entire ecosphere. These interactive connections produce primary, secondary, tertiary, and even more remote degrees of coupling between myriad systems. There is even some evidence suggesting that the ecosphere acts like an enormous living organism in modifying and regulating its own physical and chemical environment. The ecosphere in this conception is called *Gaea*. An example of interbiome coupling between Arctic tundra ecosystems and temperate zone estuaries illustrates one way such coupling may take place.

In the temperate zone, during the winter and spring large numbers of shore birds—plovers, dowitchers, etc.—are found scurrying over inter-tidal mudflats, or estuarine ecosystems. These birds crop "surplus" energy, mostly in the form of marine invertebrates inhabiting the mudflats. Energy derived from this source which is surplus to the birds' daily caloric requirements is stored as body fat. During the process much of the nutrient material locked up in the invertebrate population is returned to the estuarine ecosystem as bird droppings and recycled. A few birds die and add their accumulated nutrients to that ecosystem, or immediately contiguous ones. A great many of these shore birds summer and breed in the Arctic tundra. Energy stored from the mudflats powers their flight to the Arctic vastnesses. The breeding success on the tundra will be reflected in the number of birds appearing in the estuaries the following year, and the productivity of estuaries is a major determining factor in how many birds return to the breeding grounds on the tundra the next summer.

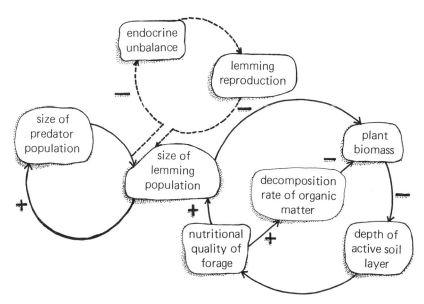

Fig. 2–1 Arctic tundra ecosystem feedback loop model (after Schultz).

Even coupling within a particular ecosystem is frequently found to be counterintuitive. Marine mammals, *e.g.* seals, appear to be a case in point. Everybody knows that seals eat fish. Therefore, fish populations sharing an ecosystem with seals will be reduced. It seems so, but the number of fish, in the first place, depends on a chain of transformable resources adequate and appropriate for each link in that chain. Large fish depend for food upon invertebrates and smaller fish. These animals are in turn dependent upon available zooplankton (tiny marine animals), which in turn are dependent upon phytoplankton (tiny marine plants). Phytoplankton require sunlight for photosynthesis and a supply of dissolved nutrient materials. One of the major reasons for spring plankton "blooms" is that a renewed supply of nutrients is brought up to the sunlit surface waters by up-welling currents from dark depths. A steady, rich supply of nutrients means that even though large numbers of phytoplankton are cropped (eaten) by zooplankton, they can be continually replaced at a rapid rate. Marine ecosystems operating in this fashion are said to have high productivity and high turnover (rapid replacement of phytoplankton). A dead fish decomposes slowly, or is carried away by wind and currents to other ecosystems, if it is not eaten on the spot. Marine mammals' feces are liquid ejecta. Thus nutrients formerly locked into their food are practically immediately available to the phytoplankton and may contribute substantially to continuing the high rate of turnover upon which the entire food chain, including the larger fish, depends. Of course, fish harvested for commercial purposes cannot contribute to this process except by the most devious and remote routes of coupling, via metropolitan sewer outfalls and the like. But commercial harvesting is a macrosystemic activity, and we are speaking for the moment of ecosystems as *natural* systems.

Natural ecosystems are a special case of systems in general. As in other systems, they are organized hierarchically—boxes within boxes, within still more boxes—and are composed of interactive sub-systems connected by feedback pathways. Internal relationships and external coupling to other ecosystems are such that resource transformations of specific types, and accomplished within a range of possible rates, became established by long evolutionary processes. Ecosystems can maintain homeostasis within those limits for resource transformations. Carrying capacities for all the species populations in ecosystems are uniquely determined by those same limits. Ecosystems, however, are not mathematically tidy. For example, there can be little argument that the vegetation established in a particular ecosystem, theoretically a dependent variable, has *some* influence on the over-all climate.

Macrosystems, ecosystems containing or influenced by the works of mankind, over the ages have become quite distinct from natural ecosystems in several respects. This divergence from natural ecosystems is especially pronounced in macrosystems occupied by technological societies. Indeed, the divergence has been accelerating steadily during the past two centuries. In technological societies, human activities superimposed on natural ecosystems transform more resources of different kinds and at much greater rates than ecosystems have evolved an ability to cope with. This destabilizes ecosystems' homeostatic mechanisms. Inevitably, the associated macrosystems are also destabilized. To make this point clear, when people transform resources (trees, fish, etc.) at rates in excess of evolved replacement possibilities, the industries associated with those excessive transformations collapse just as surely as do the populations of those resources. Typically, macrosystemic technological stressing of ecosystems results from release of prodigious amounts of energy, usually from fossil fuels, for which ecosystems have no homeostatic mechanisms. Understand that we are quite capable of drastically altering ecosystems without massive inputs of fossil fuel energy; the alteration just takes longer. Macrosystems in modern times appear to be attempting to reach new levels of homeostasis that their associated ecosystems are unable to achieve. Ecosystems can transform resources only within certain limits, and we are constantly forcing a heavier burden of transformations upon them.

Human activities are what makes macrosystems different. The effects of some human activities are what must be considered in the process of environmental impact forecasting. And now that we have discussed the kinds of systems and some of the salient properties we must deal with, we can turn our attention to environmental impact assessment and forecasting.

A major component of environmental impact documents is the portion describing the "environmental setting." The setting and the kind of activity contemplated should determine the composition of the team charged with carrying out the impact study. Final composition of the team should be postponed until some of the preliminary work has been done. Preliminary holistic studies should reveal the extent of systems-effects and in what macrosystems, other than the immediate site of the project, they are likely to occur. The initial study team should include experts familiar with the major features of the project macrosystem(s). In addition, the team should include at least one competent generalist—an interdisciplinarian capable of speaking the "language" of experts and equally capable of integrating the different aspects of the study into a coherent holistic approach.

Describing the environmental setting is the part of the process closest to meriting the appelation "assessment." What is at the site, nearby, and likely to be affected by the project must all first be assessed as it is, before any changes are made. Major components of the setting that usually require separate treatment by experts discussing both regional and local aspects are:

1. *Geology.* Pay special attention to potential geological hazards and unique features.

2. *Topography.* Relief maps should be provided, and the watershed in which the project will be located identified in addition to its geomorphology.

3. *Soils.* In addition to standard parameters important to civil engineering studies, pay attention to fertility, off-site erosion hazards, and suitability for contemplated use as opposed to other possible uses—farming, for example.

4. *Climate.* Site microclimate should also be included. There is now sufficient evidence of a world-wide cooling trend; it would be prudent to include consideration of possible effects cooling might have on contemplated uses.

5. *Hydrology.* Groundwater, run-off, drainage patterns, percolation, salinization, recharging rates, and the like are appropriate for discussion.

Studies with a major primary or secondary aquatic orientation—dams, stream channelization, irrigation, harbors, coastal development, oceanic off-shore operations, and the like—should include the services of appropriate experts: oceanographers, limnologists, marine biologists, marine geologists, engineers, and the like. Projects with major waste discharge into bodies of water are included in this category. Sections on geology and topography may still be appropriate when discussing aquatic ecosystems. Sections on soils and hydrology should be changed to suitable oceanographic or limnological considerations.

6. *Biology.* The living components of the ecosystem should be described as to species populations and *trophic relationships* between them ("trophic" refers to nutrient flow). Special attention should be given to rare and endangered species. Also, do not ignore invertebrates.

At the very minimum, the biological portion should include some idea of the major trophic structure and how it is likely to be altered by the project and its alternatives. It should also include how such changes are likely to ramify through adjacent and other ecosystems to which the ones in question are coupled. Will the ecosystems be able to handle the new demands for resource transformations thrust upon them? If not, how will their form and functions be changed?

Remember that ecology is the study of the interrelationships of an organism or a biotic community and its environment. Understanding the basic food web of an ecosystem is fundamental to disclosing ecosystemical interactions. A laundry list won't do. A taxonomic list of species is the cast of characters—not the play. Such a list is, of course, essential, but it is only a beginning, not the end of the studies that should be done.

A beginning can be made at depicting trophic relationships with a very simple modification added to taxonomic lists.* If all the entries are serially numbered, a column can be added wherein, on the same line that a particular species appears, the numbers of the animals that eat that species can be listed and the number of animals that are eaten by that species can be indicated in parentheses. Moreover the numbers contained within the parentheses are a visual clue for remembering that those are the species eaten by (contained in) that critter. Such an entry might appear thus:

#	Species	Common Name	Food Web	Pop. #
135	Spinus pasaltria	lesser goldfinch	26,30,36,87,(198,210,234)	10^2
.	. .	. .	.	.
.	. .	. .	.	.
etc.	. .			

In this fashion, at least the major dietary items could be indicated. A column could be added, as merely suggested above, to show that species' trophic position. A lesser goldfinch might be shown as both an herbivore and a sometime

* The author is indebted to Dr. P. B. Turner, Jr., for the basis of this idea.

carnivore (insects). A rough approximation of population numbers can also be added. In the example above it is given to the nearest power of ten.

One small terminological matter should be mentioned. The term "flora" is frequently used in describing the vegetation on a site. But field botanists use the term *flora* in a regional sense to indicate the total plant reservoir that could contribute *disseminules* (seeds and spores) capable of colonizing the ecosystem in question. The actual vegetation is referred to as just that—vegetation.

7. *Cultural features* include present human land use patterns, activities, and present levels of energy use. This covers public health aspects of air, water, and noise pollution. Socio-economic aspects related to the project and its alternatives should also be included. Archaeological and historical sites should be identified, and preservation or salvage considered. A more comprehensive treatment of these topics may be found in Chapter 3.

Aerial photos and maps will be invaluable aids to almost any study, but they should not be used as a substitute for actual site visits. *Go to the site and study it.* There is no substitute for direct observation. Neophyte biologists must spend part of their site-time during hours of darkness and dusk. Plan to arrive long before morning twilight, preferably alone, or with another observer who understands the need for *complete silence*. Visits during mid-day full-light are very apt to be during intermission—when the play is in abeyance. To avoid Inspector Clouseau-like encounters with the local police, inform them and the landowner of your pending night site-visits.

One of the compelling reasons for a personal site study is that ecological theory is not invariably a good predictor of what will be found in the field. And what may be true of a particular type of ecosystem *qua* ecosystem may not be at all true when that type of ecosystem is complexed as a macrosystem. As an example, it is an ecological dictum that ecosystems with high species diversity and elaborately interconnected food webs are more stable—that is, are less susceptible to and recover faster from perturbations than do less complex ecosystems. But it does not follow that similar stability is conferred when those types of ecosystems are made to serve as the base for *any and all* configurations of macrosystems. All ecosystems have what might be termed a *disruptive threshold*, determined by the limits of kind and rate of resource transformations sustainable. Tropical rain forests offer an example. Though now endangered by encroaching human activities, these rain forests have the highest species diversity to be found on this earth. They have persisted for countless thousands of years in many places. Swidden (slash and burn) agricultural communities are a common form of macrosystem based upon tropical rain forests. If swidden agriculturalists maintain between burnings fallow periods of ten years or so, transformation limits of the supporting tropical rain forest are not exceeded, and such macrosystems can endure for long periods. When for whatever reason the fallow cycle is drastically shortened, the base ecosystem's disruptive threshold is exceeded and the agricultural system collapses, as does that portion of the supporting rain forest. Thus, theoretical ecosystemic stability when coupled to incompatible human activities becomes macrosystemic fragility. Yet it is not uncommon to encounter such bland statements as appeared in a publication by a large international agency working on a huge construction complex in tropical rain forests to the effect that "viewed in the light of the basic principles of ecology, one irrefutable fact that stands out is that environmental alterations are far less likely to be disruptive in the . . . basin than in the tropical grasslands of Africa, in Europe, or in the Arctic." An accompanying photo is captioned *built-in tolerance for change.* No mention is made of the magnitude of disruption being of importance.

In general, though, ecological tenets are confirmed and reconfirmed by experimental evidence. Diversity does usually convey stability. And there is evidence that predation frequently enhances stability by encouraging diversity.

There are quite a few "standard" methods for organizing and conducting environmental impact studies. Some workers use checklists, others employ matrices such as the one suggested by Luna Leopold and published by the U.S. Geological Survey. Still others find that the complexity of macrosystems is better handled by a network of matrices, or nested matrices. Several books treating these different methods are listed in the references. Whatever method you decide to employ, do not approach the task with the concept that any method is an adequate cookbook to be followed blindly. Any method will have to be tailored to a particular task. Moreover, some method outlines may have conceptual "clinkers" that are not instantly apparent, especially if you adopt the cookbook attitude.

We can now consider in more detail the matter of being holistic. Hierarchical systems are organized in such a fashion that if you wish to know the purpose of a given system, the place to look is the next level "up." If you want to know how something works—the mechanism—look at the next lower system level. For example, the "purpose" of a species population is to be found in its interactive role at the ecosystem (or community) level. The mechanisms of how a species population reproduces, eats, is eaten, etc. is found at the individual level. Therefore, the level of resolution chosen for macrosystem studies should generally be the macrosystem-ecosystem level, to begin with. Later, when the major system functions at that level are pretty well in hand, it may be necessary to look more closely at lower levels of resolution in order to understand better a particular problem or process. Quite naturally, we can expect the study boundary to be at the macrosystem level. More than likely, this boundary will enclose more than just one type of ecosystem. As a first approximation we can consider each of the constituent ecosystems a contributor to the whole system roughly in proportion to its share of the total area, but adjusted for the type of ecosystem in each case. We can also assume that an ecosystem of a given type, say a riparian ecosystem, will be pretty much like similar ecosystems in adjacent areas—one expects mule deer, not giraffes, in the California chaparral. If there is a reason to do so, this part of the procedure can be dignified by saying that we are making an assumption of *fractional relative isomorphy.*

In systems practice, "environment" has a very special meaning. Everything inside the system boundary is something that in theory we can operate upon and change if necessary. Everything outside the system boundary is in the "system environment" and must be accepted as "given" and not to be operated upon.

Recently several colleagues and I were confronted with the task of devising environmental impact guidelines that would have universal application throughout a region extending from Iran in the west to Japan, Australia, and the Pacific Island states in the east. We came up with the concept of "resource transactions." The basic idea is that all actions of environmental significance necessarily involve resource transformations. An idea, for instance, despite the amount of energy used in thinking about it, does not have environmental significance until it is acted upon. A resource can only be transformed or *not* transformed. By following resource transformations it should be possible to satisfactorily delineate a macrosystems boundary encompassing a whole-systems perception of any proposed project. But, this is another area of the EIF process that must remain judgmental. Since everything that happens in macrosystems, and especially in ecosystems, can be viewed as resource transformations, it is necessary to be selective. We cannot hope to follow *all* that goes on, if for no other reason than that we cannot know everything.

Therefore, our goal is more modest than *complete* understanding. This method is based upon locating and following *significant* resource transformations. We can start with an *apriori* assumption that the proposed project involves significant resource transformations (RT's). Then the chain of RT's can be followed to determine to what extent our assumption seems justified. The same procedure is followed for alternatives to the project. In a very rigorous application of this method, as in the case of potentially dangerous or very damaging projects, our *apriori* assumption would be couched in the form of a series of hypotheses to be tested.

And resources have a limited range of possible future states, when viewed at the level of resolution employed for the basic method. They are:

A resource can be transformed:

1. In space. That is, it can be moved from one location to another.
2. Into other things. This can be accomplished by either adding or taking away

energy or materials or both. Water, for example, is made into ice by removing heat energy, and into steam or vapor by adding heat energy. Material addition and subtraction should be self-evident.

3. In magnitude. Living organisms are most likely to be involved in this kind of RT. Populations can grow or shrink in numbers. "Natural resource" depletion is another common case.

For our purposes these RT's are not considered mutually exclusive, with the obvious exception that no further RT's are possible, for a given resource, after its magnitude is transformed to zero. During a specified time, a resource could undergo all three forms of transformation.

The remaining possibility is that the resource is *not* transformed during the time interval we are considering.

To follow a chain of RT's, for each resource of concern we can ask a series of questions and enter the answers in a flow diagram, matrix, or whatever other recording scheme we find most suitable either to our own preferences or for the efficiency of a team. The questions to ask are:

1. *What?* What resource will be transformed? Into what? From what resources in previous steps? Be sure to account for all the transforms. Recall that in the example we gave of the furnace we said the transformation was from fossil fuel to heat, but we ignored products of combustion, stack gases, particulate matter, and the steps to get the fuel to our furnace.

2. *When?* When does the RT take place and over what time span?

3. *Where?* Where will the RT take place *and* where will the transforms go—*all* of them? Relate this to time span.

4. *Who?* In a multiple sense, who is the operator, what are the sub-system and mechanism involved? If a human activity is involved, precisely who and what? Who are the experts that know about this type of RT, for further investigation, if required at lower levels of resolution? And who is the governmental or regulatory agency, if any, concerned with this RT?

5. *How?* Again in a multiple sense. How does the RT take place? By steps? By mechanisms? How do we find out more about it, and about prior and succeeding RT's linked to this one? How does it couple to other systems, sub-systems, and RT's?

6. *Why?* Is this RT really necessary to accomplish the objectives of the project or its alternatives? Why is it necessary in ecosystemic or macrosystemic processes? What functional role does it play?

If the results of this kind of inquiry are depicted in a matrix, some useful results can be had. For example, if a resource by space (ecosystems, watersheds, airsheds, etc.) matrix is constructed for a sequence of times, one for each discrete time interval, a three-dimensional matrix is created that depicts how resources are transformed and move through space over time. This could be done on acetate overlays or some similar graphic device to get an over-all impression of how a project is most likely to ramify throughout its own and adjoining macrosystems.

Following this procedure, the initial team selected for a particular EIF should quickly determine and set appropriate boundaries for the job. Moreover, it should indicate which other specialists should be drawn upon to give expert assistance for the thorough investigation of RT's which have been discovered to present particularly important or specific problems. Also notice how the questions raised in following RT's recall the "four laws of ecology."

Following RT's generates what amounts to a functional model of the macrosystem, present and future. At each step, environmental professionals are urged to go "outside" the particular segment they are at the moment considering to see how it relates to past and future as well as adjacent systems. The same basic process is repeated over and over again for each significant RT. Once a tentative boundary is set, the investigator must go "outside" that boundary to see if it is really appropriate. Are there "side-effects" outside the boundary? If so, expand the boundary. Then repeat the process until no significant side-effects remain to be transformed. On occasion, this may well entail expanding the scope or authority, perhaps both, over that originally contemplated. If this cannot be done, then the client and public agencies should be informed in no uncertain terms that the study will be incomplete in that respect.

The kind of holistic approach we recommend can now be defined. This holistic approach is an *apperceptive, exiterative* process. It is apperceptive in that it requires one to see things from new viewpoints to better understand what is already known. It is exiterative (*exo- + iterative: to go outside of + to repeat a routine, to get closer and closer to the correct answer*) in that the process requires that one repeatedly go outside particular resource transformations and tentative boundaries, to find new significant RT's and more appropriate boundaries.

Dynamics of the EIS Process

The environmental impact process is developing a set of dynamics of its own. A few of these can be seen already:

1. No one person or group can know *all* the facts. But to be disastrously surprised is inexcusable (and probably means professional suicide).

2. A decision to take no action is an active decision to maintain the status quo and continue present trends. But present trends may result in irreversibility.

3. Delayed action will result in better decisions. But delay increases costs and difficulties.

4. Effective action is usually inversely proportional to the number of authorita-

tive decision-makers. Yet many factors and interests must be coordinated and accommodated for effective action.

5. Options should be maximized. But planning forecloses options.

6. Ecologically sound decisions should optimize benefits over the long run for the greatest number possible. But some interests must be negatively affected.

7. Protecting a natural resource can save a precious natural resource for future generations. But present demand does not evaporate. It is applied with increasing pressure to the same resource in other locations or applied to other resources.

We have attempted here to discuss some of the theoretical aspects of the environmental impact process as they apply to the practicalities of getting the job done. We have presented one way to examine macrosystems holistically in a manner we hope has sufficient clarity to be of use to environmental professionals. We have not done so with a heavy air of certitude, nor have we wished to convey to you that certitude can somehow be found in the theory and methods we recommend to you. It cannot. Certitude is a creature of 19th century science, a chimaera. We will not see its like again.

Does practicing holistic approaches to environmental problems require a different kind of mind? We think not. But almost assuredly it requires a different personality, one that does not have to rely on certitude but can cope with uncertainties and complexities in the face of the pressing requirements of our times.

Acknowledgment: The author is indebted to Drs. James N. Anderson, Edwin R. Lewis, and Arnold M. Schultz, all of the University of California at Berkeley, and to Dr. Norbert Dannhaeuser of Case Western Reserve University for many stimulating discussions of matters touched upon in this chapter. However, any egregious blunders, errors of fact, or eccentricities of opinion as may lie abasking in this text are solely due to the incapacities and general malfeasance of the author.

References

This is by no means an exhaustive or comprehensive bibliography, but it should serve as an introduction to a vast literature touching upon various aspects of "environmental science." Almost all of the works cited here have extensive references to lead interested readers to many of the prime sources. The biological sciences are emphasized, but not exclusively so. The basic ecological references can be relied upon to confirm what has been said here with respect to fundamental points about ecology. However, other authors listed here bear no responsibility for this author's views on science in general, environmental science, and methods of applying a systems-approach in particular. Such pronouncements, though unwittingly contributed to by many of these authors, are heresies perpetrated solely by this author—as are the comments which follow some of the entries below. Please read all critically. And remember that you are under no injunction to agree with this or any author.

Some General Environmental Texts

Anderson, F. R., *NEPA in the Courts: A Legal Analysis of the National Environmental Policy Act.* Resources for the Future, Johns Hopkins Univ. Press, Baltimore. 1973, 324 pp.

Oliver, J. E., *Climate and Man's Environment: An Introduction to Applied Climatology.* John Wiley & Sons, N.Y. 1973, 517 pp.

Hull, D., *Philosophy of Biological Science.* Foundations of Philosophy Series, Prentice-Hall, Englewood Cliffs, N.J. 1974, 148 pp.

An excellent introduction to the philosophy of science, concise and readable.

Krauskopf, K. B., *The Third Planet: An Invitation to Geology.* Freeman Cooper, San Francisco. 1974, 523 pp.

Fascinating and beautifully written.

McHarg, I. L., *Design with Nature.* Natural History Press, Doubleday, N.Y. 1971, 197 pp.

A classic—a regional planning perspective.

Turk, A., *et al., Environmental Science.* W. B. Saunders, Philadelphia. 1974, 563 pp.

By far the best introductory text on this subject that I have seen. Read it.

Strahler, A. N., & A. H. Strahler, *Environmental Geoscience: Interactions between Natural Systems and Man.* Hamilton (division of John Wiley & Sons), Santa Barbara. 1973, 511 pp. + appendices.

As good in geoscience as Turk *et al.* is in general.

Watt, K. E. F., *Principles of Environmental Science.* McGraw-Hill, N.Y. 1973, 319 pp.

Seen from the systems-ecologists' viewpoint; thirty-eight "principles," some indubitable, others less so. Well worth reading.

Some Ecology Texts

Colinvaux, P. A., *Introduction to Ecology.* John Wiley & Sons, N.Y. 1973, 621 pp.

Collier, B., *et al, Dynamic Ecology.* Prentice-Hall, Englewood Cliffs, N.J. 1973, 563 pp.

Emlen, J. M., *Ecology: An Evolutionary Approach.* Addison-Wesley, Reading, Mass. 1973, 493 pp.

Though it deals with evolutionary theory, it would have been better sub-titled "A Mathematical Approach."

Farnworth, E. G., & F. B. Golley, eds., *Fragile Ecosystems: Evaluation of Research &*
Applications in the Neotropics. A Report of the Institute of Ecology (TIE).
Springer-Verlag, N.Y. 1974, 258 pp.
Note especially the need for further study, (and of the discussion in this chapter
of "disruptive thresholds").

Golley, F. B., & E. Medina, eds., *Tropical Ecological Systems: Trends in Terrestrial &*
Aquatic Research. Ecological Studies 11, Springer-Verlag, N.Y. 1975, 398 pp.

Krebs, C. J., *Ecology: The Experimental Analysis of Distribution and Abundance.*
Harper & Row, N.Y. 1972, 694 pp.
One of the very best introductory texts; balanced and comprehensive.

McNaughton, S. J., & L. L. Wolf, *General Ecology.* Holt, Rinehart & Winston,
N.Y. 1973, 710 pp.
Excellent treatment of biomes.

Odum, E. P., *Fundamentals of Ecology.* 3rd Edition. W. B. Saunders, N.Y. 1971,
574 pp.
A third edition of *the* classic introductory text, greatly expanded and improved.
Excellent references.

Pianka, E. R., *Evolutionary Ecology.* Harper & Row, N.Y. 1974, 356 pp.
An excellent synthesis of much recent material in a non-mathematical approach.

Poole, R. W., *An Introduction to Quantitative Ecology.* McGraw-Hill Series in
Population Biology, McGraw-Hill, N.Y. 1974, 532 pp.
A good introduction to "mathematical ecology."

Ricklefs, R. E., *Ecology.* Chiron Press, Portland, Oregon. 1973, 861 pp.
As direct and unpretentious as the title. A biological approach with a wealth of
information.

Systems Approaches and "Modeling"

von Bertalanffy, L., *General Systems Theory: Foundations Development Applications.*
Revised Edition. George Braziller, N.Y. 1968, 295 pp.
Essays on GST by one of the founders of that field.

Jeffers, J. N. R., ed., *Mathematical Models in Ecology.* Blackwell Scientific
Publications, Oxford. 1972, 398 pp.

Laszlo, E., ed., *The Relevance of General Systems Theory.* George Braziller, N.Y.
1972 A, 213 pp.

Laszlo, E., ed., *The Systems View of the World.* George Braziller, N.Y. 1972 B,
131 pp.
The "Systems View . . ." would be rendered more accurately as "A."

Levin, S. A., ed., *Ecosystem Analysis and Prediction: Proceedings of a Conference on*
Ecosystems, Alta, Utah, July 1–5, 1974. Society for Industrial and Applied
Mathematics, Philadelphia. 1975, 337 pp.

Lewis, E. R., *Network Models in Population Biology*. Springer-Verlag, N.Y. (In preparation)

Have seen some of the early manuscript. Promises to be excellent.

May, R. M., *Stability and Complexity in Model Ecosystems*. Monographs in Population Biology #6, Princeton University Press, Princeton. 1973, 235 pp.

Pattee, H. H., ed., *Hierarchy Theory: The Challenge of Complex Systems*. George Braziller, N.Y. 1973, 156 pp.

Patten, B. C., *Systems Analysis and Simulation in Ecology, Vol. 1*. Academic Press, N.Y. 1971, 610 pp.

Patten, B. C., *Systems Analysis and Simulation in Ecology, Vol. 2*. Academic Press, N.Y. 1972, 592 pp.

Patten, B. C., *Systems Analysis and Simulation in Ecology, Vol. 3*. Academic Press, N.Y. (In preparation)

Smith, J. M., *Models in Ecology*. Cambridge University Press, Cambridge. 1974, 146 pp.

Watt, K. E. F., *Ecology and Resource Management: A Quantitative Approach*. Series in Population Biology, McGraw-Hill, N.Y. 1968, 450 pp.

Possible Futures

Calder, N., *The Weather Machine*. Viking Press, N.Y. 1975, 143 pp.

Chen, K., *Growth Policy: Population Environment and Beyond*. University of Michigan Press, Ann Arbor. 1974, 237 pp.

Cole, H. S. D., *et al.*, *Models of Doom: A Critique of the Limits to Growth*. Universe Books, N.Y. 1973, 244 pp.

Darling, F. F., *Wilderness and Plenty*. F.O.E./Ballantine Books, N.Y. 1971, 112 pp.

Editors of *The Ecologist*, *Blueprint for Survival*. Houghton Mifflin, Boston. 1972, 189 pp.

Ehrlich, P. R., & A. H. Ehrlich, *The End of Affluence: A Blueprint for Your Future*. Ballantine Books, N.Y. 1974, 307 pp.

Editors of *Fortune*, *The Environment: A National Mission for the Seventies*. Perennial Library, Harper & Row Publishers, N.Y. 1970, 220 pp.

Hardin, G., *Exploring New Ethics for Survival: The Voyage of the Spaceship Beagle*. A Pelican Book, Penguin Books, Baltimore. 1973, 273 pp.

Contains a reprint of "The Tragedy of the Commons" (*v.* pp. 250–264).

Park, C. F., Jr., *Earthbound: Minerals, Energy, and Man's Future*. Freeman Cooper, San Francisco. 1975, 279 pp.

Ridgeway, J., *The Last Play: The Struggle to Monopolize the World's Energy Resources*. A Mentor Book, New American Library, N.Y. 1973, 373 pp.

Taylor, G. R., *Rethink: Radical Proposals to Save a Disintegrating World*. A Pelican Book, Penguin Books, Baltimore. 1974, 374 pp.

Toffler, A., *The Eco-Spasm Report.* A Bantam Book, Bantam Books, N.Y. 1975, 116 pp.
  The "Eco" here is largely eco-nomic.
Watt, D. E. F., *The Titanic Effect: Planning the Unthinkable.* Sinauer Associates. Stamford, Conn. 1974, 268 pp.

Many of these books describe indicators that readers can use to determine for themselves whether or not the authors' projections of future events are being realized.

3 · Assessing Social and Economic Impacts

In this chapter, we examine social and economic impacts in general and discuss specifically some that are especially important. We also review sources of social and economic data and suggest methods of using and portraying this information.

The National Environmental Policy Act requires the use of the social sciences and mandates the consideration of unquantified values by means of a systematic interdisciplinary approach (102(A)). These requirements were expanded by the Council on Environmental Quality in its 1973 Guidelines, which specified the consideration of impacts on a list of concerns including population growth, community facilities, land use, urban congestion, threats to health, transportation, noise, neighborhood character and continuity, low income populations, recreation, and objects of historic or archeological significance.

Additionally, the internal guidelines of many federal agencies require consideration of social and economic impacts in such areas as national and regional economic development, social well-being, the distribution of impacts among population groups, economic stability, education, income distribution, aesthetic values, employment opportunities, displacement of people, housing, safety, and security.

Robert A. Johnston, born in 1945, is currently Assistant Professor of Environmental Studies at the University of California at Davis. An Associate Member of the American Institute of Planners, he has served as a planner and planning consultant to government agencies in California, Nevada, and Massachusetts. He has also worked in the fields of economic and social analysis with M.I.T.'s Joint Urban Studies Program and in the development of computer mapping programs at the University of California at Davis. He currently conducts research in planning systems, land use politics, and impact analysis.

Impact analysis, then, clearly must be comprehensive, covering as many significant impacts as possible and tracing their interrelationships.

Such a comprehensive approach requires the use and correlation of existing scientific theories and data for a number of reasons:

(*1*) If you consider long-term natural environmental impacts (as NEPA and many states' laws require), you must look at medium-term economic and population growth impacts, since the major environmental effects of projects are often the result of urban growth.

(*2*) You can then gather and interpret data in an integrated fashion.

(*3*) By the time you have considered all of the impacts required by the guidelines of most agencies, NEPA, or state laws, you have covered almost everything anyway.

While we are chiefly concerned here with economic and social impacts, we discuss natural environmental effects when they occur as elements in the social and economic impact chains. Our definition of "social" includes human psychological, biological, and physiological processes, as well as community processes. "Economic" includes the production, distribution, and consumption of goods and services.

1. A Theoretical Framework

A major failing of many EIS's is their fragmented character. No effort is made to introduce the EIS reader to the natural and cultural processes at work so that he or she can see the impacts of a project against a perspective of its surroundings. The usual reason for this fragmentation is the lack of theoretical framework. The result is that many EIS's avoid explaining what the real issues of a project are and what relationship a project may have to the environment, economy, and community. Many impact statements also give no hint of the political battles raging over certain impacts, nor of the scientific arguments concerning data interpretation. What is needed is an effort to place the impact report in a theoretical framework that organizes the information so laypersons can comprehend it. Impact reports should list and quantify not only the effects of a project on the surrounding environment, but also its political issues and economic and social ramifications. This is done by presenting data in a scientifically valid framework and focusing political attention on those impacts of the greatest scientific and political concern. In this way, an EIS can truly aid the political process and the job of the decision-makers.

There is a great body of knowledge that can be used in estimating the social and economic impacts of a policy, a plan, or a project. Economics, sociology, psychology, human physiology, anthropology, political science, geography, mathematics, geology, chemistry, engineering, medicine, and planning all contribute to our understanding of human systems. Since no one can master all of this knowledge, we must specialize in our work. The more specific your information needs are, the more experts you will require.

Someone, however, has to sit down at the beginning of the impact-reporting process and conceptualize the project's impacts in a rough sort of way to organize the research program. A panel of experts can be used at an early point to help identify the variables to be investigated. Interest groups can be similarly used to outline certain impacts of potential concern. Someone must organize this list of impact types and their relationships to give the various disjointed concepts theoretical meaning. Ordering the impacts into theoretic groupings allows for a systematic and efficient investigation of impacts and a coherent explanation of the causal processes in the EIS.

How do we organize all of these disciplines and data? We suggest two overarching concepts be used as a unifying framework for analysis:
(*1*) Regional economic growth (and decline) processes
(*2*) Community social processes
Regional economic growth processes involve primarily increases in the production of exportable goods, provision of access, water or utilities, changes in residential or recreational amenities and hazards, and changes in land tenure or zoning in a region or areas within a region. Agency plans are viewed in the context of all other development plans within the region. All growth-inducing projects, ones that could significantly change interregional or intraregional growth rates, should be examined within the regional economic growth framework.

Community social processes involve child rearing and education, employment, family formation and housing, physical and social services, shopping, and transportation. All projects developed in a region will affect some or all of these factors. Frequently the effects are cumulative and occur slowly over time, such as the change in a neighborhood from single-family housing with many elderly residents to multiple-unit housing with many children. All projects should be examined in the framework of community social processes. We will return to these two unifying concepts later in the chapter.

Organizing Information

Regional economic and social processes can provide a framework and direction for research, but the problem of organizing information still remains during an EIS investigation. Generally, social and economic data are available from a multitude of federal, state, and local agencies and are seldom organized by any one agency in a format that is useful for planning. Government offices usually carry on their activities year after year with little or no information on the people they affect or their own performance. This is reflected in the way data are gathered and organized and will be a major problem for your EIS research.

Developing a data base that adequately describes the basic structure of social and economic environments requires searching the records of dozens of local, state, federal, and private bureaus for information on fires, crimes, traffic congestion, diseases, education, housing, income, employment, welfare, parks, sewers, water supply, land use, local private financing markets, economic markets, population, government finances, political participation, construction, noise, aesthetics, transportation, zoning, natural hazards, racial and sexual equality, community cohesion, and so on.

Generally data will not be broken down by subareas, such as neighborhoods; or by cross-categories, such as age or race; or by environmental areas, such as watersheds. Often data will not be summarized, but will exist only in file cabinets. Many agencies have no need at all for the data an EIS writer requires and simply do not collect them. For example, a subdivider might wish to know about his proposed development's potential impact on city service costs. Service agencies, such as fire and police departments, are not concerned with the marginal costs of servicing various types of developments and do not collect this information.

Social and economic data have expanded dramatically in the last twenty years. Data management, however, has made much slower progress. Few cities and fewer counties have centralized automated information systems that allow an EIS researcher to get data quickly in useable formats. Different levels of government collect different data types for their own program evaluation needs and the data are coded in incompatible ways. Agencies resist the centralization of data in planning offices because it may weaken them politically.

A Basic Approach

The EIS writer is required to produce research in a limited period of time with limited funds. He can't wait for local, state, and other federal agencies to provide the needed information. Most of the secondary research (obtaining existing data from outside sources) has to be done by the EIS coordinator under pressure. Therefore, studies must be relatively fast, cheap, and contribute to an on-going data bank whenever possible.

Our focus in this chapter is on research methods that are relatively easy to perform and involve minimal primary data collection in the field (generating data through your own basic studies). As we have noted, there is no lack of data in files, reports, and computer tapes in various federal, state, and local agencies. You just have to find the information and interpret it to suit your needs.

The impact-reporting process can be accomplished by organizing the work in four steps: (*1*) organizing for the job; (*2*) identifying the impacts; (*3*) estimating (and quantifying) the impacts; (*4*) interpreting the impacts for political relevance and display in the final report. You can organize impact assessment work using the sections of this chapter during the four phases of the impact-reporting process in this order:

(*1*) *Organizing for the Job*
> Section 1. A theoretical framework

(*2*) *Identification of Impacts*
> Section 2. Four classifications of impacts
> Section 3. Impacts caused by changes in regional economic development processes
> Section 4. Impacts caused by changes in community social processes

(*3*) *Estimation (and Quantification) of Impacts*
> Section 3. Impacts caused by changes in regional economic development processes
> Section 4. Impacts caused by changes in community social processes
> Section 5. Information sources

(*4*) *Interpretation and Display of Impacts*
> Section 2. Four classifications of impacts
> Section 6. Impact portrayal

2. Four Classifications of Impacts

There are many ways of classifying and defining impacts and the selection of classifications will have an important effect on the impact-reporting process. We have selected four general fundamental classifications, or characteristics, for this chapter. Understanding them will help you *identify* social and economic impacts comprehensively and *interpret* them politically. The four we will discuss in this chapter are:

(*1*) Net and gross impacts,
(*2*) Direct and indirect impacts,
(*3*) Concentrated and dispersed impacts,
(*4*) Degree of importance of impacts.

Net and Gross Impacts

NEPA and CEQ Guidelines (August 1, 1973) do not specify whether impacts are to be considered in their gross form (future environment with the project minus *present environment without* the project), or in their net form (future environment with the project minus *future environment without* the project). The distinction is critical: Gross impacts consider not only the effects of a project itself, but also the other changes that construction and operation of the project will cause or permit. Net impact assessment ignores the secondary impacts of a project, such as induced growth, assuming they will occur anyway.

Agencies quickly adopted the net impact definition. Not only was it easier because they did not have to trace and document the secondary impacts of their projects, but they could use their own estimates of future growth and environmental change to justify proposals. They frequently claim that the changes in the environment that are not directly caused by the project over this period of time are not relevant to the EIS. This statement is true for small projects and unimportant plans and policies that do not have important economic effects. However, for large growth-inducing projects and important growth-inducing or growth-permitting plans and policies the whole process of environmental change from the present must be looked at in order to competently identify cumulative impacts.

For example, Marin County, California (just north of San Francisco) revised its Countywide General Plan in October, 1973. The plan revised the County's projected 1990 population downward from 364,000 under "current trends" to 300,000 under the new Plan. The Draft Environmental Impact Report (under the California law, similar to NEPA) claimed an "improvement" in year 1990 housing mix, water quality, air quality, and open space associated with the population "reduction." So, as described in the impact report, Marin County would go from 210,000 residents in 1974 to 300,000 in 1990 and have a better environment. "The plan's impacts on air quality, vegetation, geology, and visual conditions have been generally assessed and found to be significantly less adverse than impacts from current trends" (p. 4). Adverse environmental impacts which cannot be avoided are discussed in three paragraphs. No specific mitigative measures are proposed. The growth-inducing impact of the plan is acknowledged briefly, but never spelled out.

What is the problem here? No one ever gets to see what happens to Marin County's environment from 1974 to 1990! No agency is responsible for "current trends" (the "free market"), so gross impacts are never identified. Marin grows by 50% and the environment is better "than it would have been." Someone would have to write an EIS on the "free" market if the purposes of NEPA are to be fulfilled.

For most small projects, however, a discussion of net impacts is sufficient, since the project impacts are limited. Large projects and important plans that will significantly stimulate *or permit* growth in a region, however, should discuss the gross impacts on the environment and the regional economy of which the project is a major component. Otherwise, we never get to see what large changes are occurring over time. Without these regional gross impact assessments, the net impacts reported in many EIS's are of limited meaning. A perspective on the whole regional environment is needed.

Direct and Indirect Impacts

Much effort has gone into trying to define "direct" and "indirect" impacts. The CEQ Guidelines call indirect impacts "secondary," "stimulated," and "induced" impacts. Indirect impacts, according to the CEQ, include "associated investments and changed patterns of social and economic activities." These indirect impacts in turn affect "existing community activities and facilities" and "natural conditions." A project, according to CEQ, may induce secondary economic and population growth, which will then adversely affect the environment [sec. 1500.8(a)(3)(ii)]. Direct impacts are also frequently called "primary impacts" and either term is correct.

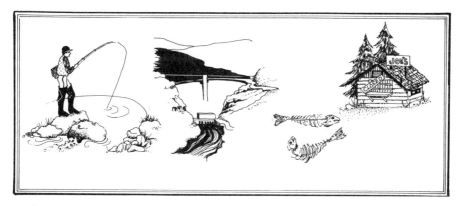

Fig. 3–1 Chain of impacts associated with dam construction.

Anyone who has tried to classify impacts as direct or indirect has come to realize how difficult this distinction is to define. If you build a highway, is the convenience experienced by the motorists a direct impact or is it an indirect impact caused by the higher speed? If you build a dam and the trout that lived in the stream in the impoundment area die, is that a direct impact or an indirect impact caused by the warming of the water caused by the dam? And so on, endlessly. Impacts don't occur in neat categories of primary, secondary, tertiary, etc. Impacts are linked in chains with more or less arbitrarily defined links in the chains. Dams impound water; impounded water warms up; warmer water kills trout; less trout provide worse trout fishing; worse trout fishing attracts fewer trout fishermen; fewer trout fishermen buy fewer hot dogs at Joe's Place; etc.

Not only are the links in the impact chains more or less arbitrary, but the chains are linked together in a net. If Joe's Place closes, his seeping septic tank won't pollute the reservoir and so on. Some scholars have drawn up elaborate matrices defining impact networks by time, space, and other factors. The point here is not the separation of impacts into "direct" and "indirect," but rather the interrelationships among the impacts. By listing the obvious, direct impacts and tracing their effects throughout the region of the project, a network or pattern will begin to appear. This network will contain the indirect impacts and their relationships to each other and to the project. Frequently, you will discover indirect impacts far greater than any of the project's direct impacts.

For example, a dam near a developing area will have a number of direct impacts, such as wildlife destruction, provision of jobs, and creation of an inexpensive water supply. The direct impact that appears to be the greatest is the destruction of the valley, which in turn will drive wildlife to other ranges, increasing competition among other wildlife populations and decreasing forage and so on.

However, a careful look at the creation of jobs and provision of a cheap water supply reveals enormous indirect impacts that will seriously, adversely affect the environment of the region. People will come to work at the dam's new construction jobs and create a demand for housing and services. But the lack of water has halted growth in the area, so no new housing and service centers can be built. However, the supply of cheap water the dam will create removes the limitation on growth, and a secondary impact of urbanization of the towns around the dam will begin. The economic base of the county expands, creating more jobs and attracting more people into the region. Schools become overcrowded and expand, shopping centers are built, adjoining counties seek to buy the water so they can cash in on the growth, air quality goes down, and so on for decades after the dam is completed.

Teams of specialists are frequently used to mathematically model these networks in natural systems and social and economic communities. However, the method is the same for small projects or reports prepared by one or a few people. First, list all the impacts of the project and trace each one's effects throughout the project's geographic region and time period of construction and operation. Then, examine the secondary effects for interrelationships and determine which of the impacts you have listed are direct, which are indirect, which are trivial, and which reinforce each other.

References such as wildlife handbooks, economic statistics, and census data can be used and should be noted as your data sources. You should interview people in the project area and others concerned with the project because they often have information and insights not available in the agencies involved.

Concentrated and Dispersed Impacts

A related characteristic of impacts is their concentration or dispersion, either within a geographical area or throughout segments of a community's population. Impacts can be concentrated in a small land area, or localized in a single economy, or affect only one population group. They can also be dispersed over many environments and areas, economies, and segments of the population. Classification of impacts as to their degree of concentration or dispersion can reveal some important factors.

Concentrated impacts, measured as output from the project, will be more important and frequently more serious. However, mitigation of the impact or compensation for its effects will also be easier because the affected elements of the environment will be easier to identify and correction of measures may be cheaper. Concentration of impacts also has important effects on project decisions. If benefits are concentrated, strong proponent groups will be involved in the politics. If, however, costs are concentrated, strong opponent groups will form, particularly if they are informed of these impacts by the EIS or by other means.

Most projects produce concentrated benefits (generally to landowners) and dispersed costs (to taxpayers and the environment). Concentrated costs occur to people displaced by projects or whose land values decline because of the project's impacts, such as increased noise and air pollution from a new freeway. The environment usually receives a concentrated cost by losing diversity and resilience. Dispersed benefits occur when travel time or water costs are reduced slightly for large populations, for example.

Tracing costs and benefits as they disperse out from the project will reveal that some costs, such as higher taxes or air pollution, and some benefits, such as lowered water costs, are passed on to other persons or parts of the environment. Other costs, such as displacement of marginal businesses or disruption of cohesive neighborhoods, rest on the first receivers and are not passed on and dispersed.

It is important to distinguish between concentrated costs and benefits and those that are dispersed. Not only should this distinction be clarified in the impact report, but mitigation measures must be proposed to disperse costs that are concentrated in one area of the environment or one segment of the population. Benefits can also be spread fairly among inhabitants by measures such as taxes, limits to subsidies, multi-purpose uses of projects, etc. These can be suggested in the EIS.

Degree of Importance of Impacts

Since NEPA is an administrative tool for increasing interagency review and citizen overview within traditional political budgetary processes, impacts should be quantified and ranked to the extent possible to allow for agency and citizen evaluation of the impacts and trade-offs of the project's alternatives.

While there can never be a rigorous system for comparing impact importance, some ranking would be very helpful in interpreting data for layperson understanding, as required by NEPA. A very useful method is ranking by duration, scale, and social importance.

The *duration* of the impacts can be scaled by five categories (among others):

(*1*) instantaneous

(*2*) one year

(*3*) five years

(*4*) twenty years

(*5*) indefinite

The *scale* of impacts should also be ranked in some general way. A useful set of levels is:

(*1*) on-site (project area)

(*2*) off-site, nearby (part of neighborhood)

(*3*) off-site, local (city or county)

(*4*) off-site, regional (airshed, watershed)

(*5*) state-multistate (or multi-watershed, airshed, etc.)

(*6*) national (river systems, coastal zones)

(*7*) hemispheric-global (oceans)

Finally, the *social importance* of impacts could be ranked as suggested by Maslow (1954):

(*1*) survival (nuclear destruction, famines, wars, violence, starvation, ecologic life-support systems, human genetic or reproductive effects)

(*2*) health and safety (poverty, pollution, housing, violence, food, noise, health)

(*3*) material well-being (employment, education, transportation, services, political-legal equity, economic and educational opportunity, displacement of jobs and people)

(*4*) psychological well-being (recreation, comfort, pleasure, joy, spirituality, self-actualization, objects of historic and aesthetic interest, growth rate and city size preferences, social involvement, privacy, community cohesion, creativity, and higher culture)

Rankings of this sort may seem pointless to many EIS writers. Indeed, most projects have only a few types of impacts. Proponents of projects and programs, however, will be required to prepare increasingly sophisticated reports in the future as the NEPA Guidelines become stronger on social and economic impacts. Urban regions are slowly building their data bases and this information is available to EIS writers. More and more in the future, a wide variety of social and economic impacts will have to be dealt with. Some way of ordering this information into conceptual categories is needed. Scaling the data by duration, scale, and social importance is one system, although others can be devised.

Summary

In Section 1 we discussed some of the general problems facing the EIS writer: the need for using an organized theory of social and economic systems, and the need for ordering what are usually disorganized data bases. In Section 2 we reviewed four characteristics of impacts which can help in conceptualizing project effects during the impact identification stage and interpreting these impacts politically in step (4). The characteristics listed were:
(1) Net or gross impacts
(2) Direct or indirect impacts
(3) Concentrated or dispersed impacts
(4) Degree of impact (duration, scale, importance)
Earlier we listed *regional economic growth* and *community social process* as overarching concepts to be used in organizing various disciplines and data into a single EIS framework. Within each of these two categories, several types of specific social and economic impacts will occur. Various methods of estimating the many types of impacts are used, along with tools to quantify them precisely when possible. In Section 3 we examine the comprehensive impacts of a project within the framework of regional growth, and then look at subregional impacts in the context of community social processes, and the methods for studying them, in Section 4.

3. Impacts Caused by Changes in Regional Economic Development Processes

Large projects and important policies or plans will often entail impacts that can affect regional economic processes. The importance of these regional processes can hardly be overstated. The development of railroads, ports, highways, airports, dams, and aqueducts are critical determinants of urbanization patterns over long periods of time. Most major cities are where rail lines meet ports because commerce is essential to industry and agriculture, the initial locators in the process of urbanization.

In this section we examine four types of actions that are important causes of regional economic impacts. We view these actions in the framework of regional economic growth (or decline). The four types of actions (see Fig. 3-2) are changes in:

(*1*) Economic base
(*2*) Access and supporting utilities
(*3*) Residential and recreational amenities and hazards
(*4*) Land tenure and zoning

Changes in Economic Base Activities

The *economic base* of a region is the sum total of economic activities that bring money (income) into the region by selling products or services outside the region. These are called "basic" activities. This income gets paid out in salaries and profits and then is spent by the entrepreneurs and workers on food, housing, transportation, etc. This second round of spending supports other entrepreneurs and workers in the retail and service sectors. The goods and services that are bought with money from within the region are called "nonbasic" activities because they do not bring money into the region. You cannot have nonbasic activities without basic ones to support them. Changes in basic economic activities (new firms moving in or old firms expanding, contracting, or moving out) are very important causes of secondary economic impacts and of environmental impacts.

For instance, in Smallville there is a mine which sells ore to a refiner a few miles away. Smallville is a "region" in economic terms. The Smallville Mining Company sells ore, gets money from the refiner (outside of the region), and pays its employees some of it. The employees live nearby in houses built by the local contractor and buy groceries in the local store. So some of the workers' income is spent in Smallville. The mine is *basic* and the contractor and store are *nonbasic*. The distinction is important. If you expand the mine by five jobs, you also expand the store and contractor by one or two jobs, since there is now more money coming into the region. If, however, the mine does not expand and you add two jobs to the store, no additional jobs in the mine are created because no more money comes *into* the region. The store is just trying to get more of the workers' money (keep it from going out of the region to the other stores down the road). The EIS writer concerned about income, employment, and growth effects of projects should be aware that a project that adds jobs in *basic economic activities* will create an expansion of secondary or *nonbasic economic activities*.

The type of secondary jobs created can be estimated. If the Smallville mine adds five employees, then the store can add, possibly, two employees. The total population increase will be seven workers and their families, or about twenty-five people. Fourteen more adults may be enough to make it profitable for someone to come into town and open up a bar or some other retail operation. If you studied other small mining towns, you would be able to estimate roughly what nonbasic activities would locate in Smallville and then estimate the impacts of this secondary economic and population growth.

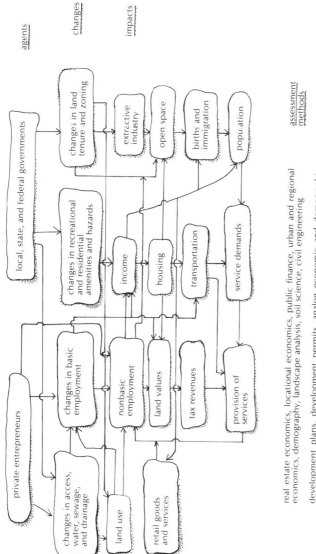

agents

changes

impacts

assessment methods

data sources

real estate economics, locational economics, public finance, urban and regional economics, demography, landscape analysis, soil science, civil engineering

development plans, development permits, analog economic and demographic data, assessment data, tax data, tenure maps, zoning maps, land use maps, employment data (census), transportation maps, trip data, income data (census), sales data (census)

Fig. 3–2 Impacts caused by changes in regional economic processes.

Estimating the amount of secondary growth quantitatively can be done most easily be extrapolating from the present economic structure of Smallville: if there are ten employees at the mine and four at the store and two construction workers, the *ratio of basic employment to nonbasic employment is 10:6*. One may crudely estimate that if the mine adds five employees, the store will add two and the contractor one, assuming a constant purchasing pattern for the mine workers.

In reality we deal with cities that are larger than Smallville, which has a minute and "leaky" economy. Much of the secondary spending occurs in other regions because Smallville does not supply a big enough market to attract most kinds of stores. Small economies have high basic/nonbasic ratios, because the money quickly leaks out of the secondary sector. Most cities have basic/nonbasic ratios in the range of 1:1 to 1:2. Since the national economy is generally moving jobs out of agriculture and mining and into services, this ratio is enlarging slowly. Larger regions have higher ratios because they are less leaky.

In practice one major difficulty is encountered in estimating the basic/nonbasic ratio. Firms do not always sell all of their products outside the region or inside it. They often sell to both areas and so the percentage of their income derived from sales outside the region must be calculated. Then the same percentage of the jobs in the firm can be said to be basic employment and the other jobs are labelled nonbasic employment. It is often very difficult to determine what percentage of a firm's goods and services are sold outside the region. Generally speaking, basic/nonbasic employment multipliers have been estimated for most large metropolitan regions of the United States. No EIS writer will ever have the time or money to do this research, so you will have to use an already calculated multiplier or estimate it theoretically. Small towns usually have basic/nonbasic employment multipliers of about 1:1, medium-sized cities (30,000–10,000) about 1:1.5, and large cities 1:2.

The ratio between total employment (basic + nonbasic) and basic employment is called the *regional employment multiplier*, which if multiplied times the number of basic jobs gives total jobs due to the development. Small cities have regional employment multipliers of about 2.0, medium-sized cities 2.5, and large cities 3.0.

As an example, the environmental impact report on the Yerba Buena Center (a redevelopment project), done by the City and County of San Francisco in 1973, calculated the employment to be created by the new convention facility (all basic, since conventioneers come almost entirely from outside the City and County) and multiplied this figure by 2.4 to get the total employment impacts. The 2.4 was the average of the range of the multiplier for San Francisco as estimated by economists (2.0 to 2.8).

Land use changes estimated to occur as a result of all these jobs include the replacement of existing uses with the convention center and sports arena and new induced retail stores and parking lots in the surrounding area. Governmental fiscal changes include rental of the facilities, sales taxes from increased retail sales, increased hotel taxes from the net addition of conventioneers, and increased property taxes from the surrounding private retail uses. Population impacts were estimated by determining the net new employment in 1983 attributable to the project (that wouldn't have occurred without it) using the employment multiplier. This figure was multiplied times the ratio of population to labor force in the San Francisco Bay Area (1.23) to get total population "attributable" to the project. [For further information on economic base techniques see Isard (1960, Ch.6 C) and Chapin (1965, Ch. 3).]

Essentially *economic base theory* states that there is a balance in a region (an employment shed or metropolitan area) between basic and nonbasic employment. A change in the number of basic jobs should lead to a change in the number of nonbasic jobs. There is also a balance in the region between jobs and housing. If more basic or nonbasic jobs are created, more housing will be needed. If you know the income levels and locations of the jobs being created you can estimate the type and general locations of the housing that should be stimulated by the new demand.

Changes in Access and Supporting Utilities

Economists study the impacts of improvements in access, water, sewers, and drainage on land use and economic and population growth through the use of *quantitative locational models* that require extensive data. The EIS writer cannot do the expensive primary research on competing sites, firms, and markets to rigorously predict what economic activities will move to certain land areas when access or supporting utilities are improved. Impact reporters can, however, estimate these future changes in land use by the qualitative use of *economic theories* of *locational advantage*.

Locational advantage provides a way to estimate what lands will develop and when as a result of the provision of access. Locational advantage, or "ripeness," takes into account the regional and local market for that type of parcel, the demand for the uses the parcel can be put to, the cost and availability of the required infrastructure (roads, rail lines, sewers, power, etc.), and the willingness of the community to allow the conversion to take place.

In some situations, future land use changes due to a proposed new road or utility are easy to estimate. Providing a road to a 100-acre parcel zoned for residential development on septic tanks that is near other utilities on the edge of a city with growing employment and a low housing vacancy rate will surely "induce" a land use change from open space (vacant) to residential, creating income in the building trades, increasing the population in the city, increasing school and other service costs, and increasing local property and sales taxes.

Likewise, providing sewers to industrially zoned land on a railroad line and a highway with good drainage in an industrial area with a low vacant land rate and a high demand for sites by firms will most likely "induce" a change in land use from vacant to industrial, with consequent effects on incomes, housing, population, services, and taxes. Impacts of increasing access or utilities to land are relatively easy to estimate if the access or utility being proposed is the sole "bottleneck" to the land's being developed, the missing ingredient necessary for development to occur, and the market for that type of parcel is good in that region. Road expansion is currently the commonest stimulant to commercial or industrial land use intensification and sewers are the most common inducer of residential growth.

To estimate demand for the land under investigation, you must use multiple sources of information. First, examine the statistics on the region's land uses over time to extrapolate average annual consumption of each land use type. Then determine the stock of vacant land in the category or categories the land is zoned for or planned for in the general plan. Next survey the other major sites with similar zoning or plan designation to estimate relative "ripeness" for development. Parcels with lower prices, lower development costs, cheaper service, closer to railroads, ports, and freeways (depending on the type of industry or business), closer to residential areas (making workers easy to attract), closer to labor pools with appropriate talents, and closer to associated activities such as banking or trucking will be sold and developed first. Many economic activities have specialized "economies of agglomeration." Their operators desire to locate near a plant that makes a product that they buy or that buys one of the products that they produce (to reduce transport costs).

Bank loan officers, larger land development firms, county economic development agencies, realtors, large landowners, and local academic economists and business administration researchers can help in estimating expected time of development. Knowing the exact time of development is not as important as determining whether the land will be developed at all and roughly when and how. Once the land use is identified and the time of development approximated, the consequent social, economic, and environmental impacts can be estimated.

An example action is the Kidwell Road Interchange proposed by the California Division of Highways in the early 1960's. The interchange was cleared for funding and a Negative Declaration filed in 1971 (stating that there were no significant impacts). The access improvement was to be on Interstate 80 about three miles southwest of the City of Davis and four miles northeast of the City of Dixon. Dixon and the proposed interchange are in Solano County, a strong promoter of industry. The area surrounding the proposed interchange was lacking freeway access but was planned by Solano County for 3,400 acres of industrial uses. Railroad access was available to about half of the acreage and it was generally felt that Dixon would run utilities out through the area since it abutted one corner of the 3,400 acre area.

The Solano County Industrial Development Agency had advertised the area for over a year as University Research Park, capitalizing on the presence of the University of California, Davis Campus, about three miles away in Yolo County. No industry was located near the University campus since Yolo County and Davis did not allow it in the area. Solano County felt that the University, with its world-wide reputation in agricultural sciences and agricultural engineering, would attract many food-processing equipment and farm machinery manufacturers. In general, Solano County was attracting industries steadily in the part of the County nearer to the San Francisco Bay Area. Industrial growth in Dixon, Woodland (fifteen miles to the north, in Yolo County), and the Sacramento metropolitan area was moderate and steady.

The City of Davis sued Solano County and the California Division of Highways for injunctive relief, claiming that an EIS was necessary. The City made a showing of environmental impact that followed this logic:

(1) The area is planned for industry and needs access. Dixon will probably provide sewers and other utilities.

(2) About 2,000 acres of the 3,400 acres planned for industry will be dependent on the Kidwell Road Interchange for freeway access.

(3) Applying a conservative ratio of workers per acre for this industrial class, about 20,000 persons eventually would be employed on-site.

(4) Assuming a family size of 4.0 for blue collar workers, total population will be around 80,000.

(5) Using a low regional employment multiplier of 1.63, the secondary population will be 50,000 persons.

(6) Of this total of 130,000 persons, most will live in Dixon, since shelter costs are higher in Davis. Davis, however, has higher perceived amenity value (nicer place to live), so we can estimate that 30,000 people will eventually come to Davis.

(7) Since the property taxes will go to Solano County and Dixon, Davis will lose money, fiscally, on the residents employed in the industrial area (about 20,000 of the 30,000 moving to Davis). The fiscal net loss was estimated to be $50–$100 per person per year or 1 to 2 million dollars annually at full development.

(8) The City of Davis will also experience a strong disturbance in its preferred (moderate) rate of growth and the location of that growth, as residential demand will pull growth to the west.

(9) Problems with air quality, ground water quality, wildlife, and recreational impacts will also affect Davis.

The California Division of Highways claimed that the interchange would not stimulate growth in the area. The case study, however, showed that the access improvements would expand the economic base affecting population affecting residential development affecting local government finances and the natural environment and so on.

Another kind of access that has a profound effect on growth is interregional transportation. When interstate freeways were built to Reno and Las Vegas in the early Sixties, for example, travel times from Los Angeles and San Francisco were cut by half. Instead of an all-day trip for truck drivers or gamblers, the Nevada cities were now only a half-day's drive from 15 million Californians. Primarily as a result of these major improvements in access, Reno and Las Vegas experienced a continued rise in gaming revenues, warehousing, and manufacturing, leading to secondary growth impacts.

More recently, access improvements to recreational resources have allowed growth to occur. The dramatic increase in population at Lake Tahoe from 1958 to 1964, for example, was primarily due to the completion of an extension of Interstate 80 to the Lake area. This reduced driving time from the San Francisco Bay area from six to three hours. The addition of modern snow removal equipment to keep the roads open all winter provided reliable year-round access. The result was an explosion of second homes and condominiums.

Second home subdivisions have become a problem throughout the nation since their first major boom in the early 60's. Often these recreational developments occur near national parks, beaches, reservoirs, forests, or ski areas. They impact on rural counties that are poorly prepared to provide the utilities and services their new residents require.

The results are higher costs in police and fire protection and utilities plus the destruction of wildlife and other natural features that attracted the development in the first place. Higher taxes soon follow, forcing landowners to sell to developers. Roads are almost always the key to these developments, whether they are in the Maine woods or on remote Hawaiian beaches.

Changes in Recreational Amenities and the Creation or Elimination of Hazards

The provision of recreational amenities and the creation or elimination of hazards have had an important effect on land use and environmental quality due largely to government public works programs and the increasing recognition of hazards such as floods and earthquakes. Recreational amenities are created by such programs as dam building, access roads to remote wilderness, creation of national and state parks or beaches, and private recreational complexes. Hazards are actually recognized more than they are created, although airports have become large hazards to residential development in recent years. Earthquake fault identification and fault zoning by states, flood plain zoning and flood control, fire control measures, and other hazard protection programs have an important effect on land use and environmental quality.

The most obvious example of these impacts is the construction of a dam that removes a flood hazard. Here a constraint to development is eliminated and economic market processes are given free play. Often flood plain lands are in the center of a city, and once a dam is built and the flood zone is narrowed, development occurs rapidly since access is good and utilities are nearby. Dam proponents, such as the Corps of Engineers, usually claim increased land values due to flood protection as a major part of the dollar benefits of their proposed construction.

Another example of an action that eliminates a residential hazard is snow avalanche prevention. Many ski areas have developed techniques for reducing avalanche hazards through the use of explosives, deflection structures, and zoning restrictions. Once the control program is underway, residential development can take place.

The development of recreational amenities has a similar effect: economic and residential activities are attracted to the high amenity area. Examples of large-scale recreational developments include national parks, recreation areas, and monuments, as well as private enterprises such as Disneyland and resorts on rivers, lakes, and seashores. These activities draw hundreds of thousands of visitors annually and employ several hundred persons on-site. Generally speaking, economic development and dependent residential construction occur on nearby private lands adjoining the access roads to the recreation area.

As we indicated above, second-home subdivisions have been attracted to remote parts of the United States by the development of national forests and parks. As incomes and vacations increase and freeways decrease time distances, more and more families are buying second homes near these recreation areas. Many mountain and coastal towns depend almost entirely on the basic income derived from summer home recreationists. Increases in local recreation due to government improvements and designation of sites can have quite predictable effects on retail sales and services, water quality, fire danger, litter along highways, air quality, and traffic congestion.

Airports frequently have drastic effects on land use by the creation of noise and landing approach zones. Federal regulations prohibit residential construction under landing patterns in many areas, and the noise caused by commercial planes often violates noise standards set by HUD. The reaction to these hazards has been to stop residential development on lands adjacent to runways, or, in the case of the Los Angeles International Airport, to buy and demolish any houses that were found to be under a landing approach or subject to excessive noise. Conflict between airport and residential uses are becoming more frequent as air travel expands and competes with housing developers for sites.

The consideration of the secondary effects of hazards or amenities should extend to growth-inducing or controlling effects, primary and secondary employment and economic effects, and potential health and property damage.

Changes in Land Tenure and Zoning

When the federal government condemns lands for use as parks or forests, the potential uses of the lands are changed dramatically. As mentioned above, the potential uses of the nearby private lands are also changed. The coast of Oregon, owned mostly by the state, is a outstanding recreation resource with many camping and picnic areas. On the other hand, the coast of California is mostly privately owned and many fine sites with recreation potential have been subdivided and closed to the public. In states with few coastal recreational sites, the acquisition of park lands by government agencies has dramatic effects. Private second homes will be eliminated as a land use and recreationists and concessions will be drawn to the site. The local government will suffer a loss in potential real property taxes from the site, now tax-exempt, but will also not have to provide services to private landowners. Motels will prosper and second homes may be attracted to nearby private lands and so on.

The most important land tenure actions in the western United States in terms of their impacts are Forest Service land trades and permits and Bureau of Land Management land disposal practices. An example of an impact due to a Forest Service tenure change is the Mammoth Lakes area in the Sierra of California. During the 1950's a permit was granted for a large ski area about six hours north of Los Angeles. Very little of the land near the ski resort was privately owned and this was soon all developed. The Forest Service traded nearby lands with several parties in exchange for lands elsewhere. Development of motels, gas stations, etc. then continued. The county zoning controls were not adequately related to service capacities in the area. The impact was a small urban area with high cyclical unemployment, service shortages, aesthetic damage, severe traffic congestion, and chronic snow removal difficulties during the winter months.

Forest Service permits for ski areas have substantial impact on nearby private lands and on local economies. This urban growth in turn affects natural systems in the region. Usual problems include avalanche hazards, road hazards, snow removal costs, high sewage treatment cost (small size, rocky ground), high heating costs, aesthetic degradation, soil erosion, fish damage, severe air quality reductions during winter inversions, and traffic congestion.

Since 1964, the Bureau of Land Management has been classifying all of the lands managed by it to determine which lands should be retained in public ownership and which lands should be disposed of by sale to private parties or gifts to state and local governments. These decisions affect the nature and scale of remote subdivisions and the ability of many cities to expand onto rural lands in the West. Disposition can allow remote development with adverse environmental impacts.

Impact was a small urban area with cyclical unemployment, service shortages, aesthetic damage, traffic congestion, snow removal difficulties, avalanche hazards, sewage treatment problems, soil erosion, fisheries damage, and air pollution.

Fig. 3–3 Impacts of remote recreation development.

Changes in land tenure brought about by the Forest Service and Bureau of Land Management have other impacts on the environment. Logging, grazing, and mining permit practices have a critical effect on fragile lands. These permits are generally granted for actions on steep and high lands where there is a short growing season or on dry lands which are poor for revegetation. The controls over these three extractive industries have a substantial impact on the local economies of the West, especially in the intermountain region.

Land zoning actions by governments also have an important impact on regional growth. One of the major political issues in the United States in the 1970's is the use of coastal resources. Many states have adopted statutes which grant state agencies authority to plan and zone land in coastal areas. Cape Cod is now a National Recreation Area with *federal* development control over many private lands.

Local governments play a central role in controlling the urbanization process. General plans and zoning maps control the location and type of development that occurs. Local government agencies may control air, water, and solid pollution in most states. The traditional practice of controlling private property to maximize personal economic gain has begun to give way to a new philosophy of land as a resource. Local planning bodies are starting to restrict development of riparian areas, steep slopes, prime agricultural soils, wildlife habitats, aquifer recharge zones, and other environmentally sensitive lands.

Local governments cannot start or stop growth processes. Natural resources, such as fertile soils or deep harbors, start urbanization, and decisions of private industrialists to create jobs speed the process. Federal, state, and local investments in water and access facilities allow the expansion to continue. Local governments can, however, determine the layout of land uses to a high degree and, in so doing, affect the quality of life greatly in urban areas.

Changes in regional economic development processes, such as alterations in basic employment, access and utilities, residential and recreational amenities and hazards, and land tenure and zoning have direct effects on the natural environment. Land preparation removes vegetation, increases surface run-off, creates erosion and sedimentation, and so on. The activities themselves create air and water pollution, harm wildlife, and consume nonrenewable resources. The greatest impacts from changes in regional economic development processes, however, occur later and are caused by the consequent economic growth. It is impossible to determine the impact of one action on the whole process of regional development. Environmental reports for large projects, however, should cover long-term regional growth.

These changes in regional economic development processes not only create regional economic and environmental impacts. They also bring about social impacts at the community level as a consequence of the induced or permitted growth. There are also many lesser governmental actions that cause community social impacts but do not have effects at the regional level. In other words, actions which have impacts on regional economic development processes are the most important in terms of the number and degree of all impacts, but actions which have impacts on community social processes are the most common. It is effects on community social processes that are the most important ones in our day-to-day lives since we *experience* impacts at this level (unless we are a major bank president or an owner of land throughout a region or of a chain of stores). We need to be able to analyze the impacts, then, of not only changes in regional economic development processes, but also changes in community social processes caused by these large-scale changes or caused by smaller governmental actions.

4. Impacts Caused by Changes in Community Social Processes

Whereas only large-scale plans and major projects will affect regional economic processes to any significant degree, almost all projects, plans, policies, and programs will in some way have a significant impact on some community and neighborhood social processes. In this section we focus our attention on intraregional impacts, but it must be remembered that many social impacts within regions are caused by larger interregional economic changes. Many of the effects discussed in this section are caused by larger events such as those we just reviewed. There are, however, many more lower-level actions taken annually by state and local governments that do not have region-wide impacts but greatly affect people's lives.

In this chapter we define "community" as an urbanized area served by one high school and "neighborhood" as a residential area served by one elementary school. Generally, neighborhoods are separated by commercial areas and major arterials and freeways. Neighborhoods generally have small parks and retail stores that serve them. Communities generally contain shopping centers and offices and are composed of several neighborhoods. Communities that are not in a large urban area contain the industries and commerce that employ their residents. They are generally incorporated as small cities. Large urbanized areas, however, contain many communities with no major economic base. The jobs for the residents of these communities are located in other parts of the metropolitan area. One or more communities form a city with its police, fire department, roads, colleges, and other services.

We will briefly review four important actions that cause community and neighborhood social impacts. These actions (see Fig. 3-4) are changes in:
(*1*) Incomes and employment
(*2*) Housing policies
(*3*) Transportation
(*4*) Schools, services, and neighborhood composition

In this discussion we view economic actions in the light of their social impacts. For example, providing employment will be seen as providing personal security and dignity; competition for taxable industries and commerce by local governments will be seen in terms of its effects on local service levels and therefore on people's quality of life. Economic skills are needed for this impact research, but the sociologist's techniques are often more useful. Understanding community social processes is fundamental in social and economic impact-reporting because all impacts, even long-term ones on the regional economy, come to rest on people in the community.

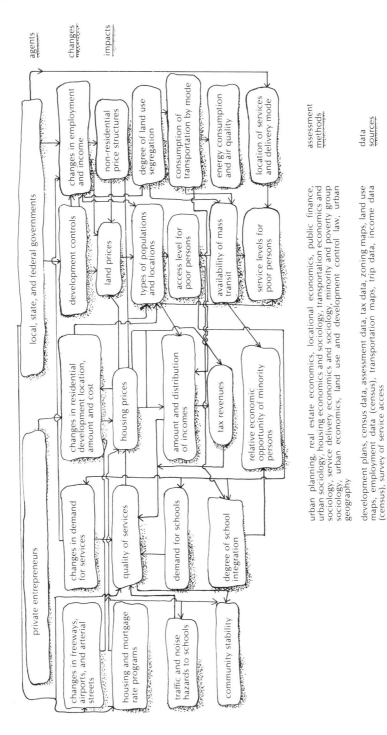

agents
changes
impacts

local, state, and federal governments

private entrepreneurs

changes in employment and income

non-residential price structures

degree of land use segregation

consumption of transportation by mode

energy consumption and air quality

location of services and delivery mode

development controls

land prices

types of populations and locations

access level for poor persons

availability of mass transit

service levels for poor persons

changes in residential development location, amount and cost

housing prices

amount and distribution of incomes

tax revenues

relative economic opportunity of minority persons

changes in demand for services

quality of services

demand for schools

degree of school integration

changes in freeways, airports, and arterial streets

housing and mortgage rate programs

traffic and noise hazards to schools

community stability

assessment methods

urban planning, real estate economics, locational economics, public finance, urban sociology, housing economics and sociology, transportation economics and sociology, service delivery economics and sociology, minority and poverty group sociology, urban economics, land use and development control law, urban geography

data sources

development plans, census data, assessment data, tax data, zoning maps, land use maps, employment data (census), transportation maps, trip data, income data (census), survey of service access

Fig. 3–4 Impacts caused by changes in community social processes.

Changes in Incomes and Employment

The character and size of a community can be significantly affected by changes in the incomes and employment of its residents. Conversely, the kind and amount of housing and other services a community supplies can affect the jobs and incomes of its citizens. Changes in income and employment that we will examine include: addition or subtraction of basic industry, new residential development and its impact on employment, and the relationship between income types and the provision of housing.

Addition or Subtraction of a Basic Industry

A commercial or industrial project that brings new *basic* employment into a community will have a beneficial financial effect on the residents in communities within commuting distance of the project site because they will have those jobs added to the total pool for which they can compete. Economic base theory also tells us that the multiplier effect of the basic employment will add nonbasic jobs and that additional nonbasic activities will be induced to locate nearby. Sometimes, minor additions of employment have an important impact in small isolated neighborhoods where there is high unemployment and no other employment within commuting distance.

In communities that are declining economically, the loss of a basic industry likewise creates a more serious impact than the loss of a nonbasic activity. Also, isolated communities are more seriously affected by declines in local employment, since alternative jobs are too far away for commuting. High unemployment in rural areas generally causes the later impact of out-migration, as people move to (urban) areas with more job opportunities. This rural-to-urban shift causes impacts in the cities.

Impacts of New Residential Development

One-time construction jobs are the first employment impact of new residential development. If projects are large enough, or if the flow of projects being approved and built in a community is steady enough over a long period of time, then construction jobs become a steady source of employment in the area. Many of the construction workers will move to the community to be close to work, causing a second round of economic impact.

Another secondary impact of continual or large amounts of construction is the secondary jobs created by suppliers and subcontractors in the region and in the community. Brick-makers, quarries, building supply houses, decorators, landscapers, and sand and gravel extraction industries all receive benefits from the construction. A major impact of new residential development is the attraction of new residents who will demand more services such as banking and shopping. This puts money in all areas of the community, with the multiplier effects noted above. Each new demand will create a certain number of new jobs, which will reduce unemployment in the area and attract new residents.

The third impact of new residential development is that the new residents will demand more government services and will pay the additional property taxes the government needs to increase service levels. This will stimulate more public sector jobs.

Many cities attempt to zone out poor people, in order to lower costs and increase revenues. Also, many cities have "urban renewed" their poor people and replaced them with upper-class people who spend more money and pay more property taxes. The impacts of these kinds of programs on low-cost housing can be identified by surveying the existing housing stock to identify housing supply by price class. Vacancy rates for each class are also estimated from HUD sources. Then you estimate the cost of constructing housing on available parcels to see how much housing may be developed in each price class. Demand for housing by price class is estimated from census information on workers by wage class in the community. In this way, supply and demand by price class can be calculated.

Since many local governments do not want lower-income residents, they try to discourage economic activities with low-paying employment from locating there. Generally, these industries are denounced as sources of air and water pollution, noise, traffic congestion, etc. As mentioned earlier, many suburbs have no industrial zoning and no moderate-income apartment zoning at all. These zoning policies have the impact of keeping blue collar families out and keeping tax revenues per capita high. Impacts on tax revenues are easily derived from estimates of the value of uses that vacant parcels can be put to multiplied by the tax rate. Impact in population mix can be estimated by calculating the number of workers by income class probable in the kinds of industries allowed by the zoning and guesstimating what percentage of each group will choose to live in the community.

Conversely, some cities and counties will practice zoning that allows for a mix of industrial job types and a mix of housing cost types. The impacts of this zoning on taxes and population mix can be estimated in a similar fashion. Service loads can also be projected for various land uses and for various populations by age, income, and family size.

Non-employment Income and the Impacts of New Housing

Income is generally considered to be derived from employment. There are, however, three types of income that are not thought of as deriving from jobs. These are income from retirement and welfare transfer payments, parental educational support, and income derived from wealth. Transfer payments include unemployment insurance compensation, aid to families with dependent children, old age assistance, Medicare, and other forms of welfare. Also included in this category are scholarships for students and retirement benefits for persons who worked in both the private and public sectors. These are all incomes based on transfers of wealth from one segment of the population to another, either through government taxes and programs or through private funds. Changes in these transfer incomes can have considerable impact in rural retirement communities, college communities, and declining rural or urban neighborhoods. The changes are usually less obvious than the effects of new basic employment.

Parental educational support, a second type of special income, is the major source of income for undergraduate college students. When a proposed university is being analyzed, the income from these parental transfers, as well as other income earned by part-time work, must be included in the estimation of impacts caused by the coming of the students.

Income from wealth must be considered as an impact when planning for upper-class communities. This is income from stocks, bonds, securities, leases, rentals, mortgages, and loans. Many persons live from these earnings and do not have a place of employment. Many of them operate investment businesses out of their homes. In upper-class suburbs and luxury apartment neighborhoods in downtown areas, this form of income can be quite significant.

The construction of moderate-income housing will allow some families on welfare (government transfers) to reside in a community. City policies that allow neighborhoods to become dilapidated will have the effect of letting shelter costs drop, allowing poverty-level families to live there. Governmental and parental transfers to college students are affected by the construction or expansion of campuses. Students demand moderate-cost housing and services. So we can see that community income is affected by changes both in employment and in the kind of housing that is built in a community. In fact, in small or even medium-size communities, the kind of housing built can determine the major type of income brought into the community. This can have long-term effects if the income type is fixed, such as social security, or dependent on changing government policies, such as welfare transfer payments.

People's incomes determine the kinds of secondary private enterprises that will probably locate in each community. Shopping centers generally try to locate in the middle of large upper-middle and upper-class areas where families have high spending power. People's incomes determine the cost of the housing they can occupy. The housing values in turn partially determine the local property tax revenues in the neighborhood or the community, the basis of local government.

All levels of governmental action affect employment. Federal investments in military bases and regional and local administrative agency field offices have substantial impacts on the economies and lives of people in large cities and in suburban neighborhoods. Military contracts to aerospace firms manufacturing airplanes or electronics can have tremendous impacts on communities. The location of a post office in a small town can have a significant effect on its employment. Federal and state investments in transportation and water systems can greatly affect the number and location of jobs in rural and urban areas. Local planning and zoning determines, to a large degree, the amount and location of jobs. The income levels of the jobs can be elevated by zoning only for "clean" (light) industry, meaning electronics, research and development, and other white collar activities.

We have discussed ways in which changes in community employment and incomes can affect communities fiscally, economically, and demographically. Now let us look at ways in which government plans and policies concerning housing can have impacts on communities.

Changes in Housing Policies

We have already examined several ways in which local governments affect housing costs through requirements on residential density, lot size, floor size, construction, and quality of improvements (utilities, streets, trees, etc.). Of these controls, those on floor size most directly affect shelter costs. Restrictions on density, lot size, construction, and improvements are more frequently used, however.

Cities can greatly affect the economic composition of their populations by zoning for various densities of residential development. Apartments tend to rent for less than the monthly payments on a detached house and therefore can be obtained by families with incomes too low to afford a house. Many suburbs in the United States exclude lower middle-class or even middle-class families through large-lot zoning: some communities have only five and ten acre zoning, effectively eliminating blue collar workers from living there. While the exclusion is economic, the results are often racial or ethnic homogeneity, since fewer Black or Spanish-surname families can afford costly homes.

Other phenomena are the "swinger" apartment and the adult trailer park. Both land uses prohibit children. Cities frequently approve these private land use decisions, because children are expensive to service educationally. Some cities, however, are contemplating prohibiting adult-only uses in areas near schools, to promote family life and transportation efficiency.

Urban renewal is a widespread program that has had tremendous impacts on housing, with long-term social and economic consequences. Urban renewal is a legal process that allows a city to take land from one owner at a fair market price and sell it to another owner, usually at a loss, on the condition that a certain kind of land use be developed there. The intent is to upgrade deteriorating areas, stimulating private industry to demolish and replace slums with more beneficial uses, such as offices and parking lots.

Many studies of redevelopment, which is taking place in cities throughout the nation, show that it:

• wipes out the very cheapest housing in declining areas of cities, often ruining the lives of the most vulnerable population groups (unemployed, old pensioners, widows, etc.)

• loses money for the city fiscally because of long periods of land vacancy due to the need for extensive demolition, legal battles by displacees, and the reluctance of new users to risk coming into the project area early

• often suppresses other private office and apartment construction, so that the net gain to the city's revenues and stock of offices and apartments is near zero

Impacts on urban renewal projects must be carefully studied to determine *who* is being moved and *to where* and *at what price*. Frequently, urban renewal projects do not relocate residents at all, or relocate them to other deteriorating areas, causing crowding and out-migration to surrounding neighborhoods. Occasionally, alternative housing provided for those evicted by urban renewal is too expensive for them and they eventually drift into other low-income areas. The effects of an urban renewal project on regional housing can be serious and long-term if the displacement problems are not carefully worked out. This is of major importance in environmental and economic and social assessments, because relocation is usually ignored or given lip service, and resettlement law suits are frequent in urban renewal projects.

Housing is primarily affected by local planning, zoning and code enforcement programs, commercial and federal mortgage policies, and to a lesser degree by state housing policies. A great deal of lower-income housing has been destroyed by freeways or renewal projects. Often single-family neighborhoods are indiscriminately rezoned for apartments, destroying inexpensive dwellings. Sometimes streets are made into one-way arterials, greatly decreasing the safety for the residents and increasing the noise.

Changes in Transportation

We have already discussed transportation as a mover of goods. Now we are interested in transportation as a people movement system. Two government functions affect community transportation: planning and zoning for land uses and planning and programming transportation. The first function is more important so we will discuss it first.

A city is a set of activities located in various places and connected together by communication systems. The most expensive and inflexible communication system is transportation. To connect two activities together involves two possible approaches: you can build a pathway between the uses or you can put the uses close enough together so that a shorter vehicular connection or a nonvehicular connection can be utilized.

American cities have taken the first approach. They have assumed low-cost auto transportation for everyone and allocated land uses with little thought to complementaries. The impact of this policy of freeway building is socially inefficient travel patterns with high energy and time consumption and a near-total dependence on the automobile.

This policy ignores the transport needs of the minority without cars. If you build freeways, it is desirable to locate an industry on the outskirts of a city and pay the workers the extra travel costs, because land is cheaper. This economic policy has been reinforced by the American local planning enthusiasm for segregating land uses to prevent nuisances from occurring in residential areas. The effect of this zoning policy has been to make it nearly impossible for the central city poor to get to the new jobs, which are out in the suburbs.

The alternative approach to connecting activities with roads is to group them together in communities that contain all of the basic life activities: employment, residence, schools, shopping, and recreation, connected by public transport, bicycle paths, and pedestrian walks. This ideal goes back to early European utopianism and is useful as a contrast to contemporary American planning practice; it will help us to see the impacts of present practices.

The city plan looks like this: Neighborhoods have elementary schools, recreation areas, and basic everyday shopping in their centers, all reachable by bicycle or by car on poor roads. Parking is limited to discourage the increases in distances between land uses it creates. No arterial roads go through neighborhoods, making them safer for children. Streets are built to keep traffic slow. Some are blocked completely to through traffic.

Several neighborhoods form a community with a high school, major recreation areas, and specialty shops in the center. The neighborhood centers are connected to the community center by public transit so high school students can walk or bike to a station and ride a bus or train to the high school. Near the community center, on one of its edges, are the industrial and wholesale commercial activities. Most workers can ride transit to work. Most shopping and recreating can be done by transit also.

The ideal is usually something like a maximum of one mile from any dwelling to the nearest transit stop. The neighborhood would then be roughly three square miles in area and would contain 5,000 to 15,000 people, depending on the dwelling densities and the amount of open space, preferably used liberally as a buffer along arterials and therefore between neighborhoods.

This "utopian" theory is a useful paradigm against which to evaluate the impacts of zoning projects and general plans which run arterials through neighborhoods, place elementary schools at the intersections of arterials, place all of the industrial activities in one area, scatter the commercial uses along the arterials, put the single-family homes upwind on the hills, and leave the rest of the gridiron gaps to the apartment dwellers. It is assumed that everyone has a car—indeed they need a car to live there. Apartments are placed at arterial intersections for efficient circulation and to keep the single-family areas quiet and safe. This approach gets the most people closest to the most noise and traffic hazards. The impacts of these land use planning practices are so pervasive they can only be seen when viewed against the perspective of the mixed community, described above.

As with housing impacts, transportation impacts are primarily the result of land use planning decisions, not transportation decisions. Often the problems of access are created by the combination of the plans of many cities in an urban region. Some cities are large-lot bedroom suburbs, some are strip commercial arterials and apartments, and some are freeway commercial and industrial. The transportation decisions reinforce the land use decisions and the land use decisions reinforce the transport decisions. Most large American cities have been trying to implement transit systems for several years now. Almost none of them has concluded that mixing land uses to reduce trip distances is an important part of the solution, or that aligning apartment and commercial zoning nodes along corridors will help build passenger volumes needed for transit systems.

A major impact of both fixed-rail transit systems and freeways is sprawl. When a new transit system is run through or to undeveloped land, the first impact is an increase in the land prices in the area, stimulating sprawl development.

Even worse, socially, are the effects of sending a rail transit line through an established residential neighborhood. Land values zoom, raising property taxes, and the pressure builds for rezoning to higher densities. One by one, home owners fall victim to the higher taxes and the offers from developers, and the neighborhood begins to change to high density, at first slowly and then in a rush. Neighborhood change impacts of transportation should be carefully evaluated, using information on assessed values, type of resident (fixed income or potential commuters), and land owned by commercial interests and speculators in the area.

Long-term land use and transportation plans should also be evaluated in the light of possibilities for beneficial impacts in reducing trip distances and increasing access to transit. Freeways, industrial parks on the edge of the city, remote suburbs, and any homogeneous zoning over large areas should be evaluated in terms of the transport impacts on the poor, social costs such as air pollution, neighborhood destruction, and noise hazards, personal costs such as traffic deaths and injuries, and economic operating expenses.

Short-run transportation programs can be evaluated in terms of their impacts on those without cars. Adding more buses or locating their routes in certain areas can have significant effects on the access of the poor. Zoning for apartments over stores and near industrial areas can also help in the short run. Maximum encouragement of bicycle and pedestrian travel by means of lane restrictions and new pathway creation can also have positive impacts. Large-scale bus systems will have beneficial effects on the transportationally disadvantaged, but will lose money until rezoning of the city reallocates land uses into a pattern where walking gets you somewhere and buses have somewhere to go.

Individual projects must be evaluated for the number of trips they will generate. Very large projects may fall under the EPA's "complex source" regulations and be subject to taxes or restrictions. These can include theaters, large parking lots, large subdivisions, or apartment complexes. Check with the regional office of EPA for traffic impact estimates.

For projects that do not fall under EPA regulations, a rough estimate of the number of auto trips the project will generate per day can be determined by multiplying the number of residents or users by the number of trips to and from the project each is assumed to make every day. Engineering manuals contain these estimates. This estimate of total daily trips should be compared to the design capacity and current loads of the surrounding streets and arterials and parking facilities to estimate the severity of the impact.

Changes in Schools, Community Services, and Neighborhood Composition

New development and government policies can have profound impacts on schools, community services, and on the composition of the community itself. Actions that will affect these areas should be identified and investigated both for their direct impacts on the demand and quality of services and for their long-term impacts on the demographic makeup of the community and on the community's tax structure.

Significant changes in a school district's tax base will have significant impacts on the quality of the schools and the taxes of the district's residents. The addition of a high value/low population development such as light industry or a singles apartment complex will improve the school district's tax base without increasing the demand for its services.

However, the addition of a low value/high population development to a district will increase demand without increasing revenues sufficiently to meet the increase in student population. Large withdrawals of land from the tax base, such as the creation of parks or the purchase of parcels by non-profit tax-exempt corporations or churches, will also impact negatively on the school district's ability to provide quality education without raising taxes. Increases in taxes may often cause home-owners to sell to developers for higher density uses, thereby increasing the problem. Estimates of revenue gained or lost and the number of new pupils and their costs can be obtained from the school district and the tax assessor's office.

Changes in Racial Composition of Neighborhoods

Zoning policies and consequent large developments that are economically homogenous are usually racially homogenous. When this results in or contributes to "de facto segregation," outlawed by the Supreme Court, extreme measures are required of the school district to achieve racial balance, including busing or redrawing school district lines.

When you evaluate residential projects or basic employment-generating projects that will attract large residential populations, you should measure the economic diversity of the planned housing or employment base. If economic homogeneity will be the result, an investigation of the racial balance and legal mandates of the affected school districts may be necessary to report potential impacts on the school district. Mitigation in the form of additional residential or employment diversity should be studied.

Impact of Hazards on Schools

Hazards include heavy traffic, noise from airplane landing approaches, landslides and land subject to flooding or other natural damage. By far the commonest hazard impacting upon schools is traffic. This hazard can be avoided through intelligent foresight and planning in locating schools and traffic-generating uses. New developments should be analyzed to determine if their traffic will impact on a school in the area.

Another major hazard for schools is noise, especially from airports, trains, and freeways. Coordination of long-range planning can help with this problem, but the noise level of individual projects should be estimated or measured and its impacts on any nearby schools should be determined. However, some transportation is needed near the schools, and whatever system is used, adverse noise impacts should be mitigated through insulation, muffling, or, if required, relocation of the school at the noisemakers' expense.

Community Services

Other public services, such as health care, police and fire protection, recreation programs and parks, play an important part in the lives of urban dwellers, especially those without the resources for a private car. Actions that influence the supply and quality of these services must be carefully traced and evaluated. Decisions concerning the location, level, and extent of state and municipal services can have substantial impacts on vulnerable populations, such as the old, the very young, and the poor. Development that increases the demand for these services without adding to the economic base that provides them should be evaluated carefully for any additional needs it will create and for potential mitigation measures.

Frequently, the problem is one of tailoring the services provided by local agencies to the needs of the population. Providing Spanish-speaking staff in hospitals which serve neighborhoods with a high percentage of Spanish-surname residents is a simple example that is frequently overlooked. Others include supplying city parks in those neighborhoods with soccer fields instead of tennis courts. Service requirements for different areas are often unique and should be ascertained in the analysis of any proposals that will have an impact on the service programs.

Community Demographic Structure

The character of a community is important to understand when attempting to assess the impact of a proposed project or program. People's needs for service vary by age, ethnic background, and economic status. When analyzing proposals, identify the various groups in the area and determine those that are most vulnerable, such as the old, welfare families, and any others with a special dependence on government and the community services. Transportation can change an entire community and drastically affect the vulnerable groups.

A more immediate impact of transportation plans on community infrastructure is the creation of new boundaries with arterials, freeways, and highways. Because low-income housing is the least expensive to purchase for right-of-way, it is often the principal target of highway engineers. Bringing a freeway through a stable community destroys it forever. Homes are demolished and a barrier is created dividing portions of a once unified community into separate sections. High-speed arterial streets or one-way streets can have similar effects.

Evaluation of the impacts of transportation involves careful analysis of the fiscal and social impacts of the road or transit system. The effects can be beneficial to the community, or may benefit only part of the total community, passing the costs on to the remainder. This can be estimated by analyzing a proposal for traffic loads, access to jobs and services, potential creation of barriers, and availability of parking. Questions that must be answered include: Who is going to use the transportation addition? Who is going to pay for it? Who will lose a home or property to it? Who will gain property values because of it? How does it fit in with the social and travel patterns of the established stable neighborhoods?

Community stability is an important aspect of social existence. Stability in neighborhoods is caused by relative constancy in dwelling condition and composition and in employment for neighborhood residents. Owner-occupied areas are generally relatively stable. The addition of apartments to a neighborhood, increases in taxes that will force sales, code enforcement and demolition, elimination of employment, or disturbance of social communication by freeways or creation of one-way streets will all weaken or destroy community cohesion and stability. Changes should be introduced gradually to reduce these adverse impacts. Major influxes of population and freeways should be directed away from stable areas. Generally, upzonings, redevelopment programs, and freeways go through older, often stable neighborhoods, because land values and political opposition are low.

The proposal of the McDonald's Company in 1974 to put a hamburger stand in mid-Manhattan in a stable neighborhood (Lexington Avenue and 65th Street) is an example of how fragile these balances are. The furor was dramatic. Neighborhood spokesmen demonstrated that the high volume outlet would irreparably change the stable social fabric of the small area. The traffic would increase considerably near the store and land values and rents would go up nearby, driving out locally owned shops, which would be replaced by new chain outlets. Profits would then go out of the neighborhood (to stockholders) and people's quiet lives would be changed forever by the turnover of uses. People who lived in this neighborhood worked and shopped there. The land uses were in balance and one hamburger stand could upset the neighborhood. The project was approved by the Planning Commission.

Let us assume that we are aware now of the *regional economic impacts* that large-scale projects or long-range land use plans create and that we are also aware of the *community-level social impacts* that most government plans and programs bring about. How do we go about gathering data to use in establishing the status of the present economy and social systems and to estimate future impacts? Where do we get the data and how do we organize them and use them?

5. Information Sources

The person in charge of reporting potential social and economic impacts has a rough job. Theory is abundant in the social sciences, but empirical evidence verifying specific hypotheses is scarce. Causal linkages connecting projects, plans, and programs to economic activities and social well-being are poorly defined, much less quantified.

To further complicate matters, social and economic data are voluminous, disorganized, and hard to evaluate. Regional planning agencies are often the only places where integration of information into usable sets takes place and where these data are interpreted to make them into information useful for evaluation. Data assembly is usually difficult, since sources include federal and state agencies, university research groups, banks, and consulting firms and others. Generally speaking, water resources agencies have the most comprehensive data for large rural regions, and transportation agencies have the most data for metropolitan areas.

First you must develop a picture of past trends and the present state of the regional economy and the community social systems which the proposed project or plan may affect. Maximum reliance must be placed on secondary (already gathered) data. After the hard data about the past and present are assembled, economic and social projections made by government agencies and banks can be examined. Let us first discuss secondary sources of data before outlining several studies that could be performed to gather primary data.

Secondary Data

Census

Every ten years the federal government performs a population and housing census throughout the United States. These data are made available about one year later in reports and on computer tape. Data include: population, age, sex, race, family status, income, wealth, residence, nativity, migration, employment status, education attained, transportation mode used to get to work, place of work, skills, automobiles owned, housing tenure and condition, dwelling value and vacancy status, and hundreds of other similar data concerning housing and population characteristics.

These data are cross-tabulated for individuals, families, and dwellings and summarized by census tract, an area containing about 6,000–8,000 people. These cross-tabulations are very useful in determining the social status of different racial or income groups. Some basic data such as population, age, and race are available for block groups and blocks. Data are summarized for cities, counties, Standard Metropolitan Statistical Areas (SMSA's—contiguous urban counties), states, and the United States. Data are available in tabular form which will serve most purposes. Heavy data users who need to perform analysis of data or to computer-map them will need to purchase the tapes for each county of interest.

Other censuses are conducted on government activities, business, manufacturing, construction industries, mining, transportation, agriculture, and exports every few years. Every five years a *City and County Data Book* is produced by the Bureau of the Census. It contains important data totals for counties, SMSA's, and cities of over 25,000 inhabitants. The Bureau also produces a *Dictionary of Non-Federal Statistics for States and Local Areas*, broken down by states (380 pages), and a *Directory of Federal Statistics for Local Areas* (162 pages). The annual *Statistical Abstract of the United States*, which summarizes data for states and the United States, has in it a guide to sources of statistics (by topic, about 50 pages). The Census Bureau also publishes frequent topical reports. In recent years, data relating to the problems of the poor have been published in special analyses of topics such as substandard housing and employment status by race, sex, and age.

Employment Data

Employment and unemployment data come from the Bureau of Statistics, the Manpower Administration, and the Social Security Administration. Education data come from HEW's Office of Education. Welfare and vocational education data are produced by the Social Security Administration and the HEW Social and Rehabilitation Service. Vital statistics are provided by the Public Health Service. Conspicuously missing from federally provided data is information about personal health beyond certain diseases recorded per county. In some states this information is compiled by regional comprehensive health-planning organizations funded by federal planning grants.

State agencies add greatly to the federal data, especially in the unemployment, welfare, and government revenues areas. Most states have departments of employment or manpower training that report unemployment insurance claims, earnings, and other employment data. State boards of equalization and franchises list tax revenues for jurisdictions by year. State departments of welfare, public health, education, motor vehicles, corrections, and transportation also produce annual reports. Banks do market studies that are often useful compilations of data concerning demand for goods and services, employment, land values, tax revenues, and other similar information.

City and county agencies provide data concerning their functions, such as police and crime, land values, zoning, planning of land, utilities, roads, construction starts and values, housing, financing, education, health, and public assistance. Special districts produce data concerning their operations, such as bus service, schools, and recreation. Quasi-public businesses, such as utilities, also report on their activities annually.

Many of the federal and state agency reports also make projections into the future, which are useful for estimating net or gross impacts of projects. The

Census Bureau projects population by states. Most states have an agency that projects populations for cities and counties for five or ten year intervals, twenty or twenty-five years into the future. Banks also perform economic projections.

Primary Data

Some social and economic processes cannot be defined adequately with secondary data, and studies must be done by the EIS team. If your budget is limited, a "quick and dirty" study with help from some experts is better than nothing at all. Hopefully, these basic research projects can be improved over a period of time. We will outline two studies useful in estimating social and economic impacts, an *economic base study* and a *social services survey*. Others are possible.

Economic Base Study

We covered economic base theory in Section 3 and explained basic and nonbasic employment, ratios of basic to nonbasic jobs, and employment multipliers. These techniques are brought together in an economic base study to develop a picture of a region's economy so that one can estimate the economic effects of a proposed project.

After you have developed a picture of the basic and nonbasic employment for the region with data from government agencies, chambers of commerce, and banks, interview affected firms to determine what percentage of their income is derived from outside the economic region of interest in the study. This area is called a tradeshed or employment shed and refers to the economic area from which the region's jobs are supplied. This is expensive research, but it is fundamental to performing an analysis of growth-inducing impacts.

If you are on a low budget, you can use accepted regional employment multipliers or make a guesstimate as we demonstrated in Section 3. This multiplier will allow you to determine what the short- and long-term employment effects of a project will be and what groups will benefit or lose. This data will tell you what population growth will result from the project. This crude method is useful for most impact studies. If you are evaluating an economic development plan, you need to determine the multiplier empirically.

Social Services Study

A survey of social service levels is another study that requires considerable expense to do accurately. Service levels can be inferred, however, from departmental budgets and other management data on calls, cases, etc. To identify specific groups, families, or persons that are underserved by public assistance, public health, public transportation, education, police, fire, and other services necessitates door-to-door interviewing, an immensely expensive under-taking. Data at this scale are seldom gathered, because people move frequently and the data are valid for only a year or two. Generally speaking, you would do a detailed survey only for an intensive social planning effort in a small area, such as a Model Cities Area, or for a single regional service, such as transportation. Even then, you would do a sample only and you would ask other questions useful in planning, to share the research cost with other programs. Research on social service adequacy is of most use in low income areas where people need public services more and impacts of changes in these services, such as bus rerouting, are important to the residents.

Once you have assembled your data to describe the regional economy and the community and neighborhood social processes, you have attempted to predict the future population, employment income, crime, transportation, and other trends, and you have estimated gross and net impacts where relevant, you are faced with the final impact-reporting problem: how to portray this information to maximize citizen understanding. Making the data accurate and complete and yet comprehensible to laypersons is a challenge.

6. Impact Portrayal

In this final section we will outline several methods for making impact information politically relevant and socially meaningful. These techniques include:
• proper emphasis of intangible data
• portrayal of impacts as they fall on population groups
• comparison of social and economic impacts with natural environmental impacts
• making the report understandable to laypersons
• evaluating impact importance in a social context

Intangible Data

NEPA explicitly requires that agencies develop impact-reporting proce-dures to "ensure environmental amenities and values may be given appropriate consideration in decisionmaking along with economic and technical considera-tions" [Sec. 102(B)]. The Act emphasizes non-economic values in the policy section (101) and requires the use of the "social sciences and the environmental design arts in planning and in decisionmaking" [102(A)]. The CEQ Guidelines also stress the need to estimate nonquantifiable effects.

Engineers and economic planners have long been criticized for relying almost exclusively on dollar values in evaluating plans and programs. Basically, critics argue that benefit-cost analysis and related techniques bias heavily toward projects that produce positive effects that can be measured in economic market terms. They also maintain that environmental and social costs of public works projects are generally non-economic or intangible, and therefore underweighted in analysis. Economists and engineers have in the past smugly ignored these arguments. However, severe budgetary cutbacks and hundreds of court injunctions in recent years are forcing highway and water development agencies to consider intangible values in their plans.

Planners interested in performing politically relevant policy analysis realize that broader plan evaluation frameworks are needed which incorporate data which are: quantified in dollars, quantified in units other than dollars, and nonquantified. The most articulate and ardent advocate of plan evaluation against multiple values is Nathaniel Lichfield. His "planning balance sheet" is a double entry account sheet for entering the benefits and costs of each plan. All important impacts are entered. Since many of the items are nonmonetary, the benefit and cost columns for each alternative plan cannot be totalled as is done in benefit-cost analysis. Instead of a pseudo-objective benefit-cost ratio to determine whether a project should be built, the balance sheet merely portrays the data, leaving the decision to the policy makers.

Impact Incidence

Making population groups aware of the effects projects or plans will have on them will increase the democratic utility of impact-reporting. Social impacts are often merely the effects of the distribution of economic impacts on various groups of people. Frequently, distributional battles are fought over whose land values will be increased and whose taxes will be raised. Many contemporary researchers have abandoned the idea of portraying impacts according to planning objectives and instead advocate displaying impacts by major interest groups, such as industry, recreationists, taxpayers, home-owners, etc. The most complete scheme has been developed by Lichfield in evaluating town expansion plans in England. He breaks impacts down by two major population groupings, producers (the development agencies) and consumers (the occupiers or users of buildings or facilities). This scheme is made quite exact by describing "instrumental objectives" for each group and developing criteria against which to measure impacts. This analysis usually requires a detailed understanding of economic and social processes in the project or planning area.

Comparison with Natural Environment Impacts

Awareness of the political and technical meaning of impacts can be increased by also portraying impacts in a fashion that allows understanding of the trade-offs among various basic political values associated with the different alternative plans. A good way to show these basic trade-offs is to categorize impacts into three types: social, economic, and natural environmental. The CEQ Guidelines suggest these categories, but are not explicit. Major political battles are being fought along these lines: Does economic progress impose too many social and environmental costs? Does environmental protection require too many economic sacrifices? Are social programs too expensive economically? And so on. Adequate first-level value distinctions such as these allow intelligent debate over project impacts if the three categories are defined in a mutually exclusive fashion. Special attention should be paid to exclude economic effects, such as recreation, from the natural environmental category to avoid muddling the trade-off analysis with a double counting of effects.

Making the Report Understandable

NEPA and the Guidelines require agencies to seek out, and to respond to, citizen review of EIS's. The Guidelines stress the need for making impact reports understandable to laypersons and recommend that technical analyses and raw data be put into appendices. Reports should begin with a brief summary that gives the bird's-eye view of the existing environment, the trends, the project, the future it will create, and the impact it will have. It is sometimes a good idea to have someone not involved in the project write the summary after reading the EIS because such a person may be able to see the whole picture better.

Controversial impacts should be emphasized in the introductory summary section of the EIS and in the responses to the comments section (of the Final EIS). These are the impacts that readers are interested in. Maximum use should be made of clear layout, graphics, and illustrations. Tables of contents should be detailed. Comments should be topically indexed and responded to individually in topical groups.

The preceding three techniques, *emphasis of intangibles, portrayal of impact incidence,* and *description* of *trade-offs,* should be used to increase citizen understanding of the meaning of the impact estimates. These portrayal formats can be displayed in schematic form as well as in charts, graphs, and text explanations.

Evaluative Impact Importance

Agency staffs do not have the final judgment in the evaluation of a proposal's impacts. They do have the responsibility to provide the context needed for decision-makers to determine the impacts and their importance and to make informed judgments on the proposal.

Impacts of greatest importance are those that are: long in duration, large in scale, or damaging to processes basic to human existence (famines, genetic changes, violence, health, safety). Identification and estimation of cumulative impacts and the long-term effects of projects that modify regional growth such as highways are difficult because these impacts are also caused by other projects. In this case, a gross impact report should be done on all of the growth-inducing and growth-permitting projects and plans.

Identification of similar projects in the region, their individual impacts on common services and amenities, such as sewers, air quality, water quality, parks, etc. should be noted. This may reveal that the cumulative impact of a given project, when combined with others in the region, will overtax a resource of the region, such as sewage capacity or water supply. By looking at the regional picture, the effect of single projects or programs that do have widespread impacts can be traced and measured.

In general, agencies and private consultants frequently stress the medium impacts, those that deal neither with the region nor with the individual, but rather with a generalized sphere of influence around the project. Frequently, these medium impacts are the chief concerns of the environmental, civic, commercial, and labor groups of the area. However, we really need to look at the larger and smaller pictures, paying attention to the ways projects and plans incrementally and mutually reinforce long-term trends that may prove damaging to the region as a whole and to individuals within each community.

Bibliography

Arrow, Kenneth J., *Social Choice and Individual Values*, John Wiley and Sons, Inc. (New York, 1951).

Barlowe, Raleigh, *Land Resources Economics*, Prentice-Hall, Inc. (Englewood Cliffs, N.J., 1958).

Bauer, Raymond A. (ed.), *Social Indicators*, The MIT Press (Cambridge, 1966).

Baxter, McDonald and Smart, Inc., "Socioeconomic Impacts of Environmental Policies," California State Office of Planning and Research (Sacramento, December, 1973).

Bolan, Richard S., "Generalist with a Specialty—Still Valid? Educating the Urban Planners: An Expert on Experts," in *Planning 1971*, American Society of Planning Officials (Chicago, 1971), pp. 373–388.

Bromley, Daniel W., A. Allan Schmid, and William B. Lord, "Public Water Resource Planning and Evaluation: Impacts, Incidence, and Institutions," Center for Resource Policy Studies and Programs, School of Natural Resources, University of Wisconsin (Madison, September, 1971), Working Paper No. 1.

Brubaker, Sterling, *To Live on Earth*, The Johns Hopkins Press (Baltimore, 1972).

California Department of Transportation, Division of Transportation Planning,

"Environmental Analysis and Reporting for Transportation Plans" (Sacramento, July, 1974).

Chapin, F. Stuart, *Urban Land Use Planning*, University of Illinois Press (Urbana, 1965).

Cox, Harvey, *The Secular City*, The Macmillan Co. (New York, 1965).

Coy, John G., Robert A. Johnston, and Peter J. Richerson, "Critique of Water Resources Council's Proposed Principles and Standards for Planning Water and Related Land Resources," in *Water Development and Environmental Quality*, Charles R. Goldman, (ed.), W. H. Freeman and Company (San Francisco, 1973), pp. 478–494.

Daedalus 97:4 (Fall, 1968), American Academy of Arts and Sciences, edition titled, "The Conscience of the City."

Dickert, Thomas G. (ed.), *Environmental Impact Assessment: Guidelines and Commentary*, University Extension, University of California, Berkeley (Berkeley, California, 1974).

Dubos, René, *Man Adapting*, Yale University Press (New Haven, 1965).

Duhl, Leonard J., *The Urban Condition*, Basic Books, Inc. (New York, 1963).

Ewald, William R., *Environment for Man*, Indiana University Press (Bloomington, 1967).

Gans, Herbert J., *People and Plans*, Basic Books, Inc. (New York, 1968).

Goodman, Paul, and Percival Goodman, *Communitas*, Random House, Inc. (New York, 1960).

Gruen Associates, *Transportation Plan Evaluation Process*, Southern California Association of Governments (Los Angeles, July, 1973).

Highway Research Record, No. 410 on "Use of Economic, Social, Environmental Indicators in Transportation Planning," Highway Research Board, National Research Council (Washington, D.C., 1972).

Holling, C. S., and M. A. Goldberg, "Ecology and Planning," *Journal of the American Institute of Planners* (July, 1971), pp. 221–230.

Hufschmidt, Maynard M., "Environmental Quality as a Policy and Planning Objective," *Journal of the American Institute of Planners* (July, 1971), pp. 231–242.

Ingram, Helen, "The Changing Rules in the Politics of Water Development," *Water Resources Bulletin* 8:6 (December, 1972), pp. 1177–1188.

Isard, Walter, *Methods of Regional Analysis: An Introduction to Regional Science*, The MIT Press (Cambridge, 1960).

Journal of the American Institute of Planners. Various issues contain articles on social and economic theory and the impacts of plans on these processes.

Kaplan, Abraham, *The Conduct of Inquiry*, Chandler Publishing Company (San Francisco, 1964).

Kaplan, Marshall, Gans and Kahn, Inc., "Social Characteristics of Neighborhoods as Indicators of the Effects of Highway Improvement," U.S. Department of

Transportation, Federal Highway Administration (Contract DOT/FH 11-7789, 1972).

Klaasen, Leo H., *Social Amenities in Area Economic Growth*, Organization of Economic Co-operation and Development (Paris, 1968).

Leopold, Aldo, *A Sand County Almanac*, Oxford University Press (London, 1949).

Lichfield, Nathaniel, "Cost-Benefit Analysis in City Planning," *Journal of the American Institute of Planners* (Vol. 3, 1960), pp. 273–279.

Lichfield, Nathaniel, "Economics in Town Planning," *Town Planning Review 39:1* (April, 1968), pp. 5–20.

Lichfield, Nathaniel, "Cost-Benefit Analysis in Urban Expansion," *Regional Studies 3* (1969), pp. 123–155.

Lichfield, Nathaniel, "Cost-Benefit Analysis in Planning: A Critique of the Rockhill Commission," in *Regional Studies 5* (1971), pp. 157–183.

Little, Charles E., "The Environment of the Poor: Who Gives a Damn," *Conservation Foundation Letter* (Washington, D.C., July, 1973).

Los Angeles City, Planning Department, Los Angeles Region Goals Project, "Social and Human Goals for the Los Angeles Region" (Inter-Religious Committee, 817 W. 34th St., Los Angeles, CA 90007, n.d. (1968?)).

Los Angeles City, "1970 Census: Selected Social and Economic Characteristics for the Geographic Divisions of the City of Los Angeles" (Los Angeles, 1973).

Lynch, Kevin, *The Image of the City*, The MIT Press (Cambridge, 1960).

Mannheim, Marvin L., et al., "Community Values in Highway Location and Design: A Procedural Guide," Urban Systems Laboratory, Massachusetts Institute of Technology, Report No. 71-4 (1971).

Marcuse, Herbert, *One-Dimensional Man*, Beacon Press (Boston, 1964).

Marin County, California, "Draft Environmental Impact Report on the Marin Countywide Plan" (San Rafael, April 3, 1973).

Marin County, California, "The Marin Countywide Plan" (San Rafael, October 30, 1973).

Maslow, Abraham H., *Toward a Psychology of Being*, D. Van Nostrand Company (New York, 1962).

Merewitz, Leonard, and Stephen H. Sosnick, *The Budget's New Clothes*, Markham Publishing Company (Chicago, 1971).

Mishan, E. J., "What Is Wrong with Roskill?" *Journal of Transport Economics and Policy* (September, 1970), pp. 221–234.

Murphy, Raymond E., *The American City*, McGraw-Hill (New York, 1966).

"National Environmental Policy Act," 42 U.S. Code, Secs. 4321–4347. Statutes, Volume 83, pp. 852 and following (Public Law 91-190).

Perloff, Harvey S., et al., *Regions, Resources and Economic Growth*, The Johns Hopkins Press (Baltimore, 1960).

Perloff, Harvey S. (ed.), *The Quality of the Urban Environment*, The Johns Hopkins Press (Baltimore, 1969).

Platt, John, "What We Must Do," *Science* 166 (November, 1969), pp. 1115–1121.

Reiner, Thomas A., *The Place of the Ideal Community in Urban Planning*, University of Pennsylvania Press (Philadelphia, 1962).

Richerson, Peter J., and Robert A. Johnston, "Environmental Values and Water Quality Planning," *Journal of the Hydraulics Division, ASCE*, Vol. 101, No. HY2, Proceedings Paper 11136 (February, 1975), pp. 259–276.

San Francisco City and County, "Draft Environmental Impact Report on Yerba Buena Center" (San Francisco, May, 1973).

Sax, Joseph L., "The (Unhappy) Truth about NEPA," *Oklahoma Law Review 26* (Vol. 26, 1973), pp. 239–248.

Self, Peter, "Nonsense on Stilts: The Futility of Roskill," *New Society* (July 2, 1970), pp. 8–11.

Selye, Hans, *The Stress of Life*, McGraw-Hill (New York, 1956).

Stockton City, California, "Neighborhood Analysis Program" (Stockton, California, March, 1973).

Tabb, William K., "Alternative Futures and Distributional Planning," *Journal of the American Institute of Planners* (January, 1972), pp. 25–32.

U.S. Army Corps of Engineers, "Final Environmental Impact Statement: Warm Springs Dam and Lake Sonoma Project, Russian River Basin, Sonoma County, California" (Washington, D.C., November, 1973).

U.S. Council on Environmental Quality, "Preparation of Environmental Impact Statements: Guidelines," in *Federal Register 38:147 Part II* (August 1, 1973).

U.S. Department of Commerce, Bureau of the Census, *Directory of Non-Federal Statistics for States and Local Areas: 1969* (Washington, D.C., 1970).

U.S. Department of Interior, "Guidelines for Implementing Principles and Standards for Multiobjective Planning of Water Resources," Review Draft (Washington, D.C., December, 1972).

U.S. Department of the Interior, "Final Environment Statement for the Prototype Oil Shale Leasing Program" (Washington, D.C., August, 1973).

U.S. Environmental Protection Agency, *The Quality of Life Concept* (Washington, D.C., March, 1973).

U.S. Environmental Protection Agency, *Alternative Futures and Environmental Quality* (Washington, D.C., November, 1973).

U.S. Water Resources Council, "Water and Related Land Resources: Establishment of Principles and Standards for Planning," in *Federal Register 38:174* (September 10, 1973).

Webber, Melvin M., et al., *Explorations into Urban Structure*, University of Pennsylvania Press (Philadelphia, 1964).

4 · Warm Springs Dam
A Case Study: Social and Economic Impacts

In this chapter we examine the Warm Springs Dam project proposed for northern California as an illustration of a broad array of social and economic impacts. This case study will allow us to examine in some detail the growth-inducing impacts of a major public works project. As stated in the previous chapter, growth-inducing impacts are an important class of project effects because economic growth is generally the cause of the most substantial social and natural environmental impacts which occur after a project's completion.

1. History of the Project

The Army Corps of Engineers received approval for the Dry Creek (also called Warm Springs) Lake and Channel in northern California's Russian River basin as part of the Flood Control Act of 1962. The project, located about 90 miles north of San Francisco, involves the construction of an earth-filled dam 3,000 feet long and 319 feet high, impounding 381,000 acre-feet of water. The major benefits claimed by the Corps for the project included flood control, water supply, and recreation. About 20,500 acres of land would be protected from floods by the dam for an annual benefit of about $3 million. The Corps calculated that 115,000 acre-feet of water would be available annually for residential and other uses in Marin and Sonoma Counties, with an estimated value of $2 million a year. The Corps also calculated recreation benefits of the dam at $1 million a year. Total annual benefits were claimed to be $7 million by the project's proponents. Total project costs were estimated to be $113 million.

The Corps had spent about $1.2 million on the project by January 1, 1972, when NEPA went into effect, about one per cent of the total estimated project cost. A Draft EIS was distributed for comment in June of 1973, and that September an organized opponent group, the Warm Springs Task Force, commented unfavorably with 70 pages of detailed, well referenced remarks.

The Final EIS was distributed in December of 1973. In February of 1974, the Council on Environmental Quality commented unfavorably on the EIS, citing as weaknesses the treatment of growth-inducing impacts, alternative sources of water supply, seismic damage potential, and faulty benefit-cost calculations. The CEQ requested that the Corps further consider these questions before deciding to continue with the project. The Corps released a contract for bids the next day to cover the following year's construction.

A mélange of plaintiffs sued the Corps in March of 1974 in the U.S. District Court for violating NEPA, the National Historic Preservations Act, the Administrative Procedure Act, and the Fifth and Ninth Amendments to the U.S. Constitution. A Temporary Restraining Order was granted, preventing the opening of bids by the Corps or the undertaking of any development. The plaintiffs sought a permanent injunction and lost in the District Court. The U.S. Supreme Court stayed construction pending appeal, however.

Before we examine the social and economic impacts of this project, we should mention the natural environmental impacts alleged by experts for the plaintiffs and by various government agency personnel commenting on the Draft and Final EIS's. Potential seismic hazards were overlooked, according to state geologists, who recommended major reassessments of the dam before continuing construction. Problems specifically included potential weaknesses of the rock under the dam's abutments, a potentially active fault under the dam's right abutment, and lack of consideration of regional seismicity. The dam site is two miles from the Healdsburg Fault, which the state geologists claimed could be expected to shake the dam five times harder than it could stand. Also, the dam is about twenty miles from the San Andreas Fault, which they estimated would experience a quake of magnitude 8 or greater (the 1906 San Francisco quake was 8.3) every 100 to 200 years. This potential earthquake would result in ground-shaking at the site three times stronger than the dam was designed to withstand.

The impacts of 25 miles of stream and river channelization below the dam were also not sufficiently accounted for in the EIS, according to scientists. The possibility of poisoning of aquatic life from a mercury mine and mercury-bearing hot springs to be inundated by the reservoir was rejected by the Corps without adequate substantiation, according to several experts. Other problems alleged included recreational traffic and resultant air quality reductions, loss of fish and wildlife, and destruction of scenic values.

2. Social and Economic Impacts of the Dam

The Corps claimed a 5 to 1 benefit-cost ratio for the project. The Corps used the $3\frac{1}{8}\%$ discount rate (the amount of interest the money used for the

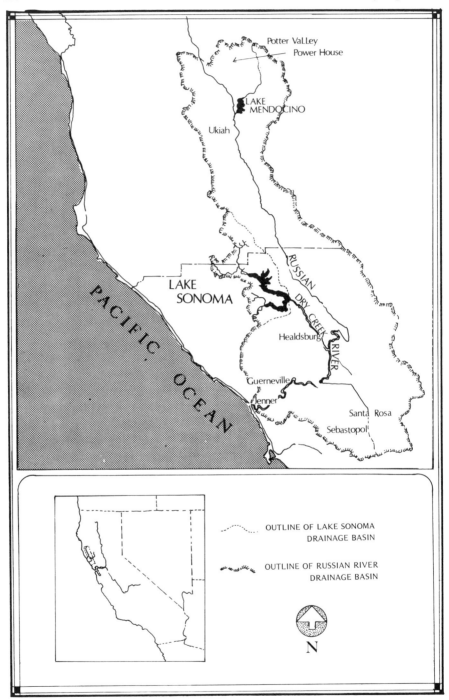

Fig. 4–1 Map of Warm Springs Dam, Sonoma County, California.

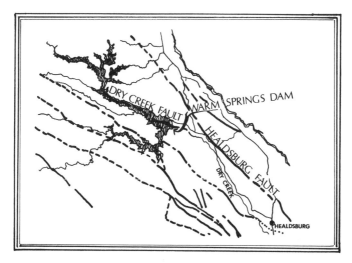

Fig. 4–2 Earthquake fault zone map, Warm Springs Dam vicinity.

project could theoretically have been drawing had it not been spent to build the dam) in effect in 1962 by order of Congress. The plaintiffs maintained that the EIS should also list a benefit-cost calculation based on the rate authorized for 1974, $6\frac{7}{8}\%$ (or even a higher rate that was actually being paid by banks at that time), which would give a ratio of .83 to 1. If this were done the EIS would show the actual economic viability of the project by using a discount rate that approximated the federal borrowing cost of money in the current market. In this way, readers of the EIS could see that the project was not financially beneficial to the nation. Also, the EIS did not indicate the true cost of the water to users. Distribution costs (pumps, pipelines, storage tanks, etc.) should be added to the dam costs.

Another weakness of the Corps' calculations was the lack of quantification of environmental costs, such as loss of hiking, hunting, habitat, etc. Even tangible costs such as the loss of gravel mining in the area were not quantified and considered in the Corps' economic analysis. Whereas the beneficial impacts were quantified to a high degree and included in the benefit-cost calculations, many adverse impacts were not quantified and were, therefore, left out of the analysis.

A third problem with the economic calculations of the Corps was the inadequate consideration of alternative projects that might be more efficient and result in a higher benefit-cost ratio. One alternative that the plaintiffs noted was not included in the EIS was the project that Congress originally authorized in 1962, a much smaller dam and storage reservoir. The project the Corps had finally decided to build would create 381,000 acre-feet of water storage, 33,000 acre-feet more than was authorized by Congress and much greater in environmental, economic, and growth-inducing impacts.

The availability of groundwater to meet future needs was also given insufficient study, according to a geologist testifying for the plaintiffs. Groundwater costs nationwide average about $\frac{1}{20}$th of the cost of the water to be delivered from the proposed dam, and yet this alternative was dismissed by the Corps.

The alternative of expanding the nearby Coyote Dam, another potential source of water supply (70,000 acre-feet), was overlooked by the Corps in its EIS. The cost of this dam addition would have been about 10% of the cost of the Warm Springs Dam. Also, the Corps failed to mention that almost half of the Coyote Dam water supply (30,000 acre-feet) was not being used in 1974.

The Corps did not discuss the significant probability that demand for municipal and industrial water would be considerably less than its projections. Thirty-five per cent of the proposed project's water supply was expected to be used by the Marin Municipal Water District. The voters in this district rejected by decisive margins bonds to build an aqueduct to carry the project water to them.

Alternatives for flood protection were also overlooked. The possibility of purchasing the flood plain below the dam site, or of using local zoning to keep the land in open space, was not considered in the EIS. This led to charges by the dam's opponents that the partial protection provided by the dam would be an incentive for building on the flood plain. The result would be greater economic damage and potential loss of life when a flood exceeding the dam's capacity did occur. Opponents pointed to the experience of other communities with increases in flood damage below flood control dams.

The inundation of Pomo Indian archaeologic sites was passed off as insignificant in the EIS. Many authorities disagreed in the trial. One of the plaintiffs was a descendant of the Dry Creek band of Pomo Indians.

Finally, the EIS did not identify the incidence of benefits and costs on various groups and persons, as required by the CEQ Guidelines of 1972 (and later versions). The main beneficiaries are, of course, the owners of flood plain lands. The losers would be the taxpayers, according to opponents.

In this particular case, the benefits were concentrated, as explained in Chapter 3, and the costs were spread. The benefits accrued to the adjacent landowners, the contractors who might build the dam, and the suppliers of water distribution and pumping equipment that might be purchased for the project. Some benefit would accrue to the workers employed on the project, but they might have worked elsewhere instead, so this is hard to measure. Costs, of course, were spread among the national and local taxpayers.

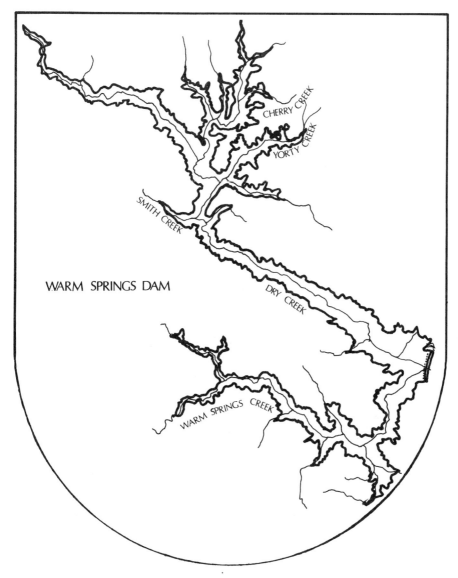

Fig. 4–3 Lake Sonoma as proposed by the Army Corps of Engineers.

3. Growth-Inducing Impacts: Whose Responsibility?

The most significant impact of a large public works project is generally the growth induced *by* the development. Individual projects do not "cause" growth, *per se.* Growth is "caused" by the presence of natural resources, such as minerals, timber, good farming soils, ports and routes for commerce, and recreational amenities, combined with a population to exploit these resources. Public works projects are the present-day means for facilitating this economic growth by permitting it to occur or by stimulating it through reducing the cost of essential production factors, such as water, power, sewers, drainage, and transportation.

As regions grow, various production factors can become overused and inefficient (water shortages, power blackouts, traffic congestion), causing a slowdown or cessation of growth. Government bodies, implementing the general desire for economic expansion in the past, have acted to remove these resource "bottlenecks" by building new dams and water systems, power sources and distribution networks, sewers and drainage lines, and freeways and roads. Each of these public works development projects may be thought of as "permitting" growth.

Each of these agencies should not have to prepare its own EIS on the growth-inducing impacts of its particular projects, repeating the same analysis of secondary impacts over and over again. The logical approach would be to have a regional body do this analysis when it adopts a plan for regional development. This EIS would account for the combined impacts of the plan, consequent local government rezonings and development permits, and the public works projects of all of the local, state, and federal agencies involved.

The catch, however, is that there isn't any regional agency controlling the growth in the service area of the dam. The locals are still going at it on their own, fighting to get industry in and to keep poor people out. Since there is no agency with jurisdiction encompassing the broader economic region, the next best agencies for doing a meaningful study of the impacts of growth are the highway engineers and the dam builders. These two agencies (State Department of Transportation and U.S. Army Corps of Engineers) build the most expensive and influential public works, without which continual regional growth could not occur. Local governments can generally not afford to pay for these major pieces of infrastructure. Furthermore, these two agencies have the largest staffs and the greatest capability for undertaking complex research of this sort. Logically, these agencies would jointly do a major EIS of their combined long-range plans for the San Francisco Bay area, showing the social, economic, and natural environmental impacts of growth. These studies could be detailed for each subregion, such as the Warm Springs Dam's service area, which includes parts of two counties.

Barring this approach by governmental bodies, the task of estimating the impacts of regional growth falls on the shoulders of whichever body proposes a major public works project that will allow substantial regional growth to occur.

The Army Corps has this responsibility, because of the importance of the dam.

The 115,000 acre-feet of water from the Warm Springs Dam is enough for about 570,000 more people in Sonoma and Marin Counties, according to the Corps' own figures. They also state in their EIS that not building the dam would result in a cessation of population growth in the area. They then state that the impacts of the additional half million people do not have to be accounted for in the EIS because the growth is "anticipated by regional population forecasts," ignoring the fact that these demographic projections assume that there will be no shortage of a resource, such as water.

After absolving themselves from causing growth, the EIS writers then proceed to describe the impacts of growth in the service area, presumably as a public service effort on their part. In this analysis, they briefly review increased wastewater and solid wastes, traffic congestion, and reduced air quality. None of the economic or health costs of these impacts are discussed.

Many significant growth impacts are not identified at all, such as crime due to increasing city size, loss of agricultural businesses, especially vineyards, due to conversion of lands to nonagricultural uses, loss of open space amenities near to residents, increased tax rates due to city growth, the disproportionate increase in school-aged children in newly developing areas, and loss of small town character for many of the area's villages.

Now that we understand the general significance of the Warm Springs Dam in terms of its natural environmental impacts and its growth-inducing impacts, we can use the framework developed in the preceding chapter to identify classes of social and economic impacts that would result from the provision of water from the dam. We will try to indicate methods for estimating (quantifying) these impacts as we proceed.

4. The Growth Impacts of the Dam

The dam will permit growth in three ways: by inducing development in the zone of reduced flood hazard below the dam, by providing a recreational resource (boating and fishing), and by providing 115,000 acre-feet of water for new growth. There will probably be more nonagricultural development in the flood plains below the dam, resulting in more economic damage in the event a flood occurs that exceeds the dam's capacity.

The impacts of providing recreation are more significant. The Corps figures 200,000 angler-days annually at the reservoir. These 200,000 anglers will spend about $2–5 each per day in the vicinity of the dam and in nearby Healdsburg buying food, beer, gas, and fishing gear. This 400,000 to 1 million dollar income would directly support about 5 to 50 jobs in stores, and the respending of this income would create roughly the same number of jobs in the Healdsburg area.

The recreation-seekers would increase the traffic on the low-quality two-lane access road from the present average of 290 cars per day to about 1,200 per day. This traffic would peak to 2,100 cars per day on summer days and have holiday peaks as high as 9,000 cars per day. Since a narrow, curvy two-lane road can only carry about 500–700 cars per hour each way and the recreation traffic will be rather unevenly distributed through the day, it is obvious that the road will have to be rebuilt at a good two-lane standard or wider. The visual impact of reconstructing this scenic rural road will be adverse. The noise impacts of the increased traffic will also be substantial.

By far the largest impacts of the dam will be caused be the provision of the 115,000 acre-feet of water supply, however. This water will essentially permit southern Sonoma County and northern Marin County to grow from a 1975 population of 450,000 to around 820,000 in the 1990's. The 570,000 new residents will require about 200,000 dwellings, which will absorb about 60,000 acres of land. Other urban uses will concomitantly consume another 450,000 acres. The total amount of land converted to urban uses would be 510,000 acres, of which about 35,000 would have been irrigated farmlands and roughly another 400,000 acres would have been dry grazing lands.

The region will continue its trend of becoming a bedroom suburb of San Francisco. Whereas in 1970 there were 106,500 jobs in the region, the number would increase only to 168,000 by the year 2000. In 1970, 76% of the working persons living in the region were employed locally. In the year 2000, only 45% of the employed will work locally.

These employment estimates, made by the Association of Bay Area Governments, lead us to conclude that traffic on U.S. 101 from Santa Rosa to San Francisco will increase dramatically by the end of the planning period. The California Department of Transportation estimates a doubling of average daily traffic at the Marin-Sonoma County line, from 37,500 in 1972 to 73,000 in 1995. The 1995 figure is probably conservative, considering the region's high potential for becoming a commuter suburb area. The air quality in the region will remain quite good, by national standards, except for areas near highways and factories.

Wastewater and solid wastes will double during this period of growth. Schools, local roads, and all government services in the region will more than double. These are the anticipated impacts of the region's growth from 450,000 people to 820,000 people in 20–25 years, according to the Corps' EIS.

Referring to Fig. 3-2 in the preceding chapter, we can trace events. The federal government is creating a change in water supply with participation by the Sonoma County Water Agency. The additional 115,000 acre-feet of water will allow basic employment to rise, as new industries locate in the region, and also bring about other changes in land use, such as residential development and irrigation of dry farmlands. These changes in industrial, residential, and agricultural activities will create a market for more nonbasic (population-serving) goods and services, creating more jobs. The potential of income from these jobs will attract more people.

In the case of this particular region, many of the potential new residents who will move to the area if new housing is developed will earn their living elsewhere. This will aggravate traffic problems, and the new housing will provide opportunities for substantial numbers of city residents to retreat to the suburbs, thus worsening the financial problems of the urban areas supplying the employment.

It is not possible to predict the nature of future urban growth accurately. It is not even possible, for example, to reliably estimate the number or types of jobs, since private corporations often make decisions which change industrial location patterns. On the basis of microeconomic theory, however, it is fairly safe to say that heavy industry will not locate in the area to any significant degree and that only minor office centers will develop in Santa Rosa and San Rafael. The employment in the region will be primarily in the service sector, in commercial activities that serve the region's population.

High demand for dwellings in the two-county area, combined with its high amenity value, rather strict land use controls, low development densities, high service levels, and low age of housing stock will make for high shelter costs in general, especially for newer units. Therefore, we would expect upper-middle and upper-income families commuting from this area into San Francisco.

It is difficult to assess the fiscal impacts of this development on the local governments. The property taxes on the places of employment for over half of the population will go to another jurisdiction (San Francisco), instead of to the jurisdictions in which those families reside. However, the relatively high average value of the dwellings will offset this loss somewhat with real property taxes. Nevertheless, one would expect high real property tax rates, especially in the cities with little industry. There is a high probability that the adult newcomers to the area will be disproportionately in their 30's, with large average numbers of children, so school costs will be high.

We can now look at Fig. 3-4 in the preceding chapter to trace out social impacts at the community level. The economic nature of the region, which we just discussed, will probably screen out lower-income families from the half of the population that commutes, because of the high cost of commuting and the high cost of exurban and suburban dwellings. So poor people will be underrepresented in the year 2000 population (first box, right column to third box, next column). Assuming normal zoning, which vigorously segregates subdivisions by lot size, the level of integration of people by incomes will probably be quite low, as it already is in most parts of the region.

The degree of land use segregation (third box, right column) will be high, with over half of the workers commuting out of the region to their jobs. Therefore, traffic will be heavy and energy consumption will rise and air quality will decline. U.S. 101 from Santa Rosa to San Francisco will have to be expanded by two or three lanes. Mass transit will have to be provided, since the Golden Gate Bridge is already being used over capacity and cannot be expanded.

5. Environmental Impacts of Urbanization

The area will continue to change from the rural small town social system of the 1940's to the suburban corridor of the type found in the northeastern United States. As a consequence of this growth, the social structure will experience the changes typical to the urbanization process.

On the positive side, incomes will rise, educational levels will increase, and choice of employment will be broadened somewhat. The fiscal efficiency of the small cities should go up as they grow to the 30,000–70,000 population range. Likewise, the size and sophistication of their political structures would be expected to increase. Finally, the cultural opportunities in the region of the dam's impact will expand, as will the choice of retail goods.

On the other hand, average commuting times for workers will rise significantly and highway injuries and fatalities will increase. Crime rates will also rise. Recreational opportunities will decline in the region itself, but good sources will still exist an hour or two north, east, and west. The famous scenic character of the region will decline dramatically. The "small town" character of the scattered villages will dissolve in the standardization of the economic mainstream.

The natural environmental impacts will include the gamut of systems that are affected by substantial urban growth. Air quality will decline. Surface and groundwater quality will be reduced. Water run-off management will become essential because of the creation of large areas of impervious surface on the flood plains. These necessary concrete channels will reduce the amenity of the watercourses, large and small.

The vegetative cover disturbance which occurs in the process of land development when combined with the increased run-off velocities from impervious surfaces will result in increased soil erosion and water pollution. The soils in the region are moderately to highly erosive. Wildlife habitats will be lost. Food production will be reduced and energy consumption will be increased because of the high average commuting distances and the high proportion of detached dwellings.

All of these categories of impacts could be elaborated on at great length. We have been able only to illustrate our qualitative model with this case study to show the importance of growth-inducing impacts, especially in major public works projects. Other authors have developed models for identifying and estimating natural environmental impacts and social and economic impacts.

The Warm Springs Dam episode is a good example of the technical complexity and difficulty of trying to estimate long-term interrelated impacts of large projects. It is also a lesson in the legal and political aspects of the National Environmental Policy Act. Much of the impact analysis on this dam had to be done by opponent groups in court and by various state and federal agencies responding to the Corps' Draft and Final EIS's.

While clear guidelines for the assessment and reporting of growth-inducement and the impacts of induced growth have not been developed, the Warm Springs case demonstrates that a determined citizenry can and will force consideration of growth in the course of debate on major projects. This consideration may never appear in an EIS, and may not be part of the causes of action used by environmental attorneys to block development, but it is present in the minds of the supervisors and Congressional representatives who have to make the decisions and then run for reelection.

The consideration of the impacts of growth, however, is required by California's law and by NEPA. The Warm Springs Dam raised the issue of how thorough must the assessment of growth be, what must its parameters be, and how far into the future must it extend. These questions will most likely be decided one at a time in the courts.

References

1. "Public Works for Water and Power Development and Atomic Energy Commission Appropriation Bill, 1975," hearings before a Subcommittee of the Committee on Appropriations, House of Representatives, 93rd Congress, Second Session, Subcommittee on Public Works, Part 2, U.S. Government Printing Office (Washington, D.C., 20402), pp. 1030–34.
2. "Final Environmental Impact Statement: Warm Springs Dam and Lake Sonoma Project, Russian River Basin, Sonoma County, California," Office of the Chief of Engineers, Department of the Army (Washington, D.C., 20314), November, 1973.

5 · The Law of Environmental Impact Assessment

History and Objectives of NEPA, the Parent

The National Environmental Policy Act was passed by Congress in December of 1969 as Public Law 91-190 after one day of hearings, a voice vote in the Senate, and a few hours of meager discussion in the House. It is perhaps ironic that such a fundamental reconstruction of national priorities was subjected to such scant debate by friend or foe prior to its passage.

As the actual impacts of NEPA became apparent, many administrators began to complain of costly delays, mountains of paperwork, and undue interference with governmental decision-making. On the other hand, many environmentalists viewed the Act as a Magna Carta of environmental protection and as an effective device to further open governmental processes to public scrutiny and accountability. Thus the lack of debate prior to passage has been succeeded by vigorous and on-going analysis during the current implementation phase of NEPA.

The broad policies of NEPA are contained in its Preface and under Title 1, Section 101: Declaration of National Environmental Policy. These provisions are intended to fundamentally modify the existing basis of executive decision-making on actions affecting the quality of the environment. To this purpose

Michael H. Remy, born in 1944, is Professor of Environmental Law at California State University at Sacramento, where he directs the Environmental Studies Center. A graduate of the University of California Law School at Davis, he served as Staff Counsel to the California Department of Water Resources for four years before assuming the Directorship of the Lake Tahoe environmental Education Center Consortium. He also served on the Design Team of *Environmental Impact Reporting and Evaluation,* a television study course.

Section 101 declares: . . . it is the . . . responsibility of the Federal
Government to use all practicable means, consistent with other essential
considerations of national policy, to improve and coordinate Federal plans,
functions, programs and resources to the end that the Nation may—

> *1*) fulfill the responsibilities of each generation as trustee of the
> environment for succeeding generations;
>
> *2*) assure for all Americans safe, healthful, productive, and aestheti-
> cally and culturally pleasing surroundings;
>
> *3*) attain the widest range of beneficial uses of the environment
> without degradation, risk to health or safety, or other undesirable and
> unintended consequences;
>
> *4*) preserve important historic, cultural, and natural aspects of our
> national heritage, and maintain, wherever possible, an environment
> which supports diversity and variety of individual choice;
>
> *5*) achieve a balance between population and resource use which will
> permit high standards of living and a wide sharing of life's amenities;
> and
>
> *6*) enhance the quality of renewable resources and approach the
> maximum attainable recycling of depletable resources.

Having drafted this declaration of a broad national policy, the law-makers
realized that implementation of the policy without enforcement mechanisms
would reduce the Act to a futile exercise. In order to assure that NEPA's goals
would be translated into action, Congress gave specific instructions in Sections
102 and 103 to the federal agencies. Prior to the enactment of NEPA, agencies
had viewed themselves as "specialists" charged to perform limited and specified
tasks. Some had felt constrained by previous legislation from considering
environmental factors in calculating the costs and benefits of public works
projects. Section 103 of NEPA, in one fell swoop, "forced action" by mandating
a "generalist" responsibility of environmental considerations upon all federal
agencies. It required all federal agencies to "review their present statutory
authority, administrative regulations, and current policies and procedures for the
purpose of determining whether there are any deficiencies or inconsistencies
therein which prohibit full compliance with the purposes and provisions of this
Act." To correct any conflicts, Section 103 further required that all federal
agencies report to the President what actions might be necessary to bring their
authorities and policies in line with the intent and purposes of NEPA. Few, if
any, agencies have reported anything in their statutory authority, regulations, or
policies which required adjustment. The requirement to report needed adjustments to the President, while thus not resulting in much change, serves to
protect NEPA from claims of conflicting mandates.

A second action-forcing mechanism, contained in Section 102, has experienced greater success and a more illustrious history. Section 102(2)(C) of NEPA is the most innovative and controversial feature of the Act and requires that all agencies of the Federal Government shall:

> (C) include in every recommendation or report on proposals for legislation and other major Federal actions significantly affecting the quality of the human environment, a detailed statement by the responsible official on—
>
> (i) the environmental impact of the proposed action,
>
> (ii) any adverse environmental effects which cannot be avoided should the proposal be implemented,
>
> (iii) alternatives to the proposed action,
>
> (iv) the relationship between local short-term uses of man's environment and the maintenance and enhancement of long-term productivity, and
>
> (v) any irreversible and irretrievable commitments of resources which would be involved in the proposed action should it be implemented.
>
> Prior to making any detailed statement, the responsible Federal official shall consult with and obtain the comments of any Federal agency which has jurisdiction by law or special expertise with respect to any environmental impact involved. Copies of such statements and the comments and views of the appropriate Federal, State, and local agencies, which are authorized to develop and enforce environmental standards, shall be made available to the President, the Council of Environmental Quality and to the public as provided by Section 552 of Title 5, United States Code, and shall accompany the proposal through the existing agency review processes.

As an added underscore, Congress introduced the mandate of Section 102 with the phrase, "to the fullest extent possible." Although this book concentrates on the key "action-forcing" mechanism of Section 102(2)(C), the environmental impact statement, the reader should bear in mind that the Act provides eight "action-forcing" provisions to ensure that the federal government will consider the goals and policies of the Act in reaching specific decisions. The various provisions of the Act are mutually reinforcing and should not be interpreted out of the context of the total legislation. The declaratory statement contained in Section 101, for example, should always be kept in mind when viewing other sections of the Act.

In addition to the declaration of a national policy and the creation of various "action-forcing" mechanisms, the third major feature of NEPA was the establishment of the Council on Environmental Quality (CEQ). Title II of the Act places CEQ in the Executive Office of the President and specifies the advisory responsibilities of this body. The Council was designed to gather information on actions of government, indices of environmental quality, conditions and trends in the environment and legislation, and to interpret these data to the President for inclusion in an annual *Environmental Quality Report.* The Council was also designed to take to the President recommendations (based on data gathered by its staff and that of the Environmental Protection Agency) concerning the formulation of national policy on environmental matters. Finally, the Council was charged with the responsibility to design guidelines for the preparation of federal environmental impact statements.

Just as CEQ's purpose is to inform the executive branch, the purpose of the environmental impact statement is to inform both the decision-maker and the public. However, requiring agencies to "jump through the hoops" of procedures outlined in NEPA and its guidelines did not guarantee that meaningful change would ensue, although it was anticipated that the additional information gathered by the agencies from various sources during the process of completing their decision-making would make the responsible officials more sensitive to environmental needs.

In addition to this projected outcome (agencies becoming more aware of environmental impact), agencies have discovered, through court interpretation of NEPA guidelines and of the Act itself, that the information we have spoken of is the essence of the requirement to prepare a "detailed" statement. The information is also necessary for "full disclosure" of impacts of proposed projects. It was at first anticipated by federal officials that environmental impact statements would need to be only several pages long—a brief statement of findings and conclusions—but court interpretation of the aforementioned phrases "detailed statement" and "full disclosure" have made it essential for agencies to avail themselves of all available information.

Compilation of reams of available information on each projected action has the desired outcome of making agencies more aware, and the less desirable outcome of making disclosures very cumbersome, especially for public use. Yet it is public use and participation in the EIS process that may well make NEPA work and it is in the interest of the public agencies to make their "full disclosures" as meaningful as possible. The public also has the duty to inform itself so that it may deal with disclosed impacts to the best advantage of the involved community. This is the concept of "citizen action." The history of citizen action with regard to environmental issues will be discussed in later portions of the chapter. The point here is that the participation of the public is vital to the enforcement of NEPA doctrines. How?

One of the ways in which an EIS informs the public is by forcing full disclosure of the environmental consequences of a proposed action. The authors of NEPA perceived the difficulty of persuading federal agencies to freely disclose. In order to assure this required disclosure, NEPA drafters opened the decision-making process to public participation and scrutiny by making, in NEPA, references to the Public Information Act (Section 552 of Title 5, United States Code); NEPA may be then construed to guarantee the public the right to obtain copies of draft and final environmental impact statements, along with any comments and views pertaining.

It became clear after the enactment of NEPA that the question of enforcement of matters such as full disclosure had not been adequately addressed in the Act. More than a year after NEPA's enactment some agencies in the executive branch of government had done nothing to ensure that the required EIS guidelines had been prepared and it rapidly became obvious that the executive branch could not be counted upon to enforce NEPA. The courts moved to fill the enforcement vacuum and began to review such issues as whether a particular impact statement was required, and, once prepared, whether or not it was adequate.

Many factors contributed to the willingness of courts to hear and decide NEPA cases. Basically, the procedures required and outlined by NEPA and its guidelines were not unlike those procedures which courts generally expected to be followed in all governmental decision-making. The courts would look for an articulation of reasons behind the decision and explanations of the risks which would follow a proposed action. In addition, courts would look for a record which disclosed consideration of alternatives while indicating the real public interests involved. Finally, very significantly, the courts have been diligent in requiring evidence of increased public participation during the years leading up to the enactment of NEPA.

After passage of NEPA, it was uncertain what role the courts would choose to play in the implementation of the Act. The significance and crucial relationship of the court to the total scheme envisioned under the Act can best be illustrated in Fig. 5-1. In the illustration, NEPA constitutes the lever which will move the administrative agency toward the desired environmental policy. Success, in oversimplified terms, will depend upon three major factors: (1) the degree to which the anchors of administrative agencies can be pried, (2) the force exerted by public interest and involvement, and (3) the placement of the fulcrum, designated in the figure as the courts.

Neither the Act nor its legislative history mentions judicial review. The actual reasons for the willingness of the courts to review agency decisions under NEPA are complex and numerous. Perhaps it was even more important, however, that the courts reached the critical conclusion that Congress intended that NEPA's various requirements should be interpreted and applied in the strictest manner. Through the now-famous decision by Judge Skelley Wright in *Calvert Cliffs' Coordinating Committee v. Atomic Energy Commission* the requirement of compliance "to the fullest extent possible" has been applied with special vigor to the provisions dealing with environmental impact statements. In terms of the illustration, the courts, as the fulcrum, chose the optimum position to attain leverage toward reform of federal decision-making.

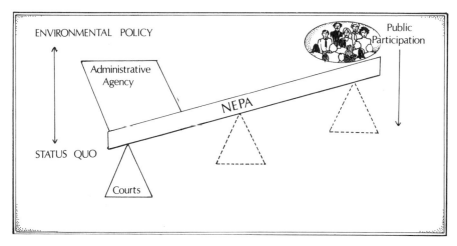

Fig. 5–1 Illustration of balance and leverage among elements of environmental decision-making.

In addition to the effective placement of the fulcrum, the rapid rise during the last four years of public interest lawsuits and the liberalization of the rules regarding "standing to sue" (right to be heard) have permitted the public to exert greater and more effective pressure upon federal agencies. In the illustration, clearly, the more public interest and participation, the greater is the force exerted through NEPA and the courts on the administrative agencies. It has, in large measure, been the judiciary and the public who, through combined efforts, have inserted teeth into this Act.

After several years of court review it became clear, according to Frederick R. Anderson in *NEPA in the Courts* (Resources for the Future: Johns Hopkins University Press, Baltimore, 1973), that the courts would scrutinize agency complicance with NEPA's provisions from start to finish. Anderson lists the key reviewable agency actions under NEPA as follows:

(*1*) The courts will review how the agencies organize (and the methods used) to decide on a course of action subject to NEPA.

(*2*) The courts will closely review whether the agency must prepare an impact statement.

(*3*) The courts will review *de novo* whether the information disclosed is adequate.

(*4*) The courts will review how the agency considered the information they developed.

(*5*) The courts will review whether the final decision made is substantively correct under Section 101.

Citizen Action

The willingness of the courts to review agency compliance with NEPA has been reinforced by the increase in citizen suits against federal agencies. In fact, history may prove the environmental movement of the 1970's one of the best examples of effective citizen action. It is a time in which citizen action has come of age. Well organized, knowledgeable, and persistent citizen action is a vital link in both NEPA and the various state acts. Through citizen monitoring, participation, and involvement, with tenacious assistance from the judicial branch, these acts have become more than "paper tigers."

In the fight to become an effective voice in environmental legislation, the first hurdle citizens had to overcome was organization. Just a decade ago, a mere three or four national environmental organizations divided up a faithful but small constituency. Today, many national, state, and local groups with increased memberships have organized under general, specific, and ad-hoc objectives.

The second major hurdle these citizen groups faced was the refusal of many private and public leaders or decision-makers to take them seriously. By and large, the record supports the assertion that citizen organizations have won this battle. Few courts are inclined to turn them away on procedural grounds today and the long list of successful court actions no longer can be scoffed at by agency administrators.

Having overcome these two obstacles, citizens are now faced with an even greater long-term challenge. The citizen will need to learn more about how things really work, how divergent views are heard and reconciled in administrative agencies, in the courts, and in the political forum. Kept on the outside so long, citizens will need time to adjust to a new role where their opinions are actually solicited and considered. Governmental agencies will benefit as well from the public's greater sensitivity to the complexities of government, the economy, and the environment. To maximize public participation, two concepts need to be adopted and utilized by governmental agencies.

(*1*) Agencies must become convinced to view their responsibility to involve the public as an "affirmative responsibility or duty," and

(*2*) Agencies will need to assist in the effort to improve the capacity and ability of citizens to deal with the complexity of environmental concerns.

Since the citizen serves such a vital function in NEPA processes, the financial and intellectual resources of schools, colleges, universities, institutes, and clubs should be made more readily available to him. Programs that will plug the private citizen into organizations with available expertise and resources should receive careful attention by federal and state funding sources.

For the citizen to be a helpful and effective partner with government, he needs to know the facts about government action, he needs the opportunity and the wherewithal to participate in decision-making, and the means to ultimately challenge governmental decisions that appear to be out of tune with legal requirements or public policy.

The environmental impact statement process under NEPA and similar state acts serves as an excellent tool to accomplish the above-stated goals. As mentioned, these acts require full disclosure in the form of an environmental impact statement of the effects of a proposed governmental action. Among several other things these acts also require are a discussion of alternatives and a description of conflicting values that may weigh for or against proceeding as planned. The requirement that any reasonable comments received by the agency from the public must be dealt with in the final environmental impact statement is of considerable significance. Environmental effects, as a rule, will be oblivious to political boundaries. Project or action decisions, on the other hand, are made by the decision-making body within a political territory. Unless a drastic reorganization of our political system were to occur, it is safe to assume that many of the project or action decisions will be made by persons who do not necessarily represent all those who will be impacted by projects or actions. However, the commenting process envisioned under NEPA and comparable state acts can and does cross artificial political boundaries. An individual affected or concerned by the environmental effects of a project can forward his concern to the governmental agency, and that agency will be required to address any reasonable issues raised. Thus, theoretically, an individual anywhere in the United States—or for that matter, the world—who expresses a particular concern or bears a particular expertise could become involved with any project proposed. Since effects on the environment are complex and interrelated and do not respect political boundaries, an expansive commenting process would aid in bringing greater awareness to provincial decision-making.

As the courts continue to expand the concept of "standing-to-sue," individuals concerned with or affected by projects administered outside of their political enclave may even succeed in utilizing the courts to enforce consideration of their concern.

Citizen's Guide to Legal Requirements of Environmental Impact Statements

In prior discussion, it has been stressed that public participation is of the utmost importance to the workings of NEPA. For purposes of this section, the role of the public, with assistance of the courts, needs to be more strongly emphasized: in fact, the public has become NEPA's "policeman." This charge carries with it heavy responsibility. Not all involved citizens need be lawyers, however, to utilize the legal requirements for NEPA disclosures as tools for citizen action. The following section has been designed to provide concerned people with an enumeration of agency responsibilities so that they may more completely scrutinize impact statements and procedures to intercede as necessary. The section will provide citizens with a means of entering discussion on proposed projects and their impact statement preparation. It is, of necessity, a general overview, as each state's requirements differ.

NEPA requires that agencies comply with the tenets of the Act "to the fullest extent possible." The courts decide whether the standard has been met. One of the ways in which the courts determine whether the standard has been met is by examining the "reviewable record," that is, a documented record of considerations leading to the project decision. Since the public shares access to this record, due to NEPA's requirement for full disclosure, citizens have an opportunity to evaluate whether or not the agency's documentation adequately supports its project decision prior to any judicial review or involvement. It is thus the procedural deficiency which provides the main entry for citizen intervention.

Such intervention need not and should not always be a resort to the courts. Realistically, the courts should remain a last resort after negotiations and persuasions through the administrative channels of agencies by citizens' or interest groups have been exhausted. The last few years have shown citizens and agencies facing off at opposite ends of the courtroom on controversial projects. In the future, there will need to be more citizen involvement—citizens and agencies working together around the conference table. A number of NEPA agency procedures and a few of the State Act guidelines encourage this kind of process. The development of constructive agency-citizen relationships promises to be the best hope for keeping governmental decision-making processes open and responsive to the public interest. Equally important, however, is the responsibility of the public to acquaint itself with the substantive and procedural duties that the federal and state environmental quality acts have assigned.

Although the differing duties and procedures specified by the various state acts will be subject to individual state court interpretation, the reader should note that federal court precedents may prove persuasive. The influence of federal court precedents will be especially strong for state acts which have borrowed many of the procedures and terms from NEPA.

The first question in the federal arena is: What circumstances require the preparation of environmental impact statements? The statutory language of NEPA in Section 102(2)(C) requires all agencies of the federal government to: "Include in every recommendation or report on proposals for legislation and other major Federal actions significantly affecting the quality of the human environment, a detailed statement . . . ." Thus, an important threshold issue is whether a particular action is sufficiently "Federal" for NEPA to apply. In some instances, the federal involvement may not yet have matured sufficiently, while other fact situations will determine whether the federal involvement exists at all or is sufficient to require EIS preparation. The following is a partial listing of types of actions where the federal involvement has been held sufficient by the courts:

(*1*) Federal agency services and construction programs

(*2*) Federal permits, licenses, certificates, or other regulatory activity

(*3*) Federal contracts, grants, and loans

A careful reading of Section 102 poses two closely related questions. "Major Federal action significantly affecting the environment" may require that an action first be found to be (1) "major," and then the inquiry into (2) significance of the environmental effects can follow. The two-test standard appears to be favored by the courts, but there exists considerable controversy over this point. From the citizen's point of view the controversy is important because a failure to prepare an environmental impact statement may be based upon the federal agency's assessment that their federal action is not "major." However, since the courts have generally required documentation of such threshold exemption determinations, the "reviewable record" may be obtained by citizens for scrutiny.

The second threshold determination, which deals with the significance of the environmental impact, must also be documented. If a federal agency determines that effects of its project will not be significant, the reviewable record should contain data upon which its conclusion has been based.

The CEQ guidelines interpret the phrase "major Federal actions significantly affecting the quality of the human environment" to cover consideration of:

(*1*) the overall, cumulative impact of the actions proposed and further actions contemplated

(*2*) the potential that the environment may be significantly affected even if the action is localized in impact

(*3*) any action whose environmental impact is likely to be highly controversial

(*4*) individually limited effects of many decisions about a project which become cumulatively significant, such as when

(*a*) one or more agencies over a period of years put into a project individually minor but collectively major resources

(*b*) a minor decision establishes a precedent or a decision in principle about a larger course of action

(*c*) several agencies are involved

These same guidelines also established that significant effects on the quality of the human environment include those that directly affect human beings and those that indirectly affect human beings through adverse effects on the environment. The decision, however, as to what is "major," "Federal," "significant," "cumulatively significant," "controversial," and many similar concepts, is left to the individual federal agencies to decide on the basis of their own projects and guidelines. Since these terms may be subject to a wide range of interpretation, the student should always look for documentation upon which the agency is relying in making its determination. Each one of these determinations may constitute a crucial "threshold" determination on the applicability of NEPA to the proposed activity (a "threshold" determination is the point at which the effects of an environmental impact are of such proportions as to be significant, which will vary from project to project).

The reader should bear in mind two limitations on the applicability of NEPA. Courts have traditionally been very reluctant to interfere with decisions of the executive branch which involve questions of national security. Although the courts have not held that the phrase "major Federal actions" excludes national security and military installation actions, per se, from environmental impact statement preparation, the extent of the exemption will need to await case-by-case resolution. The second limitation on NEPA applicability concerns federal temporary or emergency actions. Since the analysis called for in an environmental impact statement is time-consuming, a government's perceived need for immediate or quick action may dictate proceeding without the preparation of a statement. The resolution of the extent to which this exemption can be utilized will again need case-by-case attention from the courts.

In both of the above situations, although a great deal of uncertainty remains, the agencies should nevertheless be required to prepare the reviewable record upon which they base their exemption, and the public should have access to the reasons for the exemption.

After the preliminary issues regarding applicability of NEPA to a federal agency action have been resolved, a number of requirements must be fulfilled by the EIS preparer. These requirements concern the timing of statement preparation, the extent to which preparation can be delegated or shared, the adequacy of the statement, and the responsibilities under the commenting and consultation processes.

With regard to timing, NEPA's legislative history supports the position of the CEQ guidelines in calling for preparation of the statement "as early as possible and in all cases prior to agency decision." It is difficult for members of the public to pinpoint when the decision-making process of federal agencies has advanced sufficiently to require the formal preparation of an impact statement. Federal agencies are, of course, under an obligation to incorporate the mandates of NEPA into all their policy considerations. It is, however, the EIS which Congress looks to for assurance that an agency has considered and balanced environmental factors and has documented their significance before any major federal action is taken. The courts have provided some assistance in terms of when this critical point in time is reached. While stating that an EIS must be prepared as early in the planning process as possible, the courts have also cautioned that agencies will not be permitted to stage the decision-making process to escape or circumvent impact preparation. Logically, the timing question will be subject to a "rule of reason." The action will need to be sufficiently defined to allow discussion of the anticipated effects of and alternatives to the proposed action. It is safe to assume that the courts, in requiring compliance to the "fullest extent possible," will scrutinize agency behavior for genuine and effective procedures to initiate these statements as early as possible in the planning and decision-making process.

In addition, the EIS when finally prepared should include discussions on how the environmental factors were incorporated in the planning or feasibility study stages prior to the time when the formal EIS requirement came into being. It is important to remember that the mandate of NEPA is to use *all* practicable means to create and maintain conditions under which man and nature can exist in productive harmony (Section 101). The EIS requirement is only one method an agency must use to meet this goal. Other means, such as design changes and mitigation measures, which preceded the formal documentation should be disclosed in the Draft EIS.

The CEQ guidelines further clarify that EIS's may need to be prepared for various stages of a proposed federal action. Thus, an impact statement prepared by the Department of the Interior on opening federal lands for geothermal exploration and leasing detailed the effects and alternatives relevant to that level of federal decision-making. This comprehensive EIS did not, however, eliminate the need to prepare future environmental impact statements for particular development projects proposed on these federal lands.

Section 102(2)(C) charges a "responsible Federal official" to prepare the impact statement. Although this section appears to require such preparation by the involved federal official or agency, the court interpretations have split between permitting the use of statements prepared by other governmental agencies and requiring federal agencies to prepare their own impact statement. The matter of who prepares the statement is closely related to the question of timing discussed above. The federal agency may well be the last line of governmental approval. If such approval is permitted on the basis of environmental impact statements prepared at the state or local level, permitting the wholesale adoption of the statement by the federal agency may foster superficial consideration by the federal decision-maker.

Courts appear to favor the rationale in the case of *Greene County Planning Board v. Federal Power Commission*, which requires an agency to prepare its own impact statement. This holding does not, however, force the agency to undertake all the necessary studies and data compilation, since it can still require state governments and private parties to supply the necessary information, hire consultants, and conduct field studies. The pulling together of such information and the necessary evaluation should be done by the federal agency, however, under the *Greene County* holding.

From the point of view of obtaining accurate environmental impact assessments, allowing permit or license applicants to prepare the statement may perpetuate distortions of environmental assessments. The federal agency should retain the responsibility to frame the issues and assess the relative weight of impacts. Under the rationale of *Greene County*, the federal agency must undertake this exercise itself in order not to become vulnerable to manipulation. The issue of who should properly prepare the impact statement and what functions can be delegated is equally important to those state environmental policy acts which require impact statements for the issuance of permits or licenses by local government activities for private activities. If "full disclosure" to the decision-maker is to be effective, the decision-maker will need to genuinely evaluate rather than merely adopt information.

If a state act makes private activities subject to an EIS requirement, it becomes important to determine who can or should write the statement. In California, for example, draft statements are frequently written by developers or their consultants with the possible risk that little or no evaluation by the local agency will take place. Such "sweetheart" or "rubber-stamped" documents will do little to accomplish the decision-making reform called for by the acts.

Many major federal actions will involve multiple federal approvals or participation of several agencies. In such a situation three possible approaches could be utilized to meet the EIS requirement: (1) each agency prepares a separate EIS, (2) all federal agencies prepare a joint EIS, or (3) one federal agency (lead agency) prepares a statement to cover all other agency involvements. The CEQ, in its guidelines, chose the "lead agency" concept which assigns the responsibility to the agency with primary authority for committing the federal government to a major course of action with possible significant impact on the human environment. The CEQ chose the "lead agency" approach in order to avoid duplication of effort and information, although compliance to the "fullest extent possible" may well favor that all agencies prepare independent statements. The state acts which apply an EIS requirement to local agencies face a similar question of possible multiple agency involvement. In order for the "lead agency" concept to fulfill some of the basic functions of NEPA, the consulting and review process between involved agencies has to be adhered to diligently. State jurisdictions may find that a joint statement preparation process better fosters the needed communication between governmental agencies than the "lead agency" concept. The fear of unnecessary duplication may be unfounded if the involved agencies can plan together and ahead. If the environment is a complex system, it must be studied in an interdisciplinary fashion and this usually involves assembling a team of experts who can interact on a problem. The goal is spelled out specifically in Section 102(2)(A) of NEPA:

> All agencies of the Federal Government shall utilize a *systematic inter-disciplinary approach* which will insure the integrated use of the natural and social sciences and the environmental design arts in planning and decision-making which may have an impact on man's environment. (Emphasis added.)

To the extent that the "lead agency" concept prevents utilization of expertise spread across other involved agencies, it is the least desirable of the three options.

In addressing the adequacy of federal impact statements, the courts have attempted to balance available institutional and financial resources with the need to obtain the most complete disclosure possible. Courts have expected comprehensive and objective treatment and rejected partial or superficial analysis of the subjects required to be discussed in an EIS.

To assess whether the statement is detailed enough, the courts will look to see that:

(1) statements are understandable and nonconclusionary

(2) statements have referred to the full range of knowledge

(3) statements have covered impacts that are typical to some types of action

Since environmental impact statements are to be reviewed by both the lay public and their scientific advisors, they must be comprehensive and informative for both audiences.

A fairly frequent criticism of early NEPA statements was that they were overly conclusionary. The conclusions should, in large measure, flow from the data and facts presented. Scientific conclusions must be supported by references to relevant literature or field studies conducted.

Although a review of early federal and state impact reports shows considerable inadequacies, even in the description of known and predictable environmental effects, the coverage of two subjects has been especially troublesome and lasting: (1) uncertain or unknown effects of a proposed action and (2) the range and detail of alternatives that an agency should discuss.

Uncertain Impacts

Environmental impact statements, in their effort to forecast anticipated effects, of necessity will involve a large measure of informed guesswork. A question which will frequently confront decision-makers and the public on new or untried proposals is whether the mandates of NEPA are satisfied when the statement discloses existing gaps in knowledge. Under a narrow reading of the full disclosure requirement some courts have held that such admissions of information gaps constitute adequate compliance with the Act. On the other hand, several courts have required more from the agency by holding out for the completion of agency research programs before permitting them to proceed with the proposed action.

In order to prevent decision-making in ignorance of the consequences, several procedures have been suggested by the courts to permit agencies to proceed despite incomplete knowledge of some risks. The agency may be required to obtain testimony on the range and magnitude of the risks involved. Similar projects might be examined to ascertain anticipated impacts. Finally, some courts have suggested that the agency outline a system for monitoring the impacts after commencement of the project and disclose such a plan in the EIS.

For the public, the problem of unknown effects can be especially unsettling. It may be constructive for them to suggest during the commenting process that needed research and information procedures and subsequent monitoring be built into the project proposal. Such comments would highlight the information gap and suggest a constructive approach which the agency would be required to consider and address.

Discussion of Alternatives

Since NEPA merely states the requirement to discuss alternatives, some guidance on the scope and extent of the requirement is essential. The courts have required consideration of alternatives which may accomplish less than the proposed action. They have clearly indicated, also, that an agency must discuss alternatives beyond the power of the agency to implement. In addition, the alternatives of no action at all and of actions which might enhance environmental quality or avoid some or all of the adverse effects are mandated by the CEQ guidelines.

The courts have applied a "rule of reason" limit on the discussion of alternatives by concluding that the alternatives discussed need only be those available in the same time span as the original proposal. Just as important as the range of alternatives is the detail of discussion required for each alternative. Here the courts have indicated that the discussion in the statement should permit the reader to assess the environmental risks of each alternative in comparison to the project proposal. Many early NEPA statements included only economic data in their discussion of alternatives, which prevented balancing or any appreciation of the environmental risks.

NEPA Commenting and Consultation Process

Section 102(2)(C) of NEPA is intended not only to implement a new rational policy but also to provide for the coordination of existing policies. The concluding portion of Section 102(2)(C) states:

> Prior to making any detailed statement, the responsible Federal official shall consult with and obtain the comments of any Federal agency which has jurisdiction by law or special expertise with respect to any environmental impact involved. Copies of such statements and the comments and views of the appropriate Federal, State, and local agencies, which are authorized to develop and enforce environmental standards, shall be made available to the President, the Council on Environmental Quality and to the public as provided by Section 552 of Title 5, United States Code, and shall accompany the proposal through the existing agency review processes.

The CEQ guidelines, along with judicial interpretations of this section and executive orders, have set up a very comprehensive procedure on commenting and consultation. A "Draft" EIS should be as complete and accurate as the agency can make it: these "Draft" statements are then utilized to obtain comments from other governmental agencies, federal, state, and local, and from the public. Such consultation is encouraged even prior to the preparation of the "Draft" EIS. Since greater public involvement or exposure comes from the circulation of this document rather than the Final EIS, it should reflect the expertise from all the various involved agencies. In the first two years of the EIS process under NEPA, there was considerable temptation to prepare these statements on a "trial balloon" basis. A document was prepared and circulated to see what type of reaction it drew. By addressing the various comments or flak received, the material for the Final EIS was easily generated. This procedure could flaw full disclosure because new information obtained during the review or consultation process could significantly alter the proposed action or anticipated environmental effects. Other governmental agencies and the public would be deprived of this new information unless the draft or final statement is recirculated for consideration. The federal guidelines now recommend that in such cases the agency consult with CEQ to determine the possible need or desirability to recirculate the draft statement for another appropriate review period.

After the comments are received, the lead or preparing agency completes a "Final" EIS, which is to accompany the proposal through "existing agency review processes." The courts have required compliance "to the fullest extent possible" in statutory procedures for obtaining comments. Any omission in the procedures will result in rejection of the statement as inadequate.

While failure to obtain comments can be fatal, the courts have also indicated that the agency must respond to all relevant and reasonable comments. Thus comments must not only be obtained in accordance with procedures, they must also be treated properly in the final statement. One court has stated that the proper response to comments which are both relevant and reasonable is either to conduct the research necessary to provide satisfactory answers or to refer to those places in the statement which provide them. Another court went even further on comments received from "expert" commenting agencies. Under the rationale of this decision, an agency should be forced to accept the facts, opinions, and recommendations for further research of "environmental" agencies as virtually conclusive.

The cases have held that agencies have an obligation to seek comments from the public and that the final impact statements must take these comments into account. Thus far, the courts have not restricted the meaning of "public." The opportunity to comment has not been limited to individuals residing within the political boundaries of the project proponent. This is an important point since environmental effects do not respect political boundaries. It is at this point speculative whether the courts would permit governmental agencies to apply some form of standing restrictions on comments. The requirement that agencies address all relevant and reasonable comments would appear to suffice.

One of the best ways to assure public participation in environmental assessment is through public hearings. The question of whether to hold such hearings is delegated in the CEQ guidelines to the various federal agencies. However, where agency procedures call for hearings on some aspect of the proposal, the courts have required such hearings to extend to environmental issues and have required the preparation of an EIS in advance of the hearing.

The objective of open discussion and debate envisioned by NEPA can be attained only if the public has ready access to all agency comments on the Draft.

In addition, the vital function served by the public in the EIS process will be most meaningful if such information is made available in a timely fashion.

State Environmental Acts: The Offspring

The National Environmental Policy Act applies only to federal actions and does not cover the multitude of activities carried on by state or local governments. Although state and local governments frequently become involved in the peparation and review of federal impact statements for proposed projects in their jurisdiction, the need for state and local environmental impact programs exists independent of federal involvement. The states have relied for the most part on the federal example in setting up their own programs. The situation has become very confused and complex for officials who are trying to develop environmental impact programs for their states, and especially for citizens who are trying to utilize and participate in the process. The following summary is intended to provide some overview of the various state acts that have been adopted. The discussion is broken down by key issues involved in any impact statement program: (1) Required Content of the Environmental Impact Statement; (2) Scope and Nature of Activities to Require an Impact Statement; (3) Relationship of Impact Statement Programs to Land Use Regulation; (4) Methods of Enforcement; and (5) Citizen Participation.

Required Content of the Environmental Impact Statement

As the reader will recall, NEPA has specified that the following five points must be covered in a federal environmental impact statement:

(*i*) the environmental impact of the proposed action,

(*ii*) any adverse environmental effects which cannot be avoided should the proposal be implemented,

(*iii*) alternatives to the proposed action,

(*iv*) the relationship between local short-term uses of man's environment and the maintenance and enhancement of long-term productivity, and

(*v*) any irreversible and irretrievable commitments of resources which would be involved in the proposed action should it be implemented.

The Council on Environmental Quality guidelines for the preparation of federal impact statements added three more subjects which must be included in these statements:

(*1*) a description of the proposed action and a statement of its purposes, along with a discussion of the environment affected;

(2) an explanation of how the proposed action relates to land use plans, policies, and controls for the affected area; and

(3) an indication of what other interests and considerations of Federal policy are thought to offset any adverse environmental effects outlined in the environmental impact statement.

Generally, the various state acts and executive orders implementing environmental impact programs differ little from NEPA and its guidelines in terms of the required points to be covered.

California's Environmental Quality Act added the requirement that an environmental impact report include a discussion of "mitigation measures proposed to minimize the impact" of a project. Several other states and the Suggested State Environmental Policy Act adopted by the Council of State Governments (see Chapter 8, Part 3) have similar clauses requiring discussion of mitigation measures. In January of 1975 the California law was amended to require that the mitigation measure discussion include consideration of energy conservation measures in order to reduce inefficient and unnecessary consumption of energy. Although neither of these requirements is specifically enumerated in NEPA, the NEPA guidelines do call for similar treatment of the subjects in federal impact statements.

The California law has added the requirement that an environmental impact report contain an analysis of the "growth-inducing impact of a proposed action." The state guidelines indicate that this discussion should include ways in which the proposed project could foster economic or population growth, either directly or indirectly, in the surrounding environment. The major expansion of a waste water treatment plant is cited as an example of a project which could provide for increased residential and commercial construction within the service area of the plant. Once again, although NEPA itself does not enumerate this discussion, the NEPA guidelines place strong emphasis on discussing the effects of a proposed project on population and growth. Although a number of state acts do require the evaluation of the primary and secondary effects of a proposed project, California presently stands alone in calling for a separate evaluation of the growth-inducing impacts.

A few states require that their environmental impact statements contain a discussion of the economic impacts of the proposed activity. The Michigan act declares: "where appropriate, a discussion of the economic gains and losses, including the effect on employment, income levels, property values, taxes, and the cost of alternatives to the proposed action, should be included in the EIS." Considerable debate has taken place in the California legislature as to the wisdom of including this type of discussion in the environmental impact statement. In 1974 a measure proposing voluntary inclusion of economic impacts passed the legislature but failed to be signed by the governor. It is anticipated that economic impacts may well be added as one of the elements to be discussed in a Calfironia impact report in the near future. The federal guidelines do not specifically require such economic impact discussion except under a general consideration of the secondary consequences of a proposal.

One or two states have added the requirement that the environmental impact statement include a discussion of the "beneficial" aspects of a project. This may constitute a slight deviation from NEPA, which requires federal agencies to "assess the positive and negative effects of the proposed action" without a specific mention of beneficial aspects.

Scope and Nature of Activities Requiring an EIS

Any actions or projects undertaken directly by state agencies will require the preparation of environmental impact statements in all jurisdictions that have adopted general EIS procedures. The major differences among the various state acts are found in their application of the EIS process to local government actions and to private activity for which a governmental permit is required.

The private sector of our society is responsible for a great many activities which might result in harmful environmental impacts. Many of these same activities are subject to discretionary governmental approval at both the state and local level. In most jurisdictions the counties, cities, towns, and special-purpose units of local government exert control over private actions relating to land use. Thus, unless the environmental impact statement program includes the activities of local governments and their regulation of private activities, a large range of environmentally significant actions will not be subjected to impact analysis. Most states have thus far not extended the impact statement analysis beyond state agency actions.

Only four states seem to apply the EIS requirement to local government and to private activities which they regulate. California law is the most inclusive by requiring that impact statements be prepared on private activities involving the issuance of a "lease, permit, license, or certificate, or other entitlement for use by one or more public agencies." By defining the term "public agencies" to include local and regional agencies as well as state agencies, the California Environmental Quality Act achieves the broadest coverage of private and public actions which may affect the environment.

An individual who wishes to determine the extent to which a state act covers local governmental and/or private actions will need to research the applicable act and any guidelines issued. To the extent these acts use phrases and concepts similar to NEPA in describing the EIS requirement, the courts may utilize federal precedents to determine whether the act should be applied to private activities. Although NEPA itself does not deal directly with the issue of private activities, the NEPA guidelines require an EIS to be filed on actions "involving a Federal lease, permit, license or certificate or other entitlement."

Relationship of EIS to Land Use Regulation

The environmental impact-reporting process represents a case-by-case approach to determining the land use impacts of a proposed action. The role, if any, an EIS program will play in a land use planning and management system depends in large measure on what kind of land use regulations a particular jurisdiction is currently employing. In some jurisdictions, with strong state-level land use regulations, the case-by-case approach may be somewhat redundant. States such as Maine and Vermont thus far have expressed little interest in adopting state EIS requirements in view of their comprehensive land use control laws. If the environmental impact-reporting process is viewed as an information tool which complements existing land use regulation administration, it can still, however, serve as a useful and desirable adjunct.

California, which has one of the nation's strongest local planning laws, requires the preparation of environmental impact reports by the local agency before granting approval to private development. Used in this manner, the environmental impact report has become a vehicle for maintaining the integrity of existing comprehensive plans.

Methods of Enforcement

Thus far only Minnesota appears to have empowered an agency to veto any proposal which it finds inconsistent with the policies set forth in its environmental policy act. Other states have followed the federal example of not specifying a clear enforcement authority or mechanism. Under NEPA, the responsibility for compliance rests with the agency proposing the action, and the CEQ has no veto power over agency proposals nor can it reject an inadequate EIS.

Under NEPA, the CEQ is responsible for issuing federal guidelines and assisting the various agencies in preparing their own procedures for implementing the Act. Although the CEQ's role can be described as advisory, the fact that decisions of environmental agencies are subject to review by the President provides the CEQ with the potential to influence actions at the highest level.

The absence of a "policeman" in the federal system is probably the main reason why so many impact statements have been found inadequate. Most of the state acts have followed the federal example in designating no enforcement agency and have experienced difficulties in that many of the reports failed to:

(1) adequately discuss the identified environmental impacts; (2) adequately treat and discuss reviewing agencies' comments; (3) adequately consider alternatives and their environmental impacts.

In most states the environmental policy legislation merely requires that a copy or notice of each impact statement be furnished to specified governmental agencies and to members of the public upon request. Most of these same acts do not specify what is to happen to these statements after they are received. Until these acts require revisions of inadequate statements and possible delay of implementation of actions, the only option left open to the community is resort to the courts after the agency attempts to proceed with the action. Much of the current litigation could be eliminated if the various state acts provided for mechanisms allowing governmental agencies with particular expertise to force needed modification in another agency's statement prior to its adoption.

Currently, the Minnesota law is the strongest. It authorizes the Minnesota Environmental Quality Council not only to require revision of inadequate statements and delay implementation of an action, but to "reverse and modify the decisions or proposal where it finds, upon notice and hearing, that the action or project is inconsistent" with the stated environmental policies and standards.

Citizen Participation

Since agencies responsible for state environmental impact programs lack enforcement powers, the major burden of enforcing compliance falls on citizen groups. Although the ever-present threat of litigation has done much to sensitize the various agencies to citizen demands, much more but less visible public participation occurs prior to any resort to the courts. By bringing deficiencies to the attention of administrators or by organizing political pressure, citizens have frequently been successful in persuading agencies to prepare or revise EIS's. Agency officials are becoming increasingly responsive to the public because of the large number of court decisions supporting citizen demands and the ever-present threat of litigation.

At the federal level, the CEQ guidelines place heavy emphasis on providing mechanisms for citizen participation. To accomplish this participation, the CEQ strongly recommended that:

(*1*) Agencies should maintain lists of their impact statements under preparation, and their determinations that certain specific proposed actions do not require the preparation of an impact statement. Guideline 1500.6(e)
(*2*) The minimum period for review of draft statements should be lengthened from 30 days to 45 days. The length of the review period should be calculated from the date of publication in the *Federal Register* of

the Council's listing notifying the public of issuance of the impact statement. Guidelines 1500.9(f) and 1500.11(c)

(3) Agencies should endeavor to provide impact statement materials free of charge to the fullest extent practicable or at a fee which is not more than the agency's actual reproduction costs. Guideline 1500.9(d)

(4) A copy of the final impact statement for a proposed action should be sent to all parties who filed substantive comments on the corresponding draft statement. Guideline 1500.10(b)

In addition, federal agencies are now required to publish revisions of their NEPA procedures in the *Federal Register* and invite public comment. They must devise an "early warning" system for informing the public of decisions to prepare a draft environmental impact statement and encourage the public to provide information and opinions for use in preparing the statement. Any studies used in an environmental impact statement should be clearly identified in the statement, and the public should be told how and where they may obtain copies of such studies. Despite these developments, the burden still rests in large measure on the public to find out what is going on rather than with the various agencies to keep the public informed.

In order to become effective in the EIS process, citizens must (1) know that an EIS is being prepared and (2) have sufficient time and notice to study and comment on the document. The following are some of the mechanisms used in the various existing laws to stimulate and facilitate public participation.

At the federal level, short summaries of draft and final impact statements with information on how and where to obtain copies are published weekly in the *Federal Register* and monthly in CEQ's *102 Monitor*. Only two or three states have followed the federal example of publishing such centralized lists of impact statements. Most of the other states merely require publication of notices of the availability of these statements in newspapers, limiting the publishing requirement in some instances to areas affected by the project.

Without the requirement of a centralized, periodic list of statements or newspaper advertising, it becomes difficult for various agencies to fulfill the requirement to involve and inform the "public." The various state acts are quite divergent in defining what constitutes the relevant public. Distribution and notice range from the narrow requirement of those "who specifically have indicated an interest in the proposed action" (Washington State Guidelines) to "wide public involvement, formal and informal" (California). As a general assessment, how citizens are to be included in the EIS process, if at all, is left very vague in the various state laws and executive orders.

The second important procedural question for effective public participation is: How much time is provided for public review and comment? The NEPA guidelines specify a minimum review period of 45 days from the time notice of an EIS is published in the *Federal Register*. Most states require some minimum time period, ranging from 20 to 60 days. California has chosen to require merely "adequate" time in its guidelines, leaving local agencies to specify in their regulations what the time frame should be. This vague requirement for review time has resulted in abuse by some local governmental agencies which have narrowed the period to as few as 5 days. The lack of a uniform state standard also contributes to confusion in the participating public, who may not be aware of the severe time limitations.

One of the best means available to facilitate public participation is the public hearing. Yet, most of the state acts and executive orders have chosen to merely encourage the use of public hearings without requiring them. Only Wisconsin requires a hearing to be held on every EIS.

Thus, with few exceptions, the states have not made it easy for citizen participation. In large measure, the role of the public in the EIS process is probably not recognized for the vital function it serves. As explained earlier, public agencies may need to be convinced to view their responsibility to obtain public participation as an "affirmative" duty before procedures will be adopted which will assure meaningful and timely public participation. As long as the various agencies do not facilitate public involvement in the formulation stages it is likely that the public will continue to exert heavy pressures through the courts to challenge agency decision-making.

The Impact Statement in Perspective

As can be seen from the foregoing discussion, much of the concern has dealt with procedural and statutory requirements of environmental policy acts. These procedural and statutory requirements are useful only if they perform the function of reforming governmental agency decision-making by forcing consideration of environmental factors in all agency activities. The information produced through the environmental impact statement process must be used in reaching decisions to serve its purpose. The courts have expressed their willingness to review the record, of which the EIS is an important part, to see that agencies have properly prepared and used the document. Some courts have taken the additional step of reviewing agency decisions to determine whether they are in accord with the substantive policies of the various acts. It is in this role that the EIS is working in its most proper perspective.

Now that several years of experience have been obtained in the EIS process, much work remains to find effective mechanisms to integrate the EIS process with on-going planning processes. In addition, much of the information collected in the numerous federal, state, and local impact statements is left to collect dust. The wealth of information should be integrated into data banks or some other information retrieval system so that the planning and utilization of our scarce resources can benefit from the labor and information produced by these documents. With the experience and maturing of the impact-reporting process, a number of actions can be taken to prevent duplication and to refine the tool in the performance of its vital function of full disclosure to the decision-maker and the public.

Checklist

The following checklist is provided to assist the reader to screen the various environmental impact statement systems for key legal and procedural character-istics. Many jurisdictions have followed the federal example in enacting a basic legislative policy act which outlines only scant procedures to be followed. The procedures to be employed are usually contained in administratively issued guidelines. The reader should be careful to obtain all the relevant guidelines which may apply to a particular governmental agency. At the federal level two sets of guidelines are operative, the Federal CEQ guidelines and the various federal agency guidelines which should conform to both the CEQ guidelines and NEPA. Several states have adopted a similar approach in issuing general state guidelines and requiring the various local and state agencies to adopt individual guidelines or regulations.

(1) Determine to which levels of government your state act or executive order applies.

Explanation: Most states apply the requirement for preparation of environ-mental impact statements only to state-level agencies. In those states the impact statement preparation is limited to activities carried out by state agencies. Some states, such as California, have made the act applicable to both state and local agencies and thus cover activities by all governmental units at both levels.

(2) Does your state act apply to regulatory activities as well as public works construction?

Explanation: Although NEPA has always applied to activities directly carried out by the federal government and to regulatory and licensing activities, many of the state acts do not include regulatory activities.

(3) Does your state act limit the environmental impact statement requirement to major actions?

Explanation: NEPA applies only to major actions which may have a significant effect on the human environment. Only large-scale or "major" activities require the preparation of such statements. California and several other states provide no size or degree limitations and require reports on all actions which may have a significant effect on the environment. You should therefore determine whether your state comes under the one- or two-test rule to determine whether an EIS is required. Check the applicable guidelines for definitions of such terms as "project," "significant effect," "major actions," and "environment."

(4) Are any activities specifically exempted from operation of the state act?

Explanation: A number of states have exempted particular actions from their acts. Typical exemptions are emergency or temporary activities and "ministerial" acts—that is, actions where the involved agency exercises no discretion. Usually when an agency is fulfilling a ministerial responsibility, it is proceeding in accordance with a strictly specified statutory or regulatory mandate. Some states also provide for "categorical exemptions" which are granted administratively. Such categorical exemptions may include such things as research and experimental projects. California is an example of a state that has adopted an extensive set of exemptions which would need to be checked to determine if the environmental impact report requirement is applicable to particular actions.

In addition, the guidelines implementing NEPA and the California act exempt regulatory actions intended to protect the environment. The setting of standards for air and water pollution control will not require environmental impact report preparation. Although the exclusion is currently the subject of litigation, the various state acts should be checked for possible utilization of this exemption.

In addition, a number of states have excluded "legislative" actions from coverage.

(5) How does the state act define the "environment?"

Explanation: The definition of "environment" can have considerable bearing on the number of impact statements that might be required. For example, the "environment" can be defined to include the totality of man's surroundings or it can be limited to physical factors. In trying to assess the scope of coverage, always check the policy statements of the legislation as well.

(6) How is significant effect defined by the act of the applicable guidelines?

Explanation: The definition of significant effect will assist in the determination of the scope of action which requires the preparation of impact statements. In addition to a possible use of the "major" concept, some jurisdictions have limited significant effects to adverse impacts. California has defined the term as a "substantial adverse impact." Some courts have attempted to assist in defining the terms, and their descriptions have ranged from "non-trivial" impacts to "serious environmental effects." Most of the federal court precedents have warned that the interpretation of this term will not be permitted to facilitate avoidance of the mandates of NEPA.

(7) Does your state act require that environmental impact statements contain discussion of economic impacts?

Explanation: A few acts require the discussion of economic impacts; California requires the discussion of growth-inducing impacts. The basic policy of the act should be inspected to see whether a balancing of socio-economic considerations is expected and, if so, whether the socio-economic effects need to be discussed in the EIS.

(8) How is public participation in the environmental impact process treated by the act?

Explanation: With few exceptions, the various state acts have not made it easy for citizens to participate. Public hearings are one means of obtaining citizen comments. Are hearings required or encouraged by the act? Another factor which determines the degree of public participation is the amount of time permitted for public review or comment. Finally, the methods employed to inform the public of prospective hearings, the availability of environmental documents, and the methodology for dissemination of such documents are important factors to check in the state acts.

(9) Are specific statutes of limitations for bringing legal actions contained in the act?

Explanation: Although the courts have expressed a general willingness to review compliance with environmental policy acts, some state legislatures have enacted time limitations on legal challenges to the need and adequacy of environmental impact documents. In California, for example, the statute of limitation runs from a mere 30 days to 180 days, depending upon the nature of the legal challenge. A great deal of variation is likely to exist in the various state acts, and individuals should be diligent since such statutes of limitation may preclude bringing a legal action.

6 · How to Prepare an EIS

The purpose of this chapter is to present a set of useful suggestions on the preparation of an EIS. It is by no means intended to be the only approach. It is simply a compendium of some of the salient results of having prepared and reviewed more than two hundred EIS's over the period of time since the passage of NEPA. Many of the ideas are not new to research or management; indeed, they may seem "old hat" to some. They are included, nonetheless, to help future writers organize their work and evaluate the work of others, and to establish at least one view of "how to" based on where we now stand in this difficult and evolving process.

The chapter is presented in six sections:

(1) The preparation process—an overview
(2) Management of the process
(3) Research and writing
(4) The product
(5) Presenting and reviewing
(6) The "sum total"

James A. Roberts, born in 1934, is currently Consulting Geographer and senior principal, James A. Roberts Associates, Inc., and was formerly President of Sasaki, Walker, Roberts Associates, Inc., both planning and environmental consulting firms. He has worked and written widely in the fields of environmental planning, management, engineering, and impact analysis. He currently teaches environmental impact analysis at the University of California at Davis and has taught in the past at the University of Virginia, University of California at Riverside, and California State College at Los Angeles.

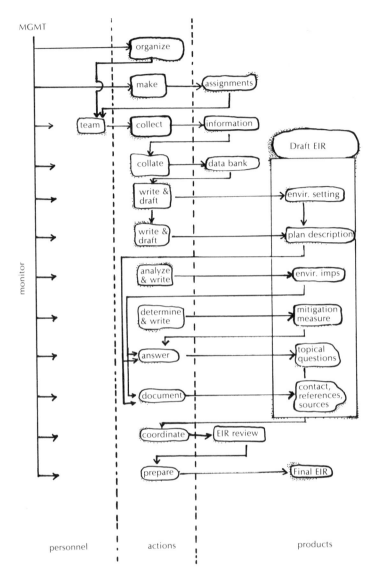

Fig. 6–1 Schematic of EIS preparation process.

1. The Preparation Process—an Overview

The essential elements in the preparation of an EIS are summarized graphically in Fig. 6-1. The process starts when management *organizes* an interdisciplinary team to undertake the actual preparation activities and ends when the team *prepares* the Final EIS. Each of the actions can be completed using the procedures outlined in the following paragraphs.

A. Organizing the Team

To be fully responsive to the intent of the laws, an EIS must be prepared by an interdisciplinary team. Management should organize a team whose members represent all required fields of study before any other steps are taken. The specific methods used to organize the team will vary from agency to agency and from project to project. In general, however, they will consist of the following steps:

Step 1. Management designates a team leader (EIS Preparation Manager)

Step 2. Management assembles specialists (experts) from each of the areas to be covered in the environmental analysis (natural, social, and economic)

Step 3. Management provides the team with staff support necessary for research, analysis, and production (both graphic and text)

Step 4. Management arranges the time and supplies the facilities required by the team

B. Making Assignments

Once a team has been organized, management should make assignments to the team members. The following steps are recommended for making the assignments:

Step 1. Management assigns over-all responsibility for the EIS to the team leader

Step 2. Either team leader or management assigns specific environmental aspects to team members

Step 3. Management assigns over-all technical quality control either (a) to team leader or (b) to a non-team member evaluator

Step 4. Management assigns the responsibility for administrative support either (a) to team leader or subordinate or (b) to a non-team member with the necessary capabilities

C. Collecting the Information

Team members should collect or direct the collection of the information needed to complete the environmental setting. We recommend the following steps:

Step 1. Team leader prepares an outline of the complete EIS

Step 2. Team leader and experts determine from the outline what data will be required for the EIS on the environmental setting of the area of your project

Step 3. Experts assemble the required information from documents and government sources

Step 4. Experts determine the nature and extent of any unavailable data

Step 5. Experts and team leader prepare a data collection work program and deadlines

Step 6. Team leader collects raw data either from direct study of the project or by surveys of primary sources

D. Collating the Data

After the basic information is assembled, the team (or supporting personnel) should put the data in a format for comparison, evaluation, and future use. The recommended steps are:

Step 1. Team leader prepares a standardized regional base map (standard scale and format)

Step 2a. Experts prepare working drafts of all environmental and plan description data on the standard map base, or

Step 2b. Experts put working data into a computer-compatible format

Step 3. Experts prepare a standardized set of draft comments on each of the environmental and description factors

Step 4. Experts prepare a standardized format for tabular data

Step 5. Team leader assembles a "package" of maps, or the tabular data for maps, and reviews draft comments

E. Describing the Environmental Setting

Once a standardized data "bank" has been prepared, the following steps are recommended for preparation of the environmental setting section of the EIS:

Step 1. Team leader and experts review and revise the EIS outline (noted above in C, Step 1)

Step 2. Experts determine what maps and/or graphics (photos, tables, etc.) are going to be needed in the draft

Step 3. Experts prepare a draft map and/or illustration needed to present the facts in the outline

Step 4. Experts write each substantive section of the environmental setting of the EIS

Step 5. Team leader edits the drafts to ensure consistency of format and accuracy of data

Step 6. Team leader reviews the edited drafts with each expert to ensure that no accidental changes were introduced in Step 5

Step 7. Prefinal: Office staff types the environmental setting text

Step 8. Prefinal: Team leader and/or staff draft the maps and/or graphics

Step 9. Team leader and/or staff make copies of text and graphics for use in impact analysis

F. Producing the Project Description

The following steps are recommended for preparation of the plan description section of the EIS:

Step 1. Team leader and experts review and revise the EIS outline noted above in C, Step 1

Step 2. Experts and team leader determine what maps and/or graphics are needed for the plan description

Step 3. Experts prepare the maps and/or graphics

Step 4. Experts write the descriptions of the plan, including maps and graphics

Step 5. Team leader edits the draft to ensure over-all accuracy and consistency of detail and form

Step 6. Team leader reviews the edited draft with experts to ensure that no accidental changes were introduced in Step 5

Step 7. Prefinal: Team leader and/or staff type the plan description text

Step 8. Prefinal: Team leader and/or staff draft the maps and/or graphics

Step 9. Team leader and/or staff make copies of text and graphics for use in impact analysis

Step 10. Team leader and experts working together review geographic scope of project to ensure that environmental setting and regional setting cover a geographic area commensurate with the project description and affected area

G. Analyzing and Writing the Environmental Impacts

After completion of the environmental setting and plan description we recommend you take the following steps to analyze and document the plan's impacts on the environment:

Step 1. Experts review each aspect of the environment to identify which are impacted by the proposed plan

Step 2. Experts evaluate the degree of impact (adverse or beneficial) on each aspect

Step 3. Experts write a statement of the impacts

Step 4. Team leader edits the statements to ensure consistency in form and in level of detail

Step 5. Team leader reviews the edited statements with the experts to ensure that no erroneous opinions or conclusions are introduced

Step 6. Experts rewrite the materials to fulfill Step 4, consistency requirements

Step 7. Team leader re-edits and reviews with experts to fulfill Step 4

Step 8. Team leader and project's planner revise the proposed plan to eliminate or reduce adverse impacts or to introduce or expand beneficial impacts

Step 9. Team leader recycles EIS to Project Description (F) and repeats subsequent steps as required

Step 10. Prefinal: Office staff types the draft analyses of the impacts

H. Determining the Mitigation Measures

After completion of impact analyses, or while the individual analysis sections are being written, determine and draft the mitigation measures for adverse impacts and the preservation measures for beneficial impacts by following these steps:

Step 1. Experts determine what potential mitigation/preservation measures are possible

Step 2. Experts review the potential measures with personnel in project design and in construction to determine economic, engineering, and environmental feasibility of the mitigation measures possible

Step 3. Experts draft a statement of the recommended mitigation/preservation measures

Step 4. Team leader edits the statements to ensure consistency in format and in level of address and detail

Step 5. Team leader determines what mitigation/preservation measures are agreeable to the management of the proposed project or plan

Step 6. Team leader and experts review results of Steps 4 and 5 to ensure that no accidental changes are introduced through those steps

Step 7. Team leader and experts repeat Steps 4 through 6, as required, to complete a technically correct and administratively acceptable statement

Step 8. Prefinal: Office staff types the draft statement of mitigation/preservation measures

I. Answering Topical Questions

Topical questions are those that must be answered to meet the specific sections of NEPA or of the various state acts. For instance, "What are the long-term impacts of the project?"

After preparation of the mitigation/preservation measures, the following steps are recommended for preparing the answers to topical questions:

Step 1. Team leader selects a sub-team to answer the questions (team should have representative experts from plan preparation and environmental experts)

Step 2. Sub-team drafts an answer to each question

Step 3. Team leader edits each answer to ensure consistency in form and in level of detail and address

Step 4. Team leader reviews edited draft answers with sub-team and experts to ensure that no accidental changes were introduced in Step 3
Step 5. Prefinal: Office staff types the draft answers

J. Documenting Contacts, References, and Sources, and Preparing the Draft EIS

Before the research on the project is begun, a uniform method and format of footnoting, referencing, and conference reports should be adopted for use by everyone involved in the EIS and in the project. You should list all references and documents quoted in the EIS throughout the entire process or wait until after the topical questions have been answered, taking your documentation from earlier notes.
Step 1. Team leader prepares a written statement of all references, contacts, and correspondence on the EIS
Step 2. Team leader reviews the statement with the appropriate experts
Step 3. Prefinal: Team leader and/or staff type and read the draft documentation

K. Reviewing the Draft EIS

After final typing, the Draft EIS should be reviewed in accordance with appropriate agency guidelines. The steps should include:
Step 1. Team leader disseminates Draft EIS's for review by all interested agencies, organizations, and/or individuals
Step 2. Team leader and experts meet with interested persons to answer questions and to obtain comments on the Draft EIS
Step 3. Team leader distributes schedule and procedures for submission of comments

L. Preparing the Final EIS

After completion of the review process, the following steps should be taken to include the results of the review and prepare the Final EIS:
Step 1. Team leader assembles all comments on the Draft EIS
Step 2. Team leader reviews each comment with the appropriate experts and project planners
Step 3a. Project planner revises the plans to reflect changes suggested during review process, or
Step 3b. Team leader resubmits EIS for rewrite of appropriate sections
Step 4. Team leader includes comments of reviewing agencies in EIS

Step 5. Team leader expands documentation section to include all comments from review process
Step 6. Office staff does final typing of the Final EIS

2. Management of the Process

Seven basic problems must be faced for successful management of the preparation of an EIS. As discussed in the following pages, they are to:
· Define the project
· Determine who prepares the EIS
· Establish the report format
· Select the team
· Budget the effort
· Allocate the effort
· Monitor the effort

A. Define the Project

In accordance with CEQA, and realistically in accordance with simple logic, three things must be considered in project definition: location and boundaries, objectives, and technical aspects.

1. Location and Boundaries

Such simple things as location and boundaries have often been a weakness in environmental studies. For example, in California law* several specific items must be considered for delineation of the actual location, and several additional items are recommended. Those items are:

> The precise location and boundaries of the proposed project shall be shown on a detailed map, preferably topographic. The location of the project shall appear on a regional map. (It is further recommended by many that the topographic map be a U.S.G.S. 7½-minute quad sheet and the regional map a 1:250,000 scale map.)

In addition to these items, and often of equal importance, is "relative location." Certainly an EIS on something as potentially significant as, for instance, a possible major new ski area should be "placed" in relation to the specific items above *and* its location relative to transportation systems, market areas, and housing areas for the employees who may one day service the skiers.

* "Guidelines for Implementation of the California Environmental Quality Act of 1970," Article 9, Section 15141(a).

Only through such a relative analysis can the boundaries of a project be fully defined.

2. Project Objectives

The California EIS "Guidelines" state that the following will be considered in project objectives*:

(*a*) A statement of the objectives sought by the proposed project

(*b*) A general description of the project's technical, economic, and environmental characteristics, considering the principal engineering proposals and supporting public service facilities

But is that all there is? What are the *real* objectives of a project; what are the *actual* or *imaginary* objectives? It would be difficult to believe that a developer's goals were exclusively to provide housing and not also to make a profitable return on his investment. Who is to say which are the real, actual, or imaginary goals? Indeed, they may all be the same. Our responsibility in preparing an EIS is to set out all of the objectives as best we can define them, not simply to present but one view.

3. The Project's Technical Aspects

What are the technical aspects of the proposed project? For a coastal area development, it is certainly likely that marine biology will be of greater significance to the understanding of possible impacts than high altitude meteorology. Every project has some unique technical or scientific aspects and these aspects should be carefully delineated in the project definition both for adequate planning and for comprehensive impact analysis.

B. Determine Who Prepares the EIS

The second basic problem that management must face is who determines who is to prepare the EIS. As noted in a previous chapter, the courts are examining this issue in depth in many states. However, in the California system, local authorities have been given a clear mandate that they can have their own staffs prepare the reports or they can contract with a consultant to have the work done. In either case, California law gives the lead agency the ultimate responsibility for the quality and comprehensiveness of the work.

What are some of the advantages and disadvantages of the various possible combinations: staff, consultant, or combined staff-consultant? In the first case, staff preparation, it is possible to bring environmental awareness into the full

* Article 9—Section 15141(b) and (c).

agency planning process; however, it is often impossible to have the full range of disciplines needed for every technical aspect of an EIS. In the second case, consultant preparation, it is often possible to obtain a broad set of technical skills; but it is also probable that little lasting contribution can be made to the agency's over-all process and that limited control can be placed on the consultant's schedules. With a combination of staff-consultants, it is possible to develop a critical mass of knowledge within the agency which can contribute to its on-going operations and help it to know when and whom to call for special expert assistance.

C. Establish the Report Format

The biggest single pitfall is that of waiting until everything is written before deciding in what format to put the material. In essence, a great many "neat" words are assembled and packed into a nice bunch of junk that the editor must unscramble to make it readable. The whole organizational process must include a management decision on: "How are you going to format the report?" There are five steps to establishing a format:

(*1*) *Select an outline:* Many agencies have adopted outlines for their EIS's. If the agency you are working with has not done so, adapt an outline for your use and develop it as a tool for scheduling and setting priorities, i.e., a device for preparing the report in an orderly form and within an orderly schedule.

(*2*) *Select graphics:* Decide before you start your project research what graphics (maps, photos, tables, etc.), what forms, what kind of content, and what kind of art work you are going to use. Determine whether you need to use oversize maps. If so, you will have to plan to go through a reducing process. How many people have started out with a beautiful map, let's say with dimensions of four feet by seven feet, decided they were going to reduce it to $8\frac{1}{2}''$ x $11''$, and discovered that the map information "disappeared"? Early on you must decide what your lettering sizes are going to be: if in your four foot by eight foot map you use half-inch lettering and reduce the map to $8\frac{1}{2}''$ x $11''$, you can't read the lettering!

(*3*) *Establish a typing procedure:* Many organizations have those wonderful "pools" that get typing done and don't have to rely on a solitary typist working through three separate typings of each EIS: (i) the draft for the expert, team leader, or planner, (ii) the Draft EIS, and (iii) the Final EIS. There are many machine typing units with memories now available on the market which are eminently well suited for the kind of typing needed for EIS's. One can almost hear the relief of the secretary who now, with a conventional typewriter, can justifiably say, "That's the third time I've typed that same sentence." But final production typing is not the only reason for using automatic typing procedures. Accuracy is an equally important, if not a more important, reason. A slip of a decimal point or a transposition of a figure—either one easily caused by retyping and commonly missed in second-editing—can be nearly fatal. Think about the typing procedure; it may be extremely helpful to go to automatic typing.

(*4*) *Establish a reproduction process:* The production of the EIS can be systematized to take advantage of any redundancies. Several agencies and consultants use automatic typing together with automatic printing machinery to produce the many copies of the Draft and Final EIS's. Some have even gone to printing Draft copy on colored paper and reserving white paper for the Final EIS printing.

(*5*) *Determine page sizes for text and graphics:* Decide before you start what page size you are going to use for the text. Certainly an 8½″ by 11″ page size for the Draft EIS is more likely to fit with more of the comments that may be received on the EIS. This size is also convenient for fold-out pages 11″ by 17″ (or other multiples of 8½); but care should be taken, as noted above, to ensure that graphics will also fit the page size.

D. Select the Team

As indicated, virtually every EIS preparation process must be a team effort. At least five different types of players are needed: specialists, generalists, draftsmen-artists, technical writers, and production personnel.

1. Specialists

All social, economic, and natural sciences will be needed at one time or another for the preparation of an EIS. In particular, specialists are often needed in areas where specific endangered animal species, rare plant materials, or unique social problems may be concerned. The need for a pool of diverse talents to be called upon as problems are identified is obvious.

2. Generalists

People who can put the over-all EIS into environmental perspective are needed in smaller numbers on a given EIS but are extremely important for its successful preparation. The role of these people, the generalists, is to bring all of the pieces together into a manageable whole, to provide balance, and to ensure that the whole can be seen for all of the parts.

3. Draftsmen-Artists

The comment was made about Fig. 6-2 by a noted County Planner that it was something "only a climatologist's mother could love." This example clearly illustrates the need for careful consideration of the needs and levels of understanding of the EIS's eventual readers when graphics are selected and designed.

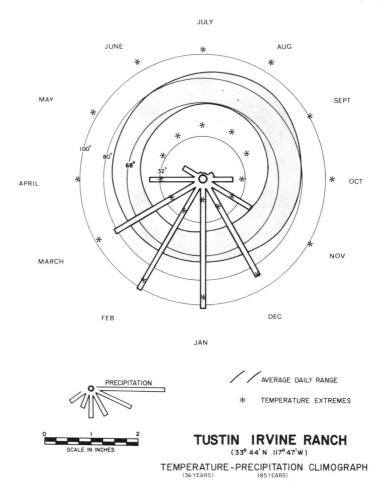

Fig. 6–2 Tustin Irvine Ranch: temperature-precipitation climograph.

4. Technical Writer

All too often the scientist is best equipped to write for scientists. It is certainly one thing to express wind information in meters per second and another to express that same information in relation to human comfort or the number of deck chairs that might be blown into a swimming pool. Of course, not all writing must or should be done by a technical writer, but that person can be a valuable contributor, along with the generalists, if he writes at the level of the readers.

5. Production Personnel

Usually the last people or group to see a report are the people who will have to work overtime to get it out on schedule: the production personnel. If they can be asked, as a regular part of the process: "What could be done at the start of the process to ease your task?" the production personnel can undoubtedly make a major, significant contribution to the timely preparation of a high quality product. Let them help particularly in establishing the over-all project schedule.

E. Budget the Effort

Every project must be thought through in relation to two budgets: money and time. In actuality, dollar budgets are the easier to determine. Either you are given a certain budget and your resulting job is to spread it to get the most for your money or you are given the summary of what must be done and have to raise the money to do it. Neither case is actually quite that simple, but either is usually more simple than time-budgeting.

Actions	%
Organize Team	2
Make Assignments	3
Collect Information	25
Collate Data Bank	5
Write and draft Setting	20
Write and draft Project Description	5
Analyze and Write Impacts	15
Determine and write Mitigation Measures	10
Answer Topical Questions	5
Document and prepare Draft EIS	10
Coordinate review of Draft EIS (Note 1)	(?)
Prepare Final EIS (Note 2)	(?)
Total	100%

Notes: *(1)* The coordination of the review of the Draft EIS may take from 30 to 90 days (or longer) which may logically be much more or less time than all of the preceding steps. *(2)* Preparation of the Final EIS usually takes almost as much time as preparation of the Draft EIS.

Caution: These percentages are approximate. Experience will vary from project to project and team to team on specific EIS's.

Fig. 6–3 Approximate time allocation for EIS preparation.

What are the natural time frames that must be used to understand impacts on an animal population? Climatically significant statistics? Demographic pattern analyses? Obviously, a field inspection in winter with a three-foot snow cover on the ground isn't going to make it possible to determine soil erosion characteristics. Equally obviously, traffic analyses at 8 p.m. on a weeknight or 7 to 8 a.m. on Saturday aren't going to provide the data needed for evaluation of traffic impact during normal rush-hour conditions. Each element, whether social, economic, or natural, has given time frames which must be understood in budgeting the time for the information collection phase of a project.

Additionally, each phase of a project must be given "time." No two projects are exactly alike, but in general the greatest portion of the time to prepare an EIS is devoted to the data collection, environmental setting, and impact analysis. A rough time frame, by percentage of project-time allocated, is shown in Fig. 6-3 assuming the flow chart described in Section 2 of this chapter.

F. Allocate Responsibilities

One of the most difficult decisions for a manager to make is to decide to allocate the responsibilities to other people and then stick by them and trust them to do the work. Select the people carefully, get a good interdisciplinary team together, and then go ahead and allocate the work. Assign the tasks to the people; assign them due dates; provide them with the technical assistance that is needed to do the work, and then let them do it. Crack the whip, of course, but allocate the work.

G. Monitor the Effort

And speaking of cracking the whip, the seventh step for management is to monitor the effort. Many local agencies are so glad to get rid of the EIS effort that they say, "You do it, and come back to us when you've got the thing done." They have just wasted most of the real value in the EIS process by making such a decision. The real value lies in learning from each EIS; the "cumulative effects" can be amazing.

The conclusion, therefore, is that management should get into the monitoring not just to make sure that "A, B, & C" are recorded or that the work is done on schedule, but so that they can learn from each EIS. Also, if you are in an agency and choose to use a contractor to prepare the EIS, have the contractor assign a project manager to work directly with you. Get him to assign a project manager who will virtually *live* with you to provide you information on the environmental impacts and make it possible for you to communicate with the contractor's team on a regular, person-to-person basis.

3. Research and Writing

Researching and writing an EIS depend on five key items: data gathering, data assembly, data analysis, Draft EIS production, and final preparation of an EIS. Each of these items is discussed in the following paragraphs.

A. Data Gathering

Four areas must be examined in relation to data gathering: data availability, field research, agency consultation, and informal data sources.

1. Data Availability

The first step in research is to determine the availability of existing data—for example, meteorological studies. There is a large network of data available on temperature and precipitation but very little on wind or any other climatic condition. The first step, therefore, is to look for and collect the existing data. This is a task that can logically be assigned to a qualified research assistant who may research one or more of the topics to be covered in the EIS.

2. Field Research

The amount of field research that is justifiable for an EIS is relatively limited. *If* the work is done purely after the fact, it cannot be fully justified; if it is done as *part* of the planning process, the collection of original data can really be useful. No attempt will be made here to explain the steps needed for field research. Obviously, those who have tried to collect data in oceanography or in an arctic or alpine environment know that much of the "project energy" goes into survival and logistics and one "bit" of useful data has immense value, to say nothing of often untold dollar and human costs.

3. Agency Consultation

One of the best data sources for secondary-source information is consultation with existing agencies. While they have many published reports, most agencies have additional unpublished data they are willing to make available to qualified EIS preparers. The Soil Conservation Service, Forest Service, Agricultural Extension or Farm Adviser, social service agencies, Census Bureau and many other federal, state and local agencies will provide information beyond their published reports.

4. Informal Data Sources

All too often a planner or EIS team hears the comment at a public gathering, "If you had only asked me I could have told you about that seasonally flooded area. It doesn't flood every year, only when we get a heavy rain in March." Such information can be "collected" only by listening to those who know an area because they have lived there for years. What is needed on every project is a *public listening* process that allows the public to provide this knowledge before a project is designed and its impact analyzed. The "listening" refers to the project's proponents and designers—the ones who should be carefully listening.

Public listening sessions can take a wide variety of forms from a formal public meeting to an informal coffee gathering. The U.S. Forest Service (Fall 1970, Inyo National Forest), for instance, on the proposed Golden Trout Study Area (near Lone Pine, California) had three formal "listenings" to get public input: in Bishop, in Lone Pine, and in Los Angeles. They might also have held one in Bakersfield and San Francisco but had elected to invite people from these areas, as well as others, to one or all three meetings. One office of the Bureau of Land Management (as discussed at a seminar at the University of California at Davis on March 13, 1973) has used the coffee approach to meet with small groups, informally, to get their inputs. Certainly this technique has been used by many agencies.

In any case, the credibility of the agency can be established and maintained only if the public is *actually* listened to! Even the most cooperative public can become an active opponent if its ideas and information are treated with calloused indifference. The listening process is not merely a form of catharsis; it must be a means of collecting useful and used information.

B. Data Assembly

Once the research data have been collected, they must be collated into forms that are suitable for analysis. Usually this involves both tabular or text data and working maps.

1. Tabular and/or Text Data

One of the most useful tools is the organization of the written data in accordance with the outline of the report to be produced. A box, file folders, or notebook labeled with the same headings as the outline can greatly facilitate the "housekeeping" of the collected data.

2. Working Maps

Working maps are maps made specifically to store bits and pieces of collected, geographically significant data. One of the worst frustrations found in many EIS's is that the maps were done only after the analysis. Maps are the best tools for analysis of any parameters that have geographic distributions or interrelationships. As such, they should be used in the collation and analysis stage, not merely as "eye wash" for a finished report. A map scale should be adopted and base maps made and reproduced in sufficient numbers for all team members to collect their data on those maps and to organize their analysis around the geographic boundaries of the project impact area. The advantages afforded by mapped data for computer analysis by any current method are also obvious.

C. Data Analysis

Once the sorted data (or do they become sordid data in the hands of inexperienced researchers?) have been collected, it is possible to do both quantitative and qualitative analysis. What are some of the pitfalls found in data analysis for EIS's?

1. Quantitative Analysis

There are many aspects of an EIS that should be treated statistically. However, in reading many EIS's, one may be reminded of Huff's little book, *How to Lie with Statistics*. In it, he cites the almost perfect correlation between the salaries of Presbyterian missionaries in Massachusetts and the price of rum in Havana.

The lesson for EIS preparation is obvious: ensure that the statistics that are selected are meaningful, that they are treated with statistically significant methods, and presented in a form that can be readable and understandable to the lay reader as well as the professional statistician and/or scientist.

2. Qualitative Aspects

The qualitative aspects of the data may be equally important. Computer graphics are often used for analytical tools but are not generally acceptable as "aesthetic tools." In one project by the author, the analysts developed a number of views of the proposed project from several different locations. Responses to the graphics ranged from "excellent" to "something only a computer's mother could love." The data for visual impact analysis can only be treated qualitatively; much the same could be said for aesthetics, quality of life, and psychological effects on human beings.

D. Draft EIS Production

Concerning manuscript preparation, recall the earlier comments on typing. As noted, at least three typing "jobs" are needed: the preliminary (author's or expert's) manuscript, the Draft EIS, and the Final EIS. Unfortunately, though, editing can be the Achilles' heel of the EIS process. A rigorous editorial policy and board should be set up and its policies followed. No matter *how* many times you proofread something, errors can creep in and can be reintroduced by retyping. If you can find a retired or willing, active linotype operator, have that person proof the material by reading it both forward and backward; then you are most likely to get rid of the typos. Once the typos are corrected, ensure that your control policy provides a means for the experts to recheck the data to see that a technical word or words have not been incorrectly "corrected."

E. Final EIS Production

The critical "new" items that must be added to the Draft EIS for the Final EIS are the comments of the reviewers and the agencies' responses thereto. The production techniques can be the same as for the Draft EIS with a few additions. We recommend (1) that all written comments be included verbatim by reproduction of the correspondence; (2) that public comments be included by a verbatim transcript; and (3) that telephonic comments be included by a telephone summary report approved by both or all parties to the conversation. All such information should contain the dates, locations, identity, and qualifications of those quoted.

4. The Product

Let us next examine the general characteristics of the product, recognizing that the contents will vary from project to project. The final product is only as good as the material in it. You can put all kinds of "good stuff" in the EIS, and it still may not be a good product. There are certain characteristics that should be found in each EIS, in the text, the graphics, the facts, the opinions, and the conclusions.

A. The Text

Many EIS's that have been written since NEPA are simply unreadable. They are confused, poorly organized, and obscure. The writers must ask themselves, therefore, "Is our text readable?" Is it something that the audience, for whom you are really designing this, can understand and read? And is it credible?

B. The Graphics

Are the graphics "absolutely, fantastically beautiful" but not technically correct? Or are they technically correct but totally unreadable? And are they exactly what you want to portray?

C. The Facts

Are the facts clear; are they meaningful; and are they pertinent to the problem with which you are working?

D. The Opinions

All impact reports, be they federal, state, or local, have sections in them that allow for opinions. What should the opinions be? First, are they identifiable as opinions? Are they based on facts? Secondly, are the opinions sound? Is the person who made the opinion qualified? We see people who are well versed in one field giving apparently excellent opinions about a totally different field. More often than not, they are not qualified to state such an opinion. Finally, has the opinion of the writer unduly biased the EIS?

E. The Conclusions

Is each of the conclusions in the report identified? Are they all supported in the text? And were they reached by someone qualified to review and understand the data in the text?

5. Presenting and Reviewing

For the most part, presentation and review are not given adequate consideration in the preparation of an EIS. Three key aspects should be considered:
- presentation versus reaction
- types of reviews
- administration of reviews

A. Presentation versus Reaction

What occurs at many public hearings on an impact statement is that the EIS is simply reviewed. The agency presents a statement which in essence is,

"You have seen the EIS, do you have any comments?" The balance of the time is spent answering detailed questions. We suggest that the environmental impact report be presented in a systematic, full presentation. The advantages of such an orderly review should be obvious, particularly to those who may have spent the better part of several evenings answering questions about minutiae on the "trees" without ever having a chance to present the "forest" of their work.

B. Types of Reviews

There are at least three major types of reviews: proponent reviews, consultant agency reviews, and special interest groups reviews.

1. Proponent Reviews

The review that can have the most potential for lasting change on a proposed project is the review of the EIS by the project's proponents in the presence of the EIS preparation team. The plan review process can be a valuable means to make changes in the project so that mitigation measures become part of the project. Indeed it would seem logical to expect that the ultimate intent of NEPA, CEQA, and other states' environmental quality measures can be best met through incorporation of environmental concerns *before* a project is planned.

2. Consultant Agency Reviews

While the state laws and regulations are generally very clear on the requirements for circulating an EIS, they do not include specific means to communicate comments beyond suggestions for written responses. It is recommended, therefore, that each agency preparing an EIS adopt a procedure whereby staff members can meet personally in a formal review session with "sister" agency personnel to discuss the EIS before the consulting agencies submit their written responses.

3. Special Interest Reviews

Just as with consulting agency reviews, the laws and regulations are clear as to procedures for an agency to request and receive comment from any special interest group. It is also recommended that each agency adopt a procedure to present its EIS to the various special interest groups, preferably in sessions with groups that have similar interests. One can just imagine the potentials for difference of opinion possible in a presentation of an EIS to a combination of members of the Sierra Club and Friends of the Earth on the one hand and the Building Industry Association and the National Homebuilders Association on the other!

C. Administration of Reviews

The notices, places, and timing of hearings all influence the review process.

1. Notice

Noticing (providing a public announcement) of reviews is a requirement of the law. Local jurisdictions typically must provide at least 10 days' notice for a public hearing on an EIS. That such notice should be in readily available publications and posted in accessible places is obvious.

2. Place

Locations for EIS reviews should be in the regular facilities used for plan reviews and other public hearings. As in the rest of the planning process, such reviews are often held "in the field" to provide a realistic opportunity for local, special interest groups to express themselves.

3. Timing

Currently most states have adopted a time period of 30 to 90 days for review of an EIS. Such a period follows the recommendations of NEPA. However, special consideration should be given to longer periods for those EIS's requiring long analysis periods (e.g., offshore oil drilling, major dams and canals, or other equally complex considerations).

6. The "Sum Total"

In the end, the answers to the following two questions really provide the ultimate measure of the quality of the process, management, research and writing, product, and review of the EIS:
• Is it legally sufficient?
• Is it actually useful?

The basis for answering the first is found in Chapter 5, "The Law of Environmental Impact Analysis." The basis for answering the second is examined in Chapter 7, "Making the Process Work."

7 · Making the Process Work

It is too soon to say that the EIS is working or is not working. To be sure, there are many developers who may condemn the EIS as an unnecessary interference in their otherwise unrestricted road toward continued "utilization" of the environment. There is an equally large or larger number of environmentalists who can point to one or more EIS's as the reason why some contested projects have been halted. And it is probably true that many good projects are better because of the analysis that went into them via the completion of an environmental impact analysis. What cannot yet be measured, however, is the actual "success" from any of these viewpoints of the EIS in meeting the actual intent of NEPA and the various statewide acts: to bring about better, wiser use of the environment.

Can the EIS actually be *made* to work?

The objective of this chapter is to examine this question. The chapter, therefore, is divided into the following topics:
- the real purpose of an EIS
- the people who must make it work
- the environmental management tools
- paying for the environmental report
- the role of the people

1. The Real Purpose of an EIS

The earlier chapters have each included some specific as well as general characteristics of the EIS. However, in Chapter 6, we pointed out that the document itself is not a separate entity or concept. It is part and parcel of the decision-making process and you should think of it as:
- part of the planning process
- a full-disclosure document

- a decision-making tool
- an environmental management tool

A. As Part of the Planning Process

In the planning process, as schematically diagramed in Fig. 7-1, the EIS is one of the logical by-products of the normal sequence of planning. The purpose of an EIS is to report the potential impact of a proposed change in land use. That is to say, the objective in preparing an EIS is to document the possible effects of changing a use of the land to another use *before* the change is made.

To meet this objective, an EIS can best be prepared as part of the planning process. If we recognize that the planning process requires two primary steps—identification of present land use and identification or development of alternative uses—the logical point for preparation of an EIS is immediately after completion of these two steps but *before* a decision is made on a specific alternative. Done at this time, an EIS can become a tool for planning, not merely a device to be used to oppose or justify a proposed plan. It can be used in concert with economic, engineering, and aesthetic factors to determine the over-all feasibility of a project.

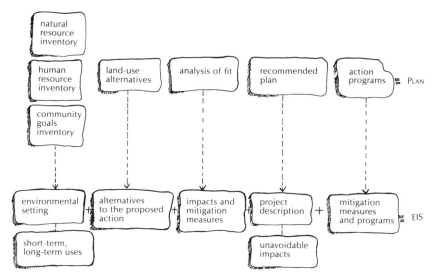

Fig. 7–1 EIS in the planning process.

For further clarification, it might be useful to take a brief look at the fundamentals of the planning process. As stated, the initial step identifies the condition of a given parcel prior to development and the second step develops alternative land uses. The first step takes inventory of the natural resources found on or affecting the property. The natural resource inventory assesses and summarizes the natural and cultural conditions of the site. Physical conditions include geology, soils, vegetation, hydrology, groundwater, climate, and wildlife; the human resources include present use of the land, transportation systems, recreation facilities, agriculture, historic factors, and utilities.

Another *cultural factor* is the goals for the given area. Such goals usually take the form of a master plan but may be no more than a loosely defined expression of what the people feel their community is or ought to be. Needless to say, these less well defined attitudes are what motivate many individuals to speak (shout?) their piece before a local planning commission. But whether defined in the form of an adopted plan or simply in the form of people's ideas, the community goals for a parcel of land are an integral part of what the land user must consider in the inventory of the resources of his area.

Most land users have at least a general range of uses in mind before they fix their sights on a given planning area. However, within certain bounds they usually are open to evaluation of alternative uses. These alternatives are determined by the natural resource inventory, human resource inventory, and community goals. In essence, the alternatives are developed from all the available facts coupled with economic reality.

Once a set of alternatives has been developed, it is possible to evaluate the effect of each on the natural and human environments and determine how well it fits the community goals. The results of this evaluation can be presented as a set of Environmental Impact Statements, one for each alternative use.

Finally, after the environmental, engineering, aesthetic, and economic aspects of each alternative have been considered, a recommended land use can be selected and action programs developed for its implementation. In short, the EIS can be a by-product of the steps of any plan:

The Plan Aspect	*Corresponding EIS Component*
• inventory	environmental setting
• goals statement	relationship between short- and long-term uses of the land
• alternatives	alternatives to the proposed action
• analysis of fit	environmental impacts and mitigation measures
• recommended plan	description of the plan or project, unavoidable adverse and beneficial effects, and irreversible changes
• action programs	mitigation measures including specific design conditions and recommended engineering and operations programs

B. As a Full Disclosure Document

It is clear from NEPA and the state laws that the intention of the legislators was to make the EIS a full disclosure document. NEPA includes the specific statement in Section 102(C), which relates to the *full disclosure* aspects of EIS's (italics added for emphasis):

(C) *include in every recommendation or report* on proposals for legislation and other major Federal actions significantly affecting the quality of the human environment, *a detailed statement* by the responsible official on—
> (*i*) the environmental impact of the proposed action,
> (*ii*) any adverse environmental effects which cannot be avoided should the proposal be implemented,
> (*iii*) alternatives to the proposed action,
> (*iv*) the relationship between local short-term uses of man's environment and the maintenance and enhancement of long-term productivity, and
> (*v*) any irreversible and irretrievable commitments of resources which would be involved in the proposed action should it be implemented.
Prior to making any detailed statement, the responsible Federal official shall consult with and obtain the comments of any Federal agency which has jurisdiction by law or special expertise with respect to any environmental impact involved. *Copies of such statement* and the comments and views of the appropriate Federal, State, and local agencies, which are authorized to develop and enforce environmental standards, shall be made available to the President, the Council on Environmental Quality and *to the public* as provided by section 552 of title 5, United States Code, and shall accompany the proposal through the existing agency review processes.

In the California case (CEQA), the statement in Section 15012 of the California Administrative Code is equally clear (again, italics are added for emphasis):

15012. Informational Document. An Environmental Impact Report is *an informational document which*, when fully prepared in accordance with the CEQA and these Guidelines, *will inform public decision-makers and the general public* of the environmental effects of projects they propose to carry out or approve. The EIR process is intended to enable public agencies to evaluate a project to determine whether it may have a significant effect on the environment, to examine and institute methods of reducing adverse impacts, and to consider alternatives to the project as proposed. These things must be done prior to approval or disapproval of the project. An EIR may not be used as an instrument to rationalize approval of a project, nor do indications of adverse impacts, as enunciated in an EIR, require that a project be disapproved. While CEQA requires that major consideration be given to preventing environmental damage, it is recognized that public agencies have obligations to balance other public objectives, including economic and social factors, in determining whether and how a project should be approved. Economic information may be included in an EIR or may be presented in whatever form the agency desires.

The very essence of both documents is the same: an EIS or EIR is ". . . a detailed statement . . . to the public . . ." (NEPA) or ". . . an informational document which . . . will inform public decision-makers and the general public . . ." (CEQA).

C. As a Decision-making Tool

Some outspoken proponents of environmental preservation wish to use the EIS as a tool to automatically stop any project or proposal that has *any* adverse aspects. This clearly was not the original intent of NEPA.

In summary, the EIS should be a document which discloses all of the relevant positive and negative environmental aspects of a proposal for public consideration in adopting a course of action in the planning process.

D. As an Environmental Management Tool

The ultimate land management use of an EIS is the ensuring of an *actual* stewardship of the property and its related natural and social resources. Mitigation measures described in the EIS and built into the project's design, construction, and operation can help guarantee this stewardship. What is required is to describe and mandate steps that reach well beyond planning and decision-making to the operation of the project and to its future relationship to the environment. Such steps would include both monitoring and management programs.

Several natural environmental monitoring programs include continual observation of the following, for example:
• water quality and quantity monitoring
• air quality monitoring
• vegetation (vitality, insect pests, etc.) monitoring
• wildlife monitoring
Obviously, changes in the natural environment may stem from a wide variety of post-project causes. Changes should be continuously observed, however, to

determine the *actual* course of the environment both to revise or enhance subsequent mitigation programs and to change or retain existing ones.

Management programs should provide for continuous, updatable programs related to:
- vegetation removal and revegetation
- fire prevention and control
- wildlife preservation and enhancement
- soils, erosion prevention and control
- water quality preservation and control
- air quality preservation and control
- pest prevention or control

Needless to say, adequate environmental management must also consider the *human* environment.
- *aesthetics*—is the place what it was expected to be as far as aesthetics are concerned?
- *social interface*—does the project provide for the expected people-to-people environment?
- *safety and health*—does the project meet the safety and/or health considerations expected?
- *quality of life*—does the project meet the life style and quality anticipations?
- *institutions*—are the effects of the project on government and other human institutions what they were expected to be?

None of these questions is easy to answer. But each aspect must be watched and considered in the operation of the place that is created by a project. In every case the essential ingredients are the same: careful monitoring to determine whether or not the anticipations for a proposal are met, and adequate active management once a project is completed.

2. The People Who Must Make It Work

Successful management of the environment must be by a *continuum* of people. No one member of that chain can be the *only* one concerned; they must all be aware and concerned to make the intent of the EIS work. Who are these people?
- the designer team
- the reviewing agencies
- the enforcing agencies
- the management agencies
- the proponent

A. The Designer Team

A project is never conceived, planned, designed, financed, and completed by a single person. On large projects—a new airport for Dallas-Ft. Worth, a major new dam in Tennessee, a new town residential project in Wisconsin—the number of people and disciplines involved may run into the hundreds before even the first shovel is turned. This section is not, however, intended as a chronicle of these people or their functions; it is meant to be a brief illustration of the people involved in the design of a project and the roles they can play in the environmental continuum.

1. Site Selection

Many different people are involved in the selection of sites for different types of land use. At this level in the continuum, the key ingredient is awareness of the relationship of the proposed use and its potential environmental effects to the natural and/or human constraints of the region. Particular care should be placed on understanding and relating with community goals. If the community is geared to accept a proposed use, the rest of the continuum has a good chance to do its job. If the community goals and the proposed use do not match, the balance of the continuum will undoubtedly spend most of its energy building "cases" or defending positions.

2. Site Utilization

When a regional location and site have been selected, a "planner" usually takes over. While these planners can be from any of a variety of disciplines, the continuum has the best chance to work if the comprehensive planning is done by a team composed of environmental scientists (typically such a team includes specialists in geography, geology, hydrology/hydrography, meteorology/climatology, soils, wildlife, and vegetation), social scientists (particularly economists, sociologists, and transportation/circulation specialists), landscape architects, architects, and site engineers. All of these people must be aware of the roles of the other disciplines, the information that can be developed, and how to use that information in designing the project.

3. Structure Siting

Usually this same team, with somewhat greater leadership roles being played by the architect/engineer, is involved in the siting and orientation of structures to optimize environmental amenities (e.g., sunlight) or to minimize environmental degradation. This effort is particularly important for future management of the site; the structures could be efficient but their location could make environmental problems more difficult for those who follow in the continuum.

4. Structure Design

Architects and/or engineers are the leaders in the design of the structures associated with most land uses. They can optimize energy use, or they can choose not to do so. They can minimize the marks of man and his buildings on the natural environment, or they can choose not to do so. They can minimize the percentage of impervious surfaces used on a site, or they can increase it. They can uglify or they can beautify.

5. Engineering

Even the best environmental considerations can go awry if the concepts cannot be converted into practical construction. To minimize run-off from a site may be an important consideration of the environmental scientists; but the facilities to do that must be engineered to fit the whole environment while not causing visual or other problems. The engineering to convert the environmental preservation notions into reality is a most serious, sensitive part of the continuum and one which takes a particularly sensitive type of engineer. Not all, indeed few, have that sensitivity.

6. Construction

"Just get out of my way and let me build it!" This has been the rallying cry for environmental chaos because construction can be the biggest step in the continuum. No matter how careful the planning, how good the design, how sensitive the engineering, a sloppy contractor can destroy all of the good efforts of those who went before him or make doubly difficult the jobs of those who come after him to repair the wounds and manage the project. There are ways to *force* a contractor into environmental awareness; what is needed, however, is his desire to do his job with environmental élan.

7. Lending Institutions

But who usually controls the *realities* of a project, private industry or a public agency? Frequently it is the lending institutions. The last five years have revealed a growing awareness of environmental responsibilities on the part of the banking and investment community. Led by men like Clarence C. Barksdale of the First National Bank in St. Louis,* who put their money into

* See the article on First National Bank of St. Louis' program for environmental education and grants in the September, 1973, issue of *Realty and Investment*, St. Louis Real Estate Publications, Inc., Maryland Heights, Missouri.

environmental awareness programs, and other members of the financial community who regularly and in growing numbers attend environmental training workshops (National Association of Home Builders, Urban Land Institute, and American Institute of Planners), the lending community is learning what requirements it should mandate for environmentally sound projects. They are not *there* yet, but they seem to be moving on the right track.

B. The Reviewing Agencies

Every level of the agency that must review and act on a proposed project can play an important part in the environmental continuum. The roles of these players are outlined briefly in the following paragraphs.

1. The Staff

Possibly the most overworked members of the continuum are the staff of the lead agency, especially of a planning agency, *the* personification of the EIS in the public's eye. Planning staffs, most often academically trained in planning or other design-related disciplines, must process every project. They must know what should be considered in each. They must know when they need specialists' help for an evaluation. They must know on whom to call, and they must have the courage and support to call on them.

2. The Agency Director

The Agency Director has to provide the support for his staff. He *must* know the meaning of environmental concerns. He must be aware of the full range of resources needed to do the job and he must honestly want to do the job. He is indeed the personification of the agency-public relationship. He can have a false or superficial concern for the environment and get a job done, but he needs a true understanding if the job is to be done right and not hypocritically. The way such a person develops that awareness is through learning it as a career grows. It cannot be learned overnight or at a three-day seminar on environmental impact statement preparation.

3. The Commissioners

But all of these people *report* to commissioners. Typically a planning staff would report through its director to a commission of the lay public, usually well-meaning but often not well informed about the environment. The commissioners have a responsibility to learn about the environment, but all who deal with them have a responsibility to provide honest, clear information to help them understand each specific project and accumulatively to educate them about all projects.

4. The Elected Officials

Commissioners usually report to elected officials, and the realities of politics or the politics of reality actually dictate the success of the environmental continuum. Officials must be given a base for decision-making, afforded the opportunity to understand the environmental ethic, and reminded by their constituents that the ethic is understood by the electorate to whom the elected officials are ultimately responsible. If it seems we have gone full circle, we have—it starts with *you*.

C. The Enforcing Agencies

Three key agencies are involved with enforcing the quality and safety aspects of man's impact on the environment:
• public works
• building inspection
• health department

1. Public Works

The city or county public works departments can take the initial enforcement steps by refusing to accept environmentally unworkable engineering. These departments can also modify their own rigid design and construction requirements when necessary in an environmental situation. An example of such a modification is allowance for flexibility in road design standards within counties encompassing both hills and flat land. Attempting to build standard straight, nearly level, and wide-shouldered roads in foothills is absurd, but not unheard of. Public works staffs should always be aware of what is right for the environmental situation in which they are working.

2. Building Inspection

Most building inspection departments are empowered to enforce the conditions of "conditional use permits" or "conditional approvals" (see discussion of "Tools"). However, manpower and training limitations frequently prevent regular enforcement of these conditions, particularly during construction. Public support for better enforcement coupled with EIS disclosure of past enforcement failures can help remedy this situation.

3. Health Departments

Just as the public works and building inspection departments usually have jurisdiction in areas of public safety, so do departments of health in the areas of health. Air quality and water quality can be the key environmental concerns of these people in the environmental continuum.

D. The Management Agencies

But who is to be the steward of the *critters* that inhabit the place? The quality of their environment is directly indicative of the quality of ours. The key agencies here, on both a national and a local scale, are:
- the Environmental Protection Agency
- air quality agencies
- water quality agencies
- forestry agencies
- fish and game agencies

1. The Environmental Protection Agency

Much has been said of EPA's growing relationship with the quality of our environment. This national agency provides the focal point for environmental awareness and monitoring. Its greatest successes have been in relation to air quality, water quality, and noise; its most recent efforts are turning to the quality of our land use and utilization of our land resources.

2. Air Quality Agencies

Both before and as a result of EPA's promulgations, most states have adopted a framework of air quality control agencies. These agencies are responsible for setting and monitoring air quality standards and enforcing abatement if those standards are not met.

3. Water Quality Agencies

All states have adopted some form of water quality management agency. Many multiple-state agencies were established under the efforts of the Federal Water Pollution Control Administration. These multi-state and single-state agencies have jurisdictional powers to set, monitor, and enforce water quality standards.

4. Forestry Agencies

The U.S. Forest Service and most state forest agencies have long been concerned with maintaining the quality of forest and rangelands for optimum productivity. Only more recently have they expanded their concerns to include the quality of vegetation as habitat for animals and man. As society has come to recognize rare and endangered species of wildlife, it has recognized that habitat management is necessary to their existence. Needless to say, we have a long way to go to understand the value of rare or endangered plant species.

5. Fish and Game Agencies

It can be said that *critters* don't vote. If they did, they might indeed unanimously agree to oppose the growth ethic, as was suggested in a pointed editorial cartoon that appeared in the *Audubon* magazine. The responsibility of the fish and game agencies has matured from one of simple hunting-husbandry to ecologic stewardship as the awareness and actions of the public have given these professionals the support so many of them had needed.

E. The Proponent

But let us go back to the question of *uglification* of the environment, to the question of the financial community's awareness of the environment, and to the reality of politics. The *ultimate* success of environmental management rests on the shoulders of the proponents. They are indeed the Tristram of the poem so beautifully quoted by Aldo Leopold in *Sand County Almanac** in explanation of the environmental ethic:

> Whether you will or not
> You are a King, Tristram, for you are one
> Of the time-tested few who leave the world,
> When they are gone, not the same place it was.
> Mark what you leave.

3. Environmental Management Tools

Several key processes and a range of environmental ordinances are the primary tools that can be used for implementation of the environmental impact statement's findings. These tools are the subject of this section. Particular emphasis is placed on the ordinances, using the practices of the Tahoe Regional Planning Agency as the primary model.

A. Processes

The most important process for implementation of environmental concerns is the planning process, the subject of the first portion of this chapter. Within that framework, there are three additional processes that are of great utility for environmental management:

* Leopold quoted from Edwin Arlington Robinson's *Tristram*, reprinted with permission of Macmillan Publishing Co. Inc. from *Collected Poems of Edwin Arlington Robinson*. Copyright 1927 by Edwin Arlington Robinson, renewed 1955 by Ruth Nivison and Barbara R. Holt.

- conditions of approval
- contractual obligations
- bonding

1. Conditions of Approval

Most EIS-approving agencies are making mitigation and management measures conditions of approval. If they are met, a project can proceed. If they are not, the project is stopped. The success of this system, widely employed by planning agencies, hinges on the agency's having a staff of sufficient number and training to pursue each project through all of the stages of the conditions.

2. Contractual Obligations

Many private developers are undertaking contractual obligations for environmental management after a project is completed or during its construction. Such contracts range from penalty payments for tree damage during construction to permanent monitoring, management, and education programs. The agents of these contracts are the owner and subcontractor in the first case and home or property owner associations in the second.

3. Bonding

The U.S. Forest Service has adopted a program of bonding for many of its users of the environment.* Under such programs, the proponents post bonds to repair any environmental damage that their projects may cause. Other agencies have adopted this procedure, particularly in the areas of road construction or resource extraction.

B. Ordinances

The most commonly adopted environmental quality implementation ordinances deal with land use, subdivision, and grading, three actions which can have the greatest impact on the environment. There are other ordinances controlling tree removal and related vegetation management, signs and exterior graphics, and architectural controls. This section will be confined to land use, subdivision, and grading. We recommend that the reader consult a local agency for examples of other environmental ordinances.

Examples of the use of ordinances to correct or prevent environmental impacts are found in the regulations of the Tahoe Regional Planning Agency. This bi-state agency was created by Congress in 1969 to protect the beauty and the water quality of Lake Tahoe, which straddles the California-Nevada border

---

* See the U.S. Department of Agriculture, Forest Service, *Forest Practices Manual.*

in the Sierra Nevada mountains. Among the key actions of this agency was the adoption of ordinances based on environmental impacts to control land use, subdivisions, and grading.

1. Land Use Ordinance

The requirement for an ordinance is summarized in the Agency's discussion of "Findings":*

> The governing body of the Tahoe Regional Planning Agency finds that in order to effectuate the adopted regional plan, it is necessary to adopt this ordinance establishing regional land use and land capability districts; providing population density controls and land coverage limitations; providing for the issuance of permits concerning land uses, structures, and land coverage; providing for non-conforming alterations, uses and structures; providing that violations of the ordinance shall constitute a misdemeanor; providing for variances; and providing for other matters properly relating thereto. The governing body further finds that the provisions of this ordinance are in accordance with the provisions and purposes of the Tahoe Regional Planning Compact.

2. Subdivision Ordinance

The need for the ordinance is summarized in the Agency's discussion of "Findings":**

> The governing body of the Tahoe Regional Planning Agency finds that in order to effectuate the adopted regional plan, it is necessary to adopt this ordinance establishing minimum standards and providing regulations governing the subdivision of land in the Tahoe Region, providing for the issuance of permits, providing for variances, and providing for other matters properly relating thereto. The governing body further finds that the provisions of this ordinance are in accordance with the provisions and purposes of the Tahoe Regional Planning Compact.

3. Grading Ordinance

The Findings of the Agency indicate the general need for a grading ordinance:†

* Tahoe Regional Planning Agency, *Land Use Ordinance*, Ordinance No. 13, amended May 24, 1973, effective July 23, 1973.

** Tahoe Regional Planning Agency, *Subdivision Ordinance*, Ordinance No. 7, adopted March 22, 1972.

† Tahoe Regional Planning Agency, *Grading Ordinance*, Ordinance No. 5, adopted February 10, 1972.

The governing body of the Tahoe Regional Planning Agency finds that in order to effectuate the adopted regional plan, it is necessary to adopt this ordinance establishing minimum standards and providing regulations for the construction and maintenance of land fills, excavations, cuts and clearing of vegetation, providing for revegetation of cleared areas, and providing for other matters properly relating thereto. The governing body further finds that the provisions of this ordinance are in accordance with the provisions and purposes of the Tahoe Regional Planning Compact.

4. Paying for the Environmental Reports

When an agency is the proponent of a project, it is evident that it should finance the preparation of an EIS as a normal function of the process it undertakes in order to plan and implement the project. Generally, however, the process is not as clear when a private development is being considered. Methods employed currently to undertake and pay for the analysis and preparation of environmental reports can be summarized under Proponent Reports, Agency Review of Proponent Reports, and Agency Reports.

A. Proponent Reports

In many cases the agencies are requiring the proponent to prepare or contract for environmental statements. An advantage of this process is that the proponent can get the benefit of the environmental information and thus make a better design if the environmental work is done as a part of the project's planning. An obvious disadvantage is that the proponent may consciously (or unconsciously at best) use the EIS as a promotional tool.

In all such cases, the agency is ultimately responsible for the quality and accuracy of the information in the report.

B. Proponent Reports—Agency Review

Several agencies, including the California county of Mono, one of the parties to the Mammoth Decision mentioned in Chapter 1, have adopted a procedure whereby the proponent can prepare the draft and submit it to the agency for staff or consultant review. In this case, the proponent pays a nominal fee upon filing the EIS (in Mono County, $300 per filing) to cover the agency's review costs.

C. Agency Reports

A number of agencies which deal with private proponents have adopted a procedure whereby the proponent submits his plans and the agency or its consultant prepares the report. Usually under this approach the proponent is billed directly by the agency for the costs of preparing the EIS or having it prepared by a consultant. As in the proponent-prepared reports, the cost for such an EIS depends on the complexity of the problem and the degree of detail required by the agency's standards and its decision-maker's requirements.

There are undoubtedly other practices that are now employed and may become widespread as the place of the EIS in the planning process matures. For the present, it is safe to conclude the following in relation to private EIS's:

(*1*) they are funded in the main by the proponents

(*2*) their cost is usually passed on to buyers or users of the project

(*3*) they tend to be most impartial when not prepared by the proponent

(*4*) their cost is usually commensurate with the complexity and significance of the problem

5. The Role of the People

In the final analysis, the people—you and I—are the only ones who can make a difference. *They* can never be held accountable, only *I* can. Making the process work requires intelligent voting coupled with support for enforcement of environmental standards. A broad range of general public actions, varying from litter cleanup to organized demands for pollution control legislation and sensible product packaging, is also required. Better public information is a very important result of the EIS process. The requirements for public notices, hearings, and review of environmental reports are a major change in the way government agencies are accustomed to operate. The concept of a "full disclosure document" is a veritable revolution for some agencies.

But the disclosure by itself will mean little if *we* are not there to monitor the information for accuracy and to ensure that it is used by our decision-makers in their deliberations.

Ultimately, we can make the EIS work by caring enough to create a human environment in which the natural environment takes at least an equal place with economics, aesthetics, and engineering in our decision-making process.

(Section 1.A. was rewritten from an article by the author that originally appeared in the May, 1973, issue of *Urban Land*.)

8 · Tools for EIS
A Practical Appendix

As we indicated in the Editors' Foreword, the EIS process is constantly changing, as are its use and administration by governmental agencies. If we look ahead at the next few years, the major developments that seem likely in the EIS process are a continual improvement in the quality of the impact analysis, and the greater integration of impact analysis with planning. Substantial effort is now being directed at these two goals and new sources of information, techniques, and administration are being developed and tested throughout the country and in a few foreign nations. The purposes of this chapter/appendix are to provide you with some of the basic tools to use in your own EIS work and to indicate some of the sources of information you can use to keep abreast of changes in the state-of-the-art of EIS. These sources range from periodicals and scientific journals to citizens' groups to government-sponsored computer models. Each has its purpose and each meets certain needs of environmental analysts, either working in the field or studying the theory of the process. Like this book and its authors, these sources are varied in their applications and emphasis.

Part 1. Information Sources for Coping with Change

1. EPA and the Institute of Ecology are conducting a joint study to develop a substantive framework for environmental analysis of government projects (i.e.,

Patrick H. Heffernan, born in 1944, is currently a graduate student in Political Science at the University of California at Santa Barbara and a principal in Resources, a public-interest consulting firm. He lectured in Environmental Planning and Impact Analysis at the University of California at Berkeley and has written in the field of employment impacts of environmental protection programs. A former news editor and writer, he edited the *Environmental Impact Review* and served as the Executive Director of the Environmental Information Clearinghouse in Berkeley.

highways, dams).

>   Contact: Institute of Ecology, University of California at Davis, Davis, California 95616.

2. The United States Geological Survey is conducting a study of the interrelationships among types of activities such as construction and environmental impacts.

>   Contact: Assistant Director of Research, USGS, Department of Interior, Interior Building, Washington, D.C. 20240.

3. The Environmental Law Institute and the International Biological Program of the National Science Foundation are conducting a study of methods of environmental impact analysis and forecasting for certain kinds of ecosystems.

>   Contact: Environmental Law Institute, Suite 614, 1346 Connecticut Ave., N.W., Washington, D.C. 20036.

4. The CEQ, EPA, the National Science Foundation (NSF), and the Energy Research and Development Agency (ERDA) have developed the MERES model for forecasting the environmental impacts of energy production.

>   Contact: EPA, Washington Research Center, Room 637, WSMW, EPA Headquarters, Washington, D.C. 20460.

5. The EPA, CEQ, Federal Energy Office, and other federal agencies are developing a reference document containing up-to-date information on the environmental impacts of energy systems and forecasting methods for use in environmental impact statements.

>   Contact: EPA, Washington Research Center.

6. The CEQ, EPA, and Department of Housing and Urban Development are sponsoring a joint analysis of the secondary impacts of providing infrastructure such as roads and sewers, and developing methods of predicting economic, social, and land use impacts of public infrastructure projects.

>   Contact: CEQ, Staff Director for Program Development, 722 Jackson Place, Washington, D.C. 20006.

7. The Strategic Environmental Assessment System (SEAS) of the EPA is a comprehensive system of special-purpose models linked to INFORUM, an input-output model of the nation's economy. SEAS is used to study the economic impacts of environmental policies, and waste generated by production and development policies, and the costs of mitigation measures.

>   Contact: EPA, Washington Research Center.

>   Also see: *Interdisciplinary Forecasts of the American Economy*, by Professor Clopper Almon, University of Maryland. Professor Almon developed the INFORUM model.

8. EPA's Technical Report No. 60015–74–005 (James E. Flinn and Robert S. Reiners, "Development of Predictions of Future Pollution Problems," 1974)

describes a technique for predicting non-quantitative short- and medium-term pollution problems.

Contact: EPA regional offices' libraries.

9. The U.S. Forest Service is currently preparing an analysis of all its environmental planning and impact analysis actions for a report entitled "The Environmental Program of the Future." The Forest Service has integrated NEPA into its planning process and adopted a *Unified Planning and Decision-Making Concept* (UPD) which describes this process.

Contact: Dr. Ross Carder and Clarkson H. Oglesby, *Unified Planning and Decision-Making: A Conceptual Framework for Forest Service Management* (Ph.D. thesis), Stanford University, October, 1973.

10. The U.S. Forest Service has involved the majority of its employees in the EIS process, especially in the field. Its guidelines and staff handbooks are quite useful for students of EIS and planning in non-urban environments.

Contact: CEQ, *An Evaluation of Implementation and Administration of NEPA by the U.S. Forest Service and the Bureau of Land Management*, February, 1974, available at EPA regional office libraries.

11. CEQ has also studied the implementation of NEPA by the U.S. Navy.

Contact: CEQ, *An Evaluation of the Implementation of NEPA by the U.S. Navy*, March, 1974, available at EPA regional libraries.

12. Roger W. Findley conducted a study of the Corps of Engineers' use of NEPA in planning its proposed Oakely reservoir in southern Illinois.

Contact: Roger W. Findley, University of Illinois, "The Planning of a Corps of Engineers Reservoir Project: Law, Economics and Politics," 3 *Ecology Law Quarterly* 1 (1973).

13. John Randolf of Stanford University compiled a study of NEPA use in the planning of the New Melones Dam in California.

Contact: *New Melones, NEPA and the Political Process: The Effect of the National Environmental Policy Act on the Planning of New Melones Lake*, prepared for incorporation into Ph.D. thesis, Stanford University, 1974.

14. EPA and CEQ have contracted for several studies of the influence and use of NEPA on the development of specific projects throughout the country and will publish them as they become available.

Contact: Publications, EPA, Waterside Mall (WSMW), Room 206, 401 M Street, S.W., Washington, D.C. 20460.

15. The Congressional Research Service of the Library of Congress has started developing environmental indices for use in EIS as required in the National Environmental Policy Act of 1969. The indices are another form of monitoring the nation's environment and are an excellent source of information for EIS and examples of continual EIS work.

Contact: Environmental Policy Division of the Congressional Research

Service of the Library of Congress, *Environmental Indices, Status of Development Pursuant to Sections 102(2)(B) and 204 of the National Environmental Policy Act of 1969*; prepared for the Committee on Interior and Insular Affairs, 1973; and the National Academy of Sciences, Environmental Studies Board, "Planning for Environmental Quality," 1974.

16. Other specific environmental indices are available from the EPA and the NSF, covering topics such as air pollution and water quality.

17. The OBERS program of the Washington-based Water Resources Council is an excellent source of information on basic population and economic activity (by SMSA) for the entire nation. It is also a model of these activities for the nation, given certain assumptions, and can be used as a basis against which to test impact analysis in larger projects.

Contact: EPA, *Population and Economic Activity in the United States and Standard Metropolitan Statistical Areas*, historical and projected 1950–2020 (available from EPA).

States with Environmental Impact Statement Requirements

California
Statutory Source: California Environmental Quality Act of 1970, Cal. Pub. Res Code §§21000–21174 (Supp. 1972), as amended by Ch. 56, Stat. of 1974 (March 4, 1974).
Guidelines: 14 Cal. Adm. Code Ch. 3, "Guidelines for the Implementation of the California Environmental Quality Act of 1970" (Register 73, No. 50-12-15-73), as amended by order of the Secretary of Resources, March 22, 1974, and Jan. 30, 1975; amended by statute to include energy considerations, January, 1975.

Contact: Norman E. Hill, Special Assistant to the Secretary for Resources, 1414 Ninth St., Sacramento, California 95815, (916) 445-9134.
Connecticut
Statutory Source: Connecticut Environmental Policy Act of 1973, Pub. Act 73-562 (approved June 22, 1973).
Guidelines: Guidelines are prepared by the Department of Environmental Protection. Guidelines for Implementation of Executive Order No. 16 were transmitted to state agencies under Memorandum from the Governor on December 13, 1972.

Contact: Mary Ann Massey, Assistant Director of Planning and Research, Department of Environmental Protection, State Office Building, Hartford, Connecticut 06115, (203) 566-4256.

Hawaii

Statutory Source: Act 246, Sess. Laws of Hawaii (approved June 4, 1974), Hawaii Rev. Stat. Ch. 334 (1974).

Guidelines: Rules and regulations are prepared by the Hawaii Environmental Quality Control Office.

> Contact: Dr. Albert Tom, Chairman, Environmental Quality Commission, 550 Halekauwila St., Honolulu, Hawaii 96813; or Richard E. Marland, Director, Office of Environmental Quality Control, Office of the Governor, 550 Halekauwila St., Room 301, Honolulu, Hawaii 96813, (808) 548-6915.

Indiana

Statutory Source: Ind. Code 1971, 13-1-10, added by Pub. L. 98, 1972:

Guidelines: None adopted at time of writing. Draft guidelines have been prepared by Environmental Management Board.

> Contact: Ralph Pickard, Technical Secretary, Environmental Management Board, 1300 W. Michigan St., Indianapolis, Indiana 46206, (317) 633-4420.

Maryland

Statutory Source: Maryland Environmental Policy Act of 1973, Ch. 702.

Guidelines: "Revised Guidelines for Implementation of the Maryland Environmental Policy Act," June 15, 1974.

> Contact: Paul McKee, Assistant Secretary, Department of Natural Resources, Tawes State Office Bldg., Annapolis, Maryland 21404, (301) 267-5548.

Massachusetts

Statutory Source: Ch. 781, Acts of 1972, as amended by Ch. 257 of the Acts of 1974.

Guidelines: "Regulations to Create a Uniform System for Preparation of Environmental Impact Reports," dated July 6, 1973, as amended October 15, 1973, and June 20, 1974.

> Contact: Matthew B. Connolly, Jr., Chief Planner, Executive Office of Environmental Affairs, 18 Tremont St., Boston, Massachusetts 20408, (617) 727-7700.

Minnesota

Statutory Source: Minnesota Environmental Policy Act of 1973, Ch. 412, Laws of 1973, Minnesota.

Guidelines: "Rules and Regulations for Environmental Impact Statement," April 4, 1974.

> Contact: John Mohr, Environmental Quality Council, Capital Square Bldg., 559 Cedar St., St. Paul, Minnesota (612) 296-3985, or the Environmental Analysis Program of the Environmental Quality Council, (612) 296-2686.

Montana

Statutory Source: Montana Environmental Policy Act of 1971, Ch. 238, L. 1971, Rev. Code Mont. §69-6501 *et seq.* 1973.

Guidelines: Montana Environmental Quality Council "Revised Guidelines for Environmental Impact Statements Required by the Montana Environmental Policy Act of 1971," September 19, 1973.

> Contact: Director, Montana Environmental Quality Council, Capital Station, Helena, Montana 59601, (406) 449-3742.

North Carolina

Statutory Source: North Carolina Environmental Policy Act of 1971, N.C. Gen. Stat. 113A, 1973.

Guidelines: North Carolina Department of Administration, "Guidelines for the Implementation of the Environmental Policy Act of 1971," February 18, 1972.

> Contact: D. Keith Whitnight, Environmental Planning Coordinator, Department of Natural and Economic Resources, P.O. Box 27687, Raleigh, North Carolina 27611, (919) 829-3115.

South Dakota

Statutory Sources: South Dakota Environmental Policy Act, SL 1974, Ch. 245 (approved March 2, 1974).

Guidelines: Department of Environmental Protection (1974 Informal Guidelines).

> Contact: Dr. Allyn O. Lockner, South Dakota Department of Environmental Protection, Office Building No. 2, Room 415, Pierre, South Dakota 57501, (605) 224-3351.

Virginia

Statutory Source: Virginia Environmental Policy Act of 1973, Ch. 384, Laws of 1973 (approved March 15, 1973).

Guidelines: "Procedures Manual for Environmental Impact Statements in the Commonwealth of Virginia," issued by the Governor's Council on the Environment, December, 1973.

> Contact: Susan T. Wilburn, Environmental Impact Statement Coordinator, Governor's Office, Council on the Environment, Eighth Street Office Bldg., Richmond, Virginia 23219, (804) 770-4500.

Washington

Statutory Source: State Environmental Policy Act of 1971, Rev. Code Wash. Ch. 43.21C and Rev. Code Wash. Ch. 47.04.

Guidelines: "Guidelines for Implementation of the State Environmental Policy Act of 1971."

> Contact: Stephen B. Crane, State of Washington Council on the Environmental Protection, No. 5 South Sound Center, Lacey, Washington 98504, or Peter R. Haskin, Environmental Review and Evaluation, Office

of Planning and Program Development, State of Washington Department of Ecology, Olympia, Washington 98504, (206) 753-6890.

Wisconsin

Statutory Source: Wisconsin Environmental Policy Act of 1971, Ch. 274, Laws of 1971.

Guidelines: "Guidelines for the Implementation of the Wisconsin Environmental Policy Act," issued by Governor's Executive Order No. 69, December, 1973.

Contact: Farnum Alston, Office of the Governor, State Capitol, Madison, Wisconsin 53703, (608) 266-2121.

Puerto Rico

Statutory Source: Puerto Rico Environmental Policy Act, 12 Laws P.R., 1970.

Guidelines: "Guidelines for Preparation, Evaluation and Use of Environmental Impact Statements," issued by the Environmental Quality Board on December 19, 1972.

Contact: Carlos Jimenez Barber, Executive Director, Environmental Quality Board. 1550 Ponce de León Ave. 4th Fl., Santurce, Puerto Rico 09910, (809) 725-5140.

In addition to the states listed above, the following states require or suggest environmental review through the authority of executive or administrative orders:

- Michigan
- New Jersey
- Arizona (limited review by Fish and Game Commission)
- Delaware (limited review, mostly coastal)
- Nevada (limited review)
- Georgia (limited review)
- Nebraska (review limited to roads)
- New Jersey (limited review, primarily coastal and wetlands)

Two cities now require environmental impact statements:

New York City, New York. Contact: Office of Environmental Impact, N.Y. Environmental Protection, Administration of the City of New York, Room 2344, Municipal Bldg., N.Y., N.Y. 10007, (212) 566-4107.

Bowie, Maryland. Contact: Environmental Planner, City Hall, Bowie, Md. 20715, (301) 262-7900.

Information sources for EIS data and/or information on changes in the EIS process

Center for California Public Affairs. 226 W. Foothill Blvd. Claremont, California 91711.

The Center publishes a number of volumes on the state government process and on the EIS process. Principally oriented to California, but very useful for anyone in the EIS field. The Center also provides subscription information services and directories of environmental organizations and agencies covering the nation.

National Wildlife Federation. 1412 Sixteenth Street, N.W. Washington, D.C. 20036.

The Federation is primarily an environmental lobby organization but among its publications is the excellent *Conservation Directory* of citizens' organizations, private corporations, and government agencies concerned with the environment. Revised annually, the Directory contains thousands of listings.

The Bolton Institute, Inc. 1835 K. St. N.W., Suite 302 Washington, D.C. 20006

Services of the Bolton Institute include design and implementation of environmental training, education, and research programs on the interrelationships between man's actions and his impacts on nature. The Institute publishes the *Environmental Impact Statement Training Guide.*

Resources for the Future. 1755 Massachusetts Ave. N.W. Washington, D.C. 20036

Research and publications in conservation and use of natural resources, environmental impacts, and quality of life. Many publications and education programs.

This appendix is meant to be suggestive rather than exhaustive. There are literally thousands of environmental organizations and research agencies in the country. Information on your city or state can best be obtained by checking with the contact listed for your state (keep in mind that the names may change over time) or by consulting one of the directories listed above. The references provided at the ends of some chapters also are a good source of further information on environmental impact analysis.

Part 2. The National Environmental Policy Act

Purpose

Sec. 2. The purposes of this Act are: To declare a national policy which will encourage productive and enjoyable harmony between man and his environment; to promote efforts which will prevent or eliminate damage to the environment and biosphere and stimulate the health and welfare of man; to enrich the understanding of the ecological systems and natural resources important to the Nation; and to establish a Council on Environmental Quality.

TITLE I

DECLARATION OF National ENVIRONMENTAL POLICY

Sec. 101. (a) The Congress, recognizing the profound impact of man's activity on the interrelations of all components of the natural environment, particularly the profound influences of population growth, high-density urbanization, industrial expansion, resource exploitation, and new and expanding technological advances and recognizing further the critical importance of restoring and maintaining environmental quality to the overall welfare and development of man, declares that it is the continuing policy of the Federal Government, in cooperation with State and local governments, and other concerned public and private organizations, to use all practicable means and measures, including financial and technical assistance, in a manner calculated to foster and promote the general welfare, to create and maintain conditions under which man and nature can exist in productive harmony, and fulfill the social, economic, and other requirements of present and future generations of Americans.

(b) In order to carry out the policy set forth in this Act, it is the continuing responsibility of the Federal Government to use all practicable means, consistent with other essential considerations of national policy, to improve and coordinate Federal plans, functions, programs, and resources to the end that the Nation may—

(*1*) fulfill the responsibilities of each generation as trustee of the environment for succeeding generations;

(*2*) assure for all Americans safe, healthful, productive, and esthetically and culturally pleasing surroundings;

(*3*) attain the widest range of beneficial uses of the environment without degradation, risk to health or safety, or other undesirable and unintended consequences;

(*4*) preserve important historic, cultural, and natural aspects of our national heritage, and maintain, wherever possible, an environment which supports diversity and variety of individual choice;

(*5*) achieve a balance between population and resource use which will permit high standards of living and a wide sharing of life's amenities; and

(6) enhance the quality of renewable resources and approach the maximum attainable recycling of depletable resources.

(c) The Congress recognizes that each person should enjoy a healthful environment and that each person has a responsibility to contribute to the preservation and enhancement of the environment.

Sec. 102. The Congress authorizes and directs that, to the fullest extent possible: (1) the policies, regulations, and public laws of the United States shall be interpreted and administered in accordance with the policies set forth in this Act, and (2) all agencies of the Federal Government shall—

(A) utilize a systematic, interdisciplinary approach which will insure the integrated use of the natural and social sciences and the environmental design arts in planning and in decisionmaking which may have an impact on man's environment;

(B) identify and develop methods and procedures, in consultation with the Council on Environmental Quality established by title II of this Act, which will insure that presently unquantified environmental amenities and values may be given appropriate consideration in decisionmaking along with economic and technical considerations;

(C) include in every recommendation or report on proposals for legislation and other major Federal actions significantly affecting the quality of the human environment, a detailed statement by the responsible official on—

(i) the environmental impact of the proposed action,

(ii) any adverse environmental effects which cannot be avoided should the proposal be implemented,

(iii) alternatives to the proposed action,

(iv) the relationship between local short-term uses of man's environment and the maintenance and enhancement of long-term productivity, and

(v) any irreversible and irretrievable commitments of resources which would be involved in the proposed action should it be implemented.

Prior to making any detailed statement, the responsible Federal official shall consult with and obtain the comments of any Federal agency which has jurisdiction by law or special expertise with respect to any environmental impact involved. Copies of such statement and the comments and views of the appropriate Federal, State, and local agencies, which are authorized to develop and enforce environmental standards, shall be made available to the President, the Council on Environmental Quality and to the public as provided by section 552 of title 5, United States Code, and shall accompany the proposal through the existing agency review processes.

(D) study, develop, and describe appropriate alternatives to recommended courses of action in any proposal which involves unresolved conflicts concerning alternative uses of available resources;

(E) recognize the worldwide and long-range character of environmental problems and, where consistent with the foreign policy of the United States, lend appropriate support to initiatives, resolutions, and programs designed to maximize international cooperation in anticipating and preventing a decline in the quality of mankind's world environment;

(F) make available to States, counties, municipalities, institutions, and individuals, advice and information useful in restoring, maintaining, and enhancing the quality of the environment;

(G) initiate and utilize ecological information in the planning and development of resource-oriented projects; and

(H) assist the Council on Environmental Quality established by title II of this Act.

Sec. 103. All agencies of the Federal Government shall review their present statutory authority, administrative regulations, and current policies and procedures for the purpose of determining whether there are any deficiencies or inconsistencies therein which prohibit full compliance with the purposes and provisions of this Act and shall propose to the President not later than July 1, 1971, such measures as may be necessary to bring their authority and policies into conformity with the intent, purposes, and procedures set forth in this Act.

Sec. 104. Nothing in Section 102 or 103 shall in any way affect the specific statutory obligations of any Federal agency (1) to comply with criteria or standards of environmental quality, (2) to coordinate or consult with any other Federal or State agency, or (3) to act, or refrain from acting contingent upon the recommendations or certification of any other Federal or State agency.

Sec. 105. The policies and goals set forth in this Act are supplementary to those set forth in existing authorizations of Federal agencies.

Title II

Council on Environmental Quality

Sec. 201. The President shall transmit to the Congress annually beginning July 1, 1970, an Environmental Quality Report (hereinafter referred to as the "report") which shall set forth (1) the status and condition of the major natural, manmade, or altered environmental classes of the Nation, including, but not limited to, the air, the aquatic, including marine, estuarine, and fresh water, and the terrestrial environment, including, but not limited to, the forest dryland, wetland, range, urban, suburban, and rural environment; (2) current and foreseeable trends in the quality, management and utilization of such environments and the effects of those trends on the social, economic, and other requirements of the Nation; (3) the adequacy of available natural resources for fulfilling human and economic requirements of the Nation in the light of expected population pressures; (4) a review of the programs and activities (including regulatory activities) of the Federal Government, the State and local governments, and nongovernmental entities or individuals, with particular reference to their effect on the environment and on the conservation, development and utilization of natural resources; and (5) a program for remedying the deficiencies of existing programs and activities, together with recommendations for legislation.

Sec. 202. There is created in the Executive Office of the President a Council on Environmental Quality (hereinafter referred to as the "Council"). The Council shall be composed of three members who shall be appointed by the President to serve at his pleasure, by and with the advice and consent of the Senate. The President shall designate one of the members of the Council to serve as Chairman. Each member shall be a person who, as a result of his training, experience, and attainments, is exceptionally well qualified to analyze and interpret environmental trends and information of all kinds; to appraise programs and activities of the Federal Government in the light of the policy set forth in title I of this Act; to be conscious of and responsive to the scientific, economic, social, esthetic, and cultural needs and interests of the Nation; and to formulate and recommend national policies to promote the improvement of the quality of the environment.

Sec. 203. The Council may employ such officers and employees as may be necessary to carry out its function under this Act. In addition, the Council may employ and fix the compensation of such experts and consultants as may be necessary for the carrying out of its functions under this Act, in accordance with section 3109 of title 5, United States Code (but without regard to the last sentence thereof).

Sec. 204. It shall be the duty and function of the Council—

(1) to assist and advise the President in the preparation of the Environmental Quality Report required by section 201;

(2) to gather timely and authoritative information concerning the conditions and trends in the quality of the environment both current and prospective, to analyze and interpret such information for the purpose of determining whether such conditions and trends are interfering, or are likely to interfere, with the achievement of the policy set forth in title I of this Act, and to compile and submit to the President studies relating to such conditions and trends;

(3) to review and appraise the various programs and activities of the Federal Government in the light of the policy set forth in title I of this Act for the purpose of determining the extent to which such programs and activities are

contributing to the achievement of such policy, and to make recommendations to the President with respect thereto;

(*4*) to develop and recommend to the President national policies to foster and promote the improvement of environmental quality to meet the conservation, social, economic, health, and other requirements and goals of the Nation;

(*5*) to conduct investigations, studies, surveys, research, and analyses relating to ecological systems and environmental quality;

(*6*) to document and define changes in the natural environment, including the plant and animal systems, and to accumulate necessary data and other information for a continuing analysis of these changes or trends and an interpretation of their underlying causes;

(*7*) to report at least once each year to the President on the state and condition of the environment; and

(*8*) to make and furnish such studies, reports thereon, and recommendations with respect to matters of policy and legislation as the President may request.

Sec. 205. In exercising its powers, functions, and duties under this Act, the Council shall—

(*1*) consult with the Citizens' Advisory Committee on Environmental Quality established by Executive order numbered 11472, dated May 29, 1969, and with such representatives of science, industry, agriculture, labor, conservation organizations, State and local governments, and other groups, as it deems advisable; and

(*2*) utilize, to the fullest extent possible, the services, facilities, and information (including statistical information) of public and private agencies and organizations, and individuals in order that duplication of effort and expense may be avoided, thus assuring that the Council's activities will not unnecessarily overlap or conflict with similar activities authorized by law and performed by established agencies.

Sec. 206. Members of the Council shall serve full time and the Chairman of the Council shall be compensated at the rate provided for Level II of the Executive Schedule Pay Rates (5 U.S.C. 5313). The other members of the Council shall be compensated at the rate provided for Level IV of the Executive Schedule Pay Rates (5 U.S.C. 5315).

Sec. 207. There are authorized to be appropriated to carry out the provisions of this Act not to exceed $300,000 for fiscal year 1970, $700,000 for fiscal year 1971, and $1,000,000 for each fiscal year thereafter.

Part 3. Suggested State Environmental Policy Act (Developed by the Council of State Governments)

This suggested State Environmental Policy Act was drafted by workshop participants at the Second National Symposium on State Environmental Legislation on April 9–12, 1973, in Rosslyn, Virginia. It draws heavily on experience gained in administering the National Environmental Policy Act (NEPA) and the California Environmental Quality Act of 1970.

Damage to the environment has often been an unexpected and unintended consequence of governmental programs. Responding to this problem, the federal government and 11 States have enacted environmental policy acts which call for the preparation of environmental impact statements on actions of public agencies which may have a significant effect on the environment. These environmental impact statements set forth the environmental impact of a proposed project and examine alternatives and mitigation measures that could reduce the adverse effects.

The suggested Act follows the approach of the National Environmental Policy Act in its simplicity, the details to be filled in by administrative guidelines. The workshop delegates believe that individual States would need flexibility in adjusting the many minor details to their individual situations.

Issues. In considering a proposed law dealing with environmental impact statements, a State should consider the following important issues. The suggested State Environmental Policy Act represents the workshop's proposed solution to these issues. Words or passages in brackets are examples of possible alternatives, depending upon individual state structures.

1. To which levels of government should the Act apply? A State should consider whether it wants to apply the requirement for environmental impact statements only to state-level agencies or whether it wishes to apply the requirement to local agencies also. The resolution of this issue is not clear in most of the state statutes adopted to the date of this writing. The California Act applies explicitly to both state and local agencies.

2. Should the Act apply only to public works construction or should it also apply to regulatory activities and approval of private sections? NEPA has always applied to direct government operations and to regulatory and licensing activities. The California Act was amended in 1972 to make clear that it applied to regulatory activities and the granting of discretionary approvals to private activities.

3. Should the Act apply only to major actions or should it apply to all actions which may have a significant effect on the environment? NEPA applies only to major actions. This follows the belief that large activities will be the main ones that have significant effects on the environment and that government will become bogged down if it has to prepare and review too many reports. Limiting the requirement to major actions is a simple way to screen out actions which do not require the preparation of an impact statement. On the other hand, there may be many small projects which may have a large effect on the environment. It should be noted that California provides no size limitation and requires reports on all actions which may have a significant effect on the environment.

4. Are there activities which should be specifically excluded from the operation of the Act? A State may wish to exempt emergency actions because there may not be sufficient time for a governmental agency to evaluate the environmental factors before taking action. The suggested Act follows the California precedent in exempting ministerial actions. With respect to these activities it was believed that governmental powers are too narrowly confined to enable the agency to shape the activity to improve the effect on the environment. The guidelines implementing NEPA and the California Act both exclude environmentally regulatory actions such as setting standards for air and water pollution control. This exclusion under NEPA is currently the subject of litigation. The requirement for an impact statement was not thought to be necessary for these regulatory actions because the programs were conducted for the express purpose of protecting the environment, and because the programs have considered the environmental effects of their activities since their beginnings. Whatever benefits might be gained from the formal preparation of impact statements could be lost as a result of the delays in enforcement. On the other hand, opponents of these exclusions have claimed that these regulatory actions may have adverse effects on the environment which were not considered by the regulatory agency or were not known to the public at the time the actions were taken. The suggested Act provides for this exclusion.

5. Should the environment be defined to include the totality of man's surroundings or should it be limited to physical factors? In order to keep the requirement for impact statements manageable, the suggested Act limits the definition of the environment to physical factors. Once a physical effect of an action is identified, social and economic factors can be considered to determine whether that effect is significant and whether an impact statement should be prepared. Environment was not limited to natural factors because most of the country's population lives in urban areas, and man-made surroundings form a large part of the environment which affects these people.

6. Should environmental effects be weighed against social and economic considerations? The suggested Act provides that environmental protection should be given appropriate weight with social and economic considerations in overall public policy. This follows the belief that public policy calls for the balancing of many potentially competing factors and that environmental protection does not require shutting down the economy.

7. *Should the Act specifically require public hearings on environmental impact statements?* Resolution of this decision was deliberately left to guidelines to allow specific procedures to be established in conformity with individual state practices.

8. *Should the Act provide for the charging of fees to applicants or should the costs of protecting the environment be borne by the public as a whole?* The suggested Act allows for the charging of fees to the sponsors of projects which require governmental approval. Participants in the workshop believed that a project which will affect the environment should bear the costs of analyzing its effects on the environment.

9. *Should the Act provide a statute of limitations for legal actions brought under the Act?* Although workshop participants believed that a statute of limitations is necessary to provide certainty after a reasonable period, no statute of limitations was included in the Act. Due to the variation in statutes of limitation among the States, the resolution of this issue is deliberately left to each individual State. This subject was believed to be too complicated and calls for too much variation to allow a proposed solution in this suggested Act.

Suggested Legislation

Section 1. [*Short Title.*] This Act may be cited as the [State] Environmental Policy Act.

Section 2. [*Purpose.*] The purposes of this Act are: to declare a state policy which will encourage productive and enjoyable harmony between man and his environment; to promote efforts which will prevent or eliminate damage to the environment and stimulate the health and welfare of man; and to enrich the understanding of the ecological systems and natural resources important to the people of the State.

Section 3. [*Findings and Declaration of State Environmental Policy.*]
The Legislature finds and declares that:

(*1*) The maintenance of a quality environment for the people of this State that at all times is healthful and pleasing to the senses and intellect of man now and in the future is a matter of statewide concern.

(*2*) Every citizen has a responsibility to contribute to the preservation and enchancement of the quality of the environment.

(*3*) There is a need to understand the relationship between the maintenance of high-quality ecological systems and the general welfare of the people of the State, including their enjoyment of the natural resources of the State.

(*4*) The capacity of the environment is limited, and it is the intent of the

Legislature that the government of the State take immediate steps to identify any critical thresholds for the health and safety of the people of the State and take all coordinated actions necessary to prevent such thresholds from being reached.

(*5*) It is the intent of the Legislature that to the fullest extent possible the policies, statutes, regulations, and ordinances of the State [and its political subdivisions] should be interpreted and administered in accordance with the policies set forth in this Act.

(*6*) It is the intent of the Legislature that the protection and enhancement of the environment shall be given appropriate weight with social and economic considerations in public policy. Social, economic, and environmental factors shall be considered together in reaching decisions on proposed public activities.

(*7*) It is the intent of the Legislature that all agencies conduct their affairs with an awareness that they are stewards of the air, water, land, and living resources, and that they have an obligation to protect the environment for the use and enjoyment of this and all future generations.

(*8*) It is the intent of the Legislature that all agencies which regulate activities of private individuals, corporations, and public agencies which are found to affect the quality of the environment shall regulate such activities so that major consideration is given to preventing environmental damage.

Section 4. [*Definitions.*] Unless the context otherwise requires, the definitions in this section shall govern the construction of the following terms as used in this Act:

(*1*) "Agency" means the executive and administrative departments, offices, boards, commissions, and other units of the state government, and any such bodies created by the State.

[(*1*) "Agency" means any state agency, board, or commission and any local agency, including any city, county, and other political subdivision of the State.] [1]

(*2*) "Actions" include:

(*i*) new and continuing projects or activities directly undertaken by any public agency; or supported in whole or part through contracts, grants, subsidies, loans, or other forms of funding assistance from one or more public agencies; or involving the issuance to a person of a lease, permit, license, certificate or other entitlement for use by one or more public agencies;

(*ii*) policy, regulations, and procedure-making.

(*3*) "Actions" do not include:

---

[1] Use the first definition of "agency" if the Act is intended to apply only to actions of state agencies. Use the alternative definition of "agency" if the Act is intended to apply to actions of both state and local agencies.

(*i*) enforcement proceedings or the exercise of prosecutorial discretion in determining whether or not to institute such proceedings;

(*ii*) actions of a ministerial nature, involving no exercise of discretion;

(*iii*) emergency actions responding to an immediate threat to public health or safety;

(*iv*) proposals for legislation;

[(*v*) actions of an environmentally protective regulatory nature.] [2]

(*4*) "Environment" means the physical conditions which will be affected by a proposed action, including land, air, water, minerals, flora, fauna, noise, objects of historic or aesthetic significance, [existing patterns of population concentration, distribution, or growth, and existing community or neighborhood character].

(*5*) "Environmental impact statement" means a detailed statement setting forth the matters specified in Section 5(b) of this Act. It includes any comments on a draft environmental statement which are received pursuant to Section 5(c) of this Act, and the agency's response to such comments, to the extent that they raise issues not adequately resolved in the draft environmental statement.

(*6*) "Draft environmental impact statement" means a preliminary statement prepared pursuant to Section 5(c) of this Act.

Section 5. [*Environmental Responsibility of Agencies.*]

(*a*) Agencies shall use all practicable means to realize the policies and goals set forth in this Act, and to the maximum extent possible shall take actions and choose alternatives which, consistent with other essential considerations of state policy, minimize or avoid adverse environmental effects.

(*b*) All agencies shall prepare, or cause to be prepared by contract, an environmental impact statement on any [major] action they propose or approve which may have a significant effect on the environment. Such a statement shall include a detailed statement setting forth the following:

(*1*) a description of the proposed action and its environmental setting;

(*2*) the environmental impact of the proposed action including short-term and long-term effects;

(*3*) any adverse environmental effects which cannot be avoided should the proposal be implemented;

(*4*) alternatives to the proposed action;

(*5*) any irreversible and irretrievable commitments of resources which would be involved in the proposed action should it be implemented;

(*6*) mitigation measures proposed to minimize the environmental impact; and

(*7*) the growth-inducing aspects of the proposed action. Such a statement

[2] This provision is highlighted as a controversial feature which States may choose to include.

shall also include copies or a summary of the substantive comments received by the agency pursuant to subsection (c) of this section, and the agency response to such comments. The purpose of an environmental impact statement is to provide detailed information about the effect which a proposed action is likely to have on the environment, to list ways in which any adverse effects of such an action might be minimized, and to suggest alternatives to such an action.

(*c*) As early as possible in the formulation of a proposal for action that is likely to require the preparation of an environmental impact statement and in all cases prior to preparation of an environmental impact statement, the responsible agency shall prepare or cause to be prepared a draft environmental statement describing in detail the proposed action and reasonable alternatives to the action, and briefly discussing, on the basis of information then available to the agency, the remaining items set forth in the preceding subsection. The purpose of a draft environmental statement is to inform the public and other public agencies as early as possible about proposed actions that may significantly affect the quality of the environment, and to solicit comments which will assist the agency in determining the environmental consequences of the proposed action. The draft statement should resemble in form and content the environmental impact statement to be prepared after comments have been received and considered pursuant to Section 5(b) of this Act; however, the length and detail of the draft environmental statement will necessarily reflect the preliminary nature of the proposal and the early stage at which it is prepared. The draft statement shall be circulated for comment among other public agencies which have jurisdiction by law or special expertise with respect to any environmental impact involved and shall be made available for comment by relevant federal agencies and interested members of the public.

(*d*) The environmental impact statement, prepared pursuant to subsection (b) of this section, together with the comments of public and federal agencies and members of the public, shall be filed with the [Office of the Governor] and made available to the public at least 30 days prior to taking agency action on the proposal which is the subject of the environmental impact statement.

(*e*) An agency may charge a fee to an applicant in order to recover the costs incurred in preparing or causing to be prepared an environmental impact statement on the action which the applicant requests from the agency.

(*f*) When an agency decides to carry out or approve an action which has been the subject of an environmental impact statement, it shall make an explicit finding that the requirements of subsection (a) of this section have been met and that all feasible action will be taken to minimize or avoid environmental problems that are revealed in the environmental impact statement process.

Section 6. [*Guidelines and Agency Procedures.*]

(*a*) After conducting public hearings the [Governor] shall issue guidelines through regulations implementing the provisions of this Act within [90] days after the effective date of this Act.

(*b*) The guidelines issued by the [Governor] shall specifically include:

(*1*) interpretation of terms used in this Act including criteria for determining whether or not a proposed action [may be major or] may have a significant effect on the environment, with examples. Social and economic factors may be considered in determining the significance of an environmental effect;

(*2*) on the basis of such criteria, identification of those typical agency actions that are likely to require preparation of environmental impact statements;

(*3*) a list of classes of actions which have been determined not to have a significant effect on the environment and which thus do not require environmental impact statements under this Act. In adopting the guidelines, the [Governor] shall make a finding that each class of actions in this list does not have a signficant effect on the environment;

(*4*) the typical associated environmental effects, and methods for assessing such effects, of actions determined to be likely to require preparation of such statements;

(*5*) procedures for obtaining comments on environmental impact statements, including procedures for providing public notice of agency decisions with respect to preparation of a draft environmental statement, or, in the case of major or controversial actions determined not to involve a significant environmental impact, procedures for announcing the decision that no environmental impact statement will be prepared.

(*c*) Within [90] days after the [Governor] adopts the guidelines, the relevant agencies shall adopt and publish procedures for implementation of this Act consistent with the guidelines adopted by the [Governor].

(*d*) Each agency shall conduct a public hearing in connection with adopting the procedures required by this section.

Section 7. [*Limitations.*] [3]

(*a*) In order to avoid duplication of effort and to promote consistent administration of federal and state environmental policies, the environmental impact statement required by Section 5 of this Act need not be prepared with respect to actions for which a detailed statement is required to be prepared pursuant to the requirements of the National Environmental Policy Act of 1969 and implementing regulations thereto; *provided*, that such statement complies with the requirements of this Act and the guidelines adopted pursuant thereto.

---

[3] In addition to these limitations, a State may wish to include a specific statute of limitations to govern legal actions brought under this Act.

(*b*) The requirements of Section 5 of this Act shall apply to actions undertaken or approved prior to the date of enactment of this Act only if:

(*1*) the responsible agency proposes a modification of the action and the modification may result in a significant effect on the environment, or

(*2*) a substantial portion of the public funds allocated for the project has not been spent and it is still feasible either to modify the project in such a way as to mitigate potentially adverse environmental effects or to choose a feasible and less environmentally damaging alternative to the project.

Part 4. EIS Evaluation Questionnaire

The following outline and questions were written as an aid to determining the adequacy of an EIR to satisfy the California Environmental Quality Act (as amended 1972). The points covered apply to EIS's in general as reminders of the various aspects that should be considered in evaluating one of these documents, and can also be used to review what should be included in preparing an EIS. An effort was made to indicate what the replies to the questions mean in terms of evaluating the report, but some interpretation is left to the user.

References are made to sections of the "Guidelines for the Implementation of CEQA," California Administrative Code Sections 15000–15166. For the latest version of these guidelines, contact the office of the Secretary for Resources, Resources Agency, 1416 Ninth Street, Sacramento, California 95814.

The Outline

I. Preparation of the Report
A. Responsibility
B. Writers' backgrounds
C. Nature of work
D. Time and money spent

II. Overall Considerations
A. Usefulness
B. Scope of report
C. Objectivity
D. Thoroughness
E. Nature of data
F. Methods of summation

III. Specific Contents
A. Required elements

B. Project description
C. Environmental setting
D. Environmental impact of the proposed project
E. Adverse impacts which cannot be avoided
F. Mitigation measures proposed to minimize the impacts
G. Alternatives to the proposed project
H. Relationship between local short-term uses of man's environment and the maintenance and enhancement of long-term productivity
I. Any irreversible environmental changes which would be involved
J. Growth-inducing impact
K. Organizations and persons consulted
L. References and appendices
M. Comments and responses (Final EIS)

IV. Evaluation Process
A. Procedures and regulations
B. Agency review
C. Public review

Questions Suggested by the Outline

I. Preparation of the Report
A. Responsibility
    1. Who is the agency person in charge of this report's preparation?
    2. Was the report prepared by:
(*a*) Agency staff?
(*b*) Firm(s) hired by the agency?
(*c*) Applicant (see question 3)?
(*d*) Firm(s) hired by applicant (see question 3)?
    3. Did the agency staff rewrite an applicant-submitted EIS? (A public agency is responsible entirely for the adequacy and objectivity of the EIS—Section 15050. Information may be transmitted in the form of a Draft EIS, but the responsible agency must examine this draft to assure itself of its accuracy and objectivity and amend the draft if necessary. The EIS in its final form must reflect the independent judgment of the responsible agency. Section 15085(a))
    4. Who are the individuals involved in the report preparation? (The identity of the persons, firm, or agency preparing the EIS by contract or other authorization must be given—Section 15144.)
    5. Are there other state or local agencies involved in this project? (If so, the agency responsible for the EIS is the lead agency, defined as the one with the

principal responsibility for carrying out the project, or the one with the greatest responsibility for supervising or approving the project as a whole—Section 15065. The lead agency is usually the agency with the more general governmental powers, i.e. a city council as opposed to a water district board.)

B. Writers' backgrounds

6. What is the competence of the individuals preparing the report (see questions 1 and 4)?

(*a*) Field(s) of expertise, education

(*b*) Experience:

Environmental, social, economic, technical studies

Planning background

Other EIS's or environmental analyses

(*c*) Generalist training

(*d*) Reputation

7. Are there any conflicts of interest on the part of the writer(s) which would indicate bias? (I.e., firm doing EIS for agency also doing planning or project design for other project by applicant. It also might be considered that a firm doing an EIS for an agency which has the project design contract might not want to lose that contract by a showing of too much adverse impact.)

C. Nature of work

8. Within the agency, firm, or group of firms, who researched, organized, and wrote the report?

(*a*) One person

(*b*) Several individuals as a team

(*c*) Several individuals or teams coordinated by one person

(*d*) Several individuals or groups led by a team

9. Were individual sections or studies prepared separately and evaluated as a whole by a team or one person, or was there exchange of information during section preparation? (Particularly for a large project, the ideal method for identifying unknowns and interrelationships between project design and impacts is interdisciplinary teamwork.)

D. Time and money spent

10. Does the amount of time spent on the EIS seem adequate to cover all the impacts, given the size of the project? (Very roughly, one to four weeks for a small project with a single facility not involving any unusual resources; one to several months for a project involving multiple facilities on a large site, or involving several locations; additional months if the project affects a special resource requiring specific studies; up to a year or more for major projects affecting little-studied resources or areas, having broad impacts over an area, or establishing precedents for new technology. Also, some studies may require a specific time of year, which should extend an otherwise shorter preparation time.)

11. Does the cost of the report reflect the size of the project, or the ratio of known to unknown information, or the depth of research on special impact problems?

12. Who paid for the report? (Public agencies preparing EIS's for projects other than their own may charge a reasonable fee, in order to recover the estimated cost, from the person or entity carrying out the project—Section 15053.)

II. Overall considerations
A. Usefulness

13. Does this report give you as a decision-maker or concerned member of the public enough information to make an independent judgment on whether or not the project will have a significant effect on the environment, on methods for reducing adverse impacts, and on alternatives to approving this project? (This is a key question for considering the adequacy of the report.)

14. Was the report prepared early enough in the project planning process to enable environmental considerations to influence the project program or design? (Section 15015)

15. Can the EIS be used to aid in the planning process for this area?

16. Can the EIS be used as an example of impacts to be covered for this project type?

B. Scope of the report

17. How is the area of impact defined? Is the area of impact identified for different impacts and identified as on-site or off-site? (I.e., loss of vegetation may be on-site only; impact on wildlife may extend off-site to immediate project area only or may affect a much broader area if there is interference with a migratory route; air pollution may affect an entire regional airshed; water pollution may have a specific off-site impact on a downstream water supply.)

18. Are regional as well as local impacts included? (For example, regional traffic patterns, population distribution or growth, regional resource allocation.)

19. Depending on the size or nature of the project, are national or international impacts included? (A major port facility, the Alaska pipeline project, weather-modification projects are examples of projects with very broad impact areas.)

20. Does the project set a precedent for action on a larger project, or does it commit the agency to a larger project? (If so, the EIS must address itself to the scope of the larger project—Section 15069.)

21. Is mention made of related projects? (If the project is one of several similar projects, the EIS should comment upon the combined effect—Section 15069.) (See also question 64.)

22. Do other EIS's exist for related projects? If so, is this EIS related to the others? (For example, airport expansion projections in an EIS done for airport commission, related to adjacent freeway interchange capacity in EIS done for highway agency.)

23. Is this EIS on a specific project for which a more general EIS or one with a broader scope had been prepared? If so, and if reference is made to information in the broader EIS, is that information sufficiently detailed to cover the specific aspects of this project?

24. Is this EIS on a phase or segment of a larger project? (A single EIS must be prepared for the ultimate project—Section 15069.)

25. Does the EIS relate this project to policy or planning documents on the area of project type done by local, regional, or other agencies or special districts? (For example, county plan, city housing policy, regional transportation agency plans, water district study, state land use plan, national energy report.)

C. Objectivity

26. Are any controversies over the project objectively described in the report?

27. Does the language of the report tend to advocate the project or is it neutral?

28. Are opinions labelled as such and the sources indicated?

29. Are statements of fact, mentions of reports or observations, etc. sufficiently documented or substantiated so that they could be verified if necessary?

30. Do there appear to be gaps in the selection of facts to be presented; that is, are there conclusions which might be different if additional or other information were included?

31. Are there conclusory statements not backed by facts or references? (For example, "This project will not have any adverse impacts on the local wildlife.")

32. Are there contradictory conclusions? (For example, "*All services capable* of handling increase in demand caused by this project. Problem of adequate fire protection and fresh water supply, although not significant, *still must be worked out.*") (Emphasis added.)

33. Are there meaningless or dishonest statements?

D. Thoroughness

34. Is a system or method used by those who prepared the report to identify impacts? (I.e., project-type checklist, general checklists of activities and environmental conditions, matrix, network, computer model.)

35. Has the responsible agency established checklists or developed some other system for identifying the impacts of the types of projects it handles?

36. Are you given enough information about the methods used to identify impacts to be able to decide from your own knowledge whether something was left out or given too little or too much significance?

37. Is there any indication whether input from citizens, people with local expertise, and other agencies with jurisdiction or expertise was solicited early in the report preparation process?

38. Did the lead agency consult with other public agencies which will issue approvals for the project? (To be done at an early stage of the development of the EIS—Section 15066.)

E. Nature of data

39. Is the level of detail sufficient for you to draw independent conclusions?

40. Is the report padded with unnecessary lists, paragraphs copied out of references whose relevance to the project is not explained, or other irrelevant data?

41. Does the report include material from any specific studies which could aid the impact analysis?

Hydrology	Traffic counts
Soil sampling	Economic impact
Geologic analysis	Utility capacity
Climate	Schools and other service capacities
Vegetation	Air pollution
Ecosystem analysis	Noise contour mapping
Visual analysis	Growth trends
(photos, sketches)	(census data interpretation)
Open space	Energy consumption
Recreation	Utilization of resources
	Other

Are you referred to these separate studies or is sufficient information included in the report for you to be able to judge the conclusions? Are the studies readily available?

42. Are interrelationships described or illustrated (i.e., wildlife food webs, predator-prey relationships, migration habits), or is information presented in list form which requires the reader to do additional work or supply additional information in order to interpret?

43. Are the assumptions and conditions of specific studies made clear in the report and do you agree with them? (For example: the time of day, day of week, or season for traffic sampling; peak or average rainfall used in flood estimation.)

44. Do references cited in the report seem legitimate, trustworthy?

45. Are references quoted in context?

46. Are primary and secondary data distinguished?

47. Are unknowns stated as such or are they glossed over? (If an effect is unknown, the EIS should so state, in order that the decision-makers can weigh the risks of proceeding without additional information.)

F. Summary methods

48. If the report includes a summary statement, are the conclusions in the summary explained in the text?

49. Does the report include a method of summarizing the impact analysis such as magnitude/importance matrix, cost/benefit analysis, ranking of significance, weighted comparison of discrete measurements? (Summary methods are not required by law but can be useful if done well.)

50. If a summary method is used, are the bases for assigning values explained and do the assumptions appear reasonable?

51. Is an effort made to include unquantifiable impacts in the summary? (I.e., public reactions on importance of impacts, surveys of subjective rankings of impacts by decision-makers, or descriptive paragraphs on unquantifiables such as visual impact, value of wildlife, recreation enjoyment, reaction to crowding.)

52. Does the summary method legitimately put together numerical estimates and opinions?

53. Does the summary include plan or policy compliance? (See question 25.)

III. Specific Contents

A. Required elements

54. Does the table of contents list at least the following seven elements required by CEQA, as distinct sections? (Section 15085(b))

(*a*) The environmental impact of the proposed action

(*b*) Any adverse environmental effects which cannot be avoided if the proposal is implemented

(*c*) Mitigation measures proposed to minimize the impact

(*d*) Alternatives to the proposed action

(*e*) The relationship between local short-term uses of man's environment and the maintenance and enhancement of long-term productivity

(*f*) Any irreversible environmental changes which would be caused by the proposed action should it be implemented

(*g*) The growth-inducing impact of the proposed action

B. Project description

55. Is there a description of the project including the precise location on a detailed map (preferably topographic), and on a regional map? (Section 15141(a))

56. Is there a statement of the objectives sought by the proposed project? (Section 15141(b)) The project's objectives should be compared with any plans which various jurisdictions might have for the area or for meeting the same goals as those of the project (see question 25).

57. Are the objectives of a public project given in relation to assessment of the need for the project and how that need was determined?

58. Is the private project objective related to satisfaction of a public need, such as low-cost housing?

59. Is there a general description of the project's technical, economic, and environmental characteristics, considering the principal engineering proposals? (Section 15141(c))

60. Is the project described in terms of what will be occurring in each of its stages—planning, purchase, site preparation, construction, landscaping/cleanup, operation, monitoring, maintenance, disassembly or restoration, etc.?

C. Environmental setting

61. Is there a description from *both* a local and a regional perspective of the environment in the vicinity of the project as it exists before the project is started? (Section 15142)

62. Are rare or unique environmental resources mentioned? These include plants, wildlife, ecosystems (i.e., Pygmy Forest ecosystem), physical features (unusual rock formation, mineral deposit, etc.), historic or archeologic sites.

63. Does the report state whether or not a more common environmental setting has importance as a good example of a type, particularly if the setting has been impacted elsewhere, or has a trend toward disappearance, such as marshes or estuaries?

64. Is specific reference made to related projects in the region, both public and private, both existing and planned, for the purpose of examining the possible cumulative impacts? (Section 15142. See also question 21.)

D. The environmental impacts of the proposed action

65. Are impacts discussed for each of the project stages? (See question 60.)

66. Do the impacts discussed cover all of the possible concerns that this project raises? (Information based on:
• Common sense
• Knowledge of location or project type
• Planning reports, academic studies, handbooks, etc.
• Concerns of local citizens
• Knowledge of individuals with expertise
• Use of project-type checklist or other impact identification method)

67. Are indirect (secondary) as well as direct (primary) impacts discussed? (Section 15143(a))

68. Are on-site and off-site impacts covered? (See questions 17–19.)

69. Are long-term and short-term effects included? (Section 15143(a))

70. Does the discussion of impacts include the following (Section 15143(a))?

- Specifics of the area
- The resources involved
- Physical changes
- Alterations of ecological systems
- Changes induced in population distribution or concentration
- Changes in human use of the land (including commercial and residential)
- Changes in other aspects of the resource base such as water, scenic quality, and public services. (Section 15143(a))

71. Is information on the intensity of any impact given in qualitative as well as quantitative terms where appropriate?

72. Are impacts identified as permanent or temporary (and the duration described)?

73. Are cumulative impacts examined? (See questions 21 and 64.)

E. Adverse impacts which cannot be avoided

74. Are all adverse effects described, including those which can be reduced to an insignificant level but not eliminated? (Section 15143(b))

75. Are there explanations of why the project is being proposed despite adverse impacts that could be eliminated with an alternative design? (Section 15143(b))

76. Is attention given to impacts on aesthetically valuable surroundings, human health (Section 15143(b)), and on the physical and biological setting, culturally valuable surroundings, and standards of living (reminders from an earlier version of the guidelines)?

77. Is there identification of the social or economic groups who would stand to lose if this project were implemented?

F. Mitigation measures proposed to minimize the impacts

78. Is it clear that the mitigation measures are to be adopted as part of the project plan or are they suggestions made by the EIS writers?

79. Where design or construction features have been included in the project plan to reduce an adverse impact, are reasons given why such a reduction is considered acceptable? (Section 15143(c))

80. If there are several alternative mitigation measures possible and one is chosen, are the reasons for the choice given? (Section 15143)c))

81. Are the mitigation measures described sufficiently to give some indication of how they can realistically be carried out?

82. Who is to carry out the mitigation measures?

83. Who will be monitoring the project to see that mitigation measures are carried out and that they have proved to be adequate to reduce the adverse impacts?

84. Will the mitigation measures be written into the conditions of a building permit or other legal document which provides for enforcement of violation (failure to carry out mitigation methods)?

85. Are any unavoidable impacts that may be generated by the mitigation measures discussed?

G. Alternatives to the proposed action

86. Does the report include all known alternatives to the project or to the location of the project which could feasibly attain the basic objectives of the project? (Section 15143(d))

87. Is the scope of alternatives considered in relation to planning or policy objectives in fulfilling social needs (i.e., needs for open space, for low-income housing)?

88. Is the "no project" alternative considered? (Section 15143(d))

89. Are alternatives included which reduce or eliminate impacts even if they are costly or impede the attainment of the project objectives? (Section 15143(d))

90. Are alternatives outside the jurisdiction of the responsible agency considered?

91. Are alternatives broadly enough defined to include alternate social policies, application of new technology, or non-traditional methods of achieving the objectives which might involve redefining the objective? (For example, the goals of a proposed roadway might be met by rapid transit, a bus system, commuter car pools, gas rationing, creating jobs near residential areas.)

H. The relationship between local short-term uses of man's environment and the maintenance and enhancement of long-term productivity

92. Is this section a useful summary for the cumulative and long-term effects of the project? (Section 15143(e))

93. Is special attention given to impacts which narrow the range of beneficial uses of the environment or pose long-term risks to health or safety? (Section 15143(e))

94. Are the beneficial aspects of the project given more weight to justify why it should be done now instead of waiting for future alternatives? (section 15143(e))

I. Any irreversible environmental changes which would be involved

95. Does this section cover the use of nonrenewable resources during the initial and continued phases of the project? (A large commitment of such resources makes removal of material or nonuse of the project thereafter unlikely—Section 15143(f).)

96. Are impacts which would commit future generations to similar uses discussed? (Example: a highway improvement which provides access to a nonaccessible area—Section 15143(f).)

97. Are statements about reversibility and re-use of resources reasonable? (How many roadways are torn up when a greater need for the land arises? Is the cost of reversibility included?)

98. Does the report cover possible irreversible damages from environmental accidents? (Section 15143(f))

99. If irretrievable commitments of resources are to be made, is discussion included on why these resources should be used now and in this project? (Section 15143(f))

J. Growth-inducing impact

100. Does this section of the EIS serve as a useful summary of the secondary and future impacts of the project?

101. Does the report cover the ways in which the project could foster economic or population growth, either directly or indirectly, especially for projects (i.e., a major sewage plant expansion) which remove obstacles to population growth? (Section 15143(g))

102. Does the report state whether or not this project encourages or facilitates other activities which could significantly affect the environment, either individually or cumulatively? (Section 15143(g))

103. Will the impact of an increase in population from this project further tax existing community service facilities? (Section 15143(g))

104. Are the growth-inducing impacts evaluated in relation to planning and policy studies for the area or project type?

K. Organizations and persons consulted

105. Does the report identify all federal, state, or local agencies, other organizations, and private individuals consulted in preparing the EIS, as well as the persons, firm, or agency preparing the EIS? (Section 15144)

L. References and appendices

106. Are references, bibliographies, appendices, or other materials included in this EIS to give additional necessary information or sources of data?

M. Comments and responses (Final EIS)

107. Is there a section containing the comments, either verbatim or in summary, received through the consultation process with public agencies and persons with special expertise, or from the general public? (Sections 15146(a), 15161(a), 15164)

108. Has the agency responded to the comments in the form of a revision of the Draft EIS or as an attachment to the EIS? (Section 15146(b))

109. Are the responses honest answers to the points raised or are the questions avoided or glossed over?

110. Are the comments referred to the changes in the text or the appended responses so that one can easily find whether or not a reply was made?

111. Do the responses describe the disposition of significant environmental issues raised (i.e., revisions of the proposed project)? (Section 15146(b))

112. Where the responsible agency's position is at variance with recommendations or objections raised in the comments, are the issues addressed in detail giving reasons why specific suggestions or comments were not accepted, and describing what factors of overriding importance took precedence over the suggestions? (Section 15146(b))

IV. Evaluation Process

A. Procedures and regulations

113. At what stage were the following brought into the EIS evaluation process: agency staff, consultants, agency officials or elected officials, other agencies with jurisdiction, applicant? (Possible stages include initial study, threshold determination of significance (the point at which the effects of an environmental impact are of such proportions as to be significant, which will vary from project to project), preliminary draft or environmental impact assessment, Draft EIS, Final EIS.)

114. How does the responsible agency review EIS's?

- Uses new staff individual(s)
- Gives new assignments to old staff
- Relies on consultants
- Uses staff evaluation committee, hearing officer, or has other specific staff arrangement
- Uses citizen review committee
- By some combination of the above
- By other method

115. Does the responsible agency have its own procedures or regulations for handling EIS's? (CEQA Section 21082: "all public agencies shall adopt . . . objectives, criteria, and procedures for the evaluation of projects and the preparation of EIR's . . .") (Section 15050 of the Guidelines)

116. Was a Notice of Completion filed with the Secretary for Resources? (Required as soon as a public agency has completed a Draft EIS and is prepared to send out copies for review—Section 15034.)

B. Agency review

117. Does the EIS indicate that the agency consulted with and obtained comments from any public agency which has jurisdiction by law with respect to the project? (Section 15085(b))

118. How many agencies responded?

119. Did the agencies consulted provide a form response or did they make an effort to evaluate the project according to their jurisdiction and expertise?

120. Is reference to previous certification by appropriate water quality agency included in the EIS? (Required by Section 15145.)

C. Public review

121. Did the responsible agency consult with any persons who have special expertise with respect to any environmental impact involved? (Suggested but not required—Section 15161.)

122. Were opportunities for comment by the general public provided? (Section 15085(b)) Was timely notice issued?

123. Was there an unreasonable charge to the public for a copy of the EIS? (Public agencies may collect a fee for the actual cost of reproducing a copy of the EIS requested by a member of the public—Section 15053(b).)

Part 5. Sample EIS Table of Contents*

Participants (authors and contributors, agency and citizen reviewers)
I. Introduction
II. Summary
III. Project Description
   A. Location
   B. Objectives (purpose, reasons project justified now, method of predicting need, and assumptions made)
   C. Technical description (construction activities, permanent structures, routine maintenance, occasional activities, etc.)
IV. Environmental Setting
   A. Project setting
   B. Local setting
   C. Regional setting

* For a more detailed description of the possible contents, see Dickert, Thomas G., and Jens C. Sorensen, "Some Suggestions on the Content and Organization of Environmental Impact Statements," in Dickert, Thomas G., and Katherine Domeny, *Environmental Impact Assessment: Guidelines and Commentary*, University Extension, University of California, Berkeley, 1974.

(And/or by characteristics of the setting:
- Biophysical description—geologic, atmospheric, hydrologic, biotic
- Socioeconomic characteristics—population, migration trends, employment, existing land use, existing access, etc.)

V. The Environmental Impacts of the Proposed Action
  A. Geologic hazards
  B. Soils and erosion
  C. Hydrologic effects (floods, water supply, etc.)
  D. Water quality
  E. Air quality
  F. Health hazards
  G. Ecological impacts (wildlife, vegetation)
  H. Nuisance (noise, disturbance, other)
  I. Visual quality (aesthetics)
  J. Social impacts
  K. Economic impacts
  L. Potential for growth (land use, etc.)
VI. Adverse Environmental Effects Which Cannot Be Avoided If the Proposal Is Implemented
VII. Alternatives to the Proposed Action
  A. No project
  B. Alternative locations
  C. Alternative methods (i.e., of sewage treatment, providing housing, etc.)
  D. Changes in size or scope of project
  E. Mitigation measures
VIII. The Relationship between Local Short-term Uses of Man's Environment and the Maintenance and Enhancement of Long-term Productivity
IX. Irreversible and Irretrievable Commitments of Resources Which Would Be Involved in the Proposed Action if It Is Implemented
X. Comments and Responses—Final EIS
(or could be included in body of report)

Bibliography, References
Appendices (as advisable)
- Organizations and persons consulted
- Comments received (full versions of major points)
- Cost/benefit studies
- Reports on specific aspects (i.e., geologic report)

Index

Index